Rulemaking in Air Transport

Ruwantissa Abeyratne

Rulemaking in Air Transport

A Deconstructive Analysis

Springer

Ruwantissa Abeyratne
Aviation Strategies International
Montreal, Québec
Canada

ISBN 978-3-319-44656-1 ISBN 978-3-319-44657-8 (eBook)
DOI 10.1007/978-3-319-44657-8

Library of Congress Control Number: 2016950568

Printed on acid-free paper

This Springer imprint is published by Springer Nature
The registered company is Springer International Publishing AG Switzerland

To Wybo Heere for his excellent contributions and dedication to Air and Space Law

Preface

This book embarks on a discussion of rulemaking in air transport and its processes and legalities, starting with a deconstruction of work carried out at the time of writing in various fields of air transport by the International Civil Aviation Organization (ICAO) which should be at the apex of rulemaking. This initial discussion, which demonstrates the weakness of rulemaking in the air transport field for lack of direction, purpose, and structure in the development of authoritative rules and regulations that should serve as compelling directives from the main organization responsible for aviation, leads to an evaluation of the fundamental principles of rulemaking in ICAO, the Federal Aviation Administration (FAA) of the United States, and the European Commission (EC).

Essentially, rulemaking is the process where governments convert the broad policy embodied in the bilateral or multilateral treaties they ratify into rules that are applicable to their people, thus providing direction and purpose to the governance process. Rules define the mission of a government and bind people to certain conduct that accord with international and internal policy.

Rules are not legislation. They are the results of deliberations of the people in their constituent assemblies that have passed a vote. As Justice Oliver Wendell Holmes put it aptly, rules are the skin of a living policy that crystallizes an inchoate normative policy into hard words that are clear and intelligible to the ordinary person. Of course, the living policy has its genesis either in ratified treaties or enacted local laws, or even decisions of the legal hierarchy of a land.

The problem with rulemaking in air transport is that, particularly in the economic field but other fields as well, there are no global rules applicable to States that can be enforceable. This is largely because of an inherent anomaly in the realm of international civil aviation. For instance, the Convention on International Civil Aviation (Chicago Convention) in its preamble states that air services will be operated soundly and economically, giving each player equality of opportunity. At best, this statement is ambiguous as it has not been elaborated upon or defined. As a result, regional bodies such as the European Commission and local bodies such as the Federal Aviation Administration (FAA) of the United States have developed their own system of rulemaking and adopted their own rules. From a competition point of view, airlines—constrained by a curious provision in the Chicago Convention that no scheduled air service may be operated into and out of the territory of a State unless permission of that State is obtained—have adopted what is called "spontaneous private deregulation" which is essentially a process which ignores dubious or obsolete concepts such as "equality of opportunity" and apply innovation and creative marketing strategy that circumvents such restraints.

As already stated, at the apex of this anomaly is ICAO, which is neither a legislative body nor a judicial tribunal, although on the subject of legislation, ICAO can have some persuasive authority on States in terms of its policies and guidance material which may or may not be incorporated by States as their domestic rules and regulations. To make matters worse, academics (who have not worked at ICAO) often misquote the Chicago Convention or demonstrate their ignorance of the meaning, purpose, and functions of ICAO as happened at the ICAO Air Transport Symposium with the ambitious title *Addressing Competition Issues: Towards a Better Operating Environment* held at ICAO Headquarters on March 30–31, 2016. At this symposium, one academic was vocal and vehement that ICAO should proclaim a global competition law on air transport. This claim is not only both baseless and unfounded but also plain wrong. The same person advocated that ICAO should establish a judicial tribunal to adjudicate on disputes between States, only to be endorsed by another academic who misquoted ICAO's dispute resolution provisions in the Chicago Convention saying that ICAO could indeed adjudicate disputes as it was a judicial body.

The first step therefore is to know what we are talking about and determine the rulemaking process in air transport accordingly. It is hoped that this book sheds some light on the subject.

Montreal, QC, Canada Ruwantissa Abeyratne
July 2016

Contents

Chapter 1
How Not to Make Rules

1.1 Introduction

Rulemaking is intrinsically linked with the perceived inadequacy of international law, the sources of which should be the genesis of rulemaking by a State. While on the one hand the entrenched principle of sovereignty of States enable a State to make its own rules and laws, on the other hand, the Sate may be circumscribed by the ambivalence of international law. In air transport, the law which stands as the fundamental postulate is the Chicago Convention which in its Article 1 recognizes State sovereignty. The provisions of the Chicago Convention give rise to its Annexes, policies of the ICAO Council, Assembly Resolutions and guidelines issued by ICAO. At the cornerstone of international law lies the concept of State sovereignty which Jean Bodin defined as the absolute and perpetual power within a State.[1] Sovereignty, according to Bodin therefore the highest power wielded over citizens of a State and was exercised by a State on its subjects and anyone else who was present in the State's territory at the time in question. This power also included a State authority and power to make laws. Bodin however, believed that sovereignty of a State was subject to divine laws (presumably, religious tenets) and laws of nature. He also believed that the sovereignty of a State was subservient to certain human laws common to all nations.[2] The idea that a law of nations, common to all mankind, was at least theoretically applicable to all sovereign States was thus conceived.

The International Court of Justice in 1970 judicially recognized this principle in the *Barcelona Traction* case when it recognized that international law places certain obligations upon States, ***erga omnes,*** i.e. obligations owed to the international community as a whole. The Court opined:

---

[1]Bodin (1955), pp. 25–36.

[2]See Rajan (1958), p. 3.

R. Abeyratne, *Rulemaking in Air Transport*, DOI 10.1007/978-3-319-44657-8_1

> such obligations derive, for example, in contemporary international law from the outlawing of acts of aggression, and of genocide, as also from the principles and rules concerning the basic rights of the human person, including protection from slavery and racial discrimination.[3]

International law anchors its validity on two elements: The sources of international law; and the general principles of law applicable to treaties.[4] The sources of international law are reflected in Article 38 of the Statute of the International Court of Justice which provides that when the Court exercises its jurisdiction to adjudicate upon disputes according to the principles of international law, the Court shall apply:

(a) international conventions, whether general or particular, establishing rules expressly recognized by the contracting States;
(b) international custom, as evidence of a general practice accepted by law;
(c) the general principles of law recognized by civilized nations; and,
(d) subject to the provisions of Article 59,[5] judicial decisions and teachings of the most highly qualified publicists of the various nations, as subsidiary means for the determination of rules of law.

There are certain fundamental inconsistencies that are identifiable with the sources of international law when they are applied practically. Firstly, the basic techniques that are applied to any system of law in order to establish its compelling and binding nature tend to be left confused in the realm of international law. These techniques are:

1. lex superior derogat inferiori : rules derived from one source prevail over rules derived from another;
2. lex posterior derogat priori : latter rules prevail over earlier ones;
3. lex specialis derogat generali : a particular or special rule prevails over a general rule.

The problem with the application of the above techniques to international law is that sources such as international custom and the general principles of international law as recognized by civilized nations cannot be determined in a chronological sense to accord with the above since custom and the acceptance of legal principles as universal law take time and hence would be indeterminable as applicable law at a given time.[6]

The next problem to be considered is the application by the International Court of Justice of the "general principles of law recognized by civilized nations" as provided for in Article 38(c) of the Statute of the International Court. Are the general principles of law "recognized" by the civilized nations the same as those

---

[3]Case Concerning the Barcelona Traction Light and Power Co., (Belgium v. Spain) 1970 *I.C.J.* 32.

[4]Brownlie (1990), p. 1.

[5]Article 59 provides that the decision of the Court has no binding effect except between the parties and in respect of that particular case.

[6]Akehurst (1974–1975), p. 273.

that are developed and codified as principles of international law, initiated by the United Nations General Assembly by Article of the United Nations Charter? The General Assembly does not have full and universal legislative powers,[7] and any codification of the principles of international law that emanates from being initiated by the United Nations General Assembly would only be persuasive. In this environment, it would remain increasingly difficult for the International Court of Justice to determine as to what laws are "recognized" by civilized nations as the general principles of law.[8]

Over and above the customary and other principles of international law which may be considered as the "recognized" principles of international law, there is also the **jus cogens** or "compelling law" which takes precedence in the realm of international law.[9] Article 53 of the Vienna Convention on the Law of Treaties, which was adopted on 23 May 1969, (hereafter referred to as the Vienna Convention)[10] provides that treaties conflicting with a peremptory norm of general international law (jus Cogens) would be void. The Article states:

> A treaty is void, if, at the time of its conclusion, it conflicts with a peremptory norm of general international law. For the purpose of the present Convention, a peremptory norm of general international law is a norm accepted and recognized by the international community of States as a whole as a norm from which no derogation is permitted and which can be modified only by a subsequent norm of general international law having the same character.

Article 64 of the Vienna Convention runs as follows:

> If a new peremptory norm of international law emerges, any existing treaty which is in conflict with that norm becomes void and terminates.

The *jus cogens* therefore admits of no derogation by the will of the contracting parties whether in the drafting of the treaty provisions or interpretation thereof. It is also generally accepted that the *jus cogens* principle as enunciated in the Vienna Convention and accepted as a general principle of international law applies only to treaties and not to unilateral acts by States such as those that may commonly seen in instances of extradition and violation of security of one State by another.[11] This would then imply that a peremptory norm of international law or the *jus cogens*, if violated by the act of a State does not stand void ab initio at international law but

---

[7]Fawcett (1971), pp. 65–66.

[8]Lord Oliver has stated:

> a rule of international law becomes a rule – whether accepted into domestic law or not – only when it is certain and is accepted generally by the body of civilised nations; and it is for those who assert the rule to demonstrate it, if necessary before the International Court of Justice. It is certainly not for a domestic tribunal in effect to legislate a rule into existence for the purposes of domestic law and on the basis of material that is wholly indeterminate. (1989) 3 W.L.R. 969 H.L. See also generally, Robert Y. Jennings, An International Lawyer Takes Stock, *I.C.L.Q.* Vol 39, Part 3, July 1990, 513-529.

[9]Whiteman (1977), pp. 609–613.

[10]*Vienna Convention on the Law of Treaties*, U.N. Doc. A/Conf.39/27, 23 May 1969.

[11]Sztucki (1974), p. 69.

rather, requires individual action by States so that the status quo ante is restored. In such instances, logically, the International Court of Justice would, when adjudicating upon breaches of international law and consequent action by States, treat the *jus cogens* as a principle of international law under Article 36(1) of the United Nations Charter. This would, in turn, render the *jus cogens* destitute of its compelling effect on the conduct of nations and relegate it to the same level as any other norm of international law when a unilateral action of a State is adjudicated upon.

A peremptory norm of international law is presumed to be based on morality. Therefore, *jus cogens* would essentially have its origins in moral tenets—such a right of a State to its security and self-determination inter alia. There are also, in close juxtaposition to these moral principles, certain compelling concepts of customary international law such as State sovereignty which in turn are sufficiently peremptory to be considered a form of jus cogens. Where then is one to draw the line between jus cogens and customary international law? As one legal commentator observes.

Jus cogens is something of a contradictio in terminis as far as international law is concerned. For how can jus cogens, as a concept introducing morals into international law, be reconciled with the age old basis of international law, called sovereignty? It can be argued that the principle of sovereignty, which by definition has to be an absolute one in the sense of being "in principle not being accountable in law to any other authority", itself is a rule of jus *cogens* in its purest form; thus, in a way, it is a problem that bites itself in its tail.[12]

To make matters worse, the Vienna Convention in its Article 53 stipulates that a peremptory norm of general international law (jus cogens) is a norm accepted and recognized by the international community of States as a norm from which no derogation is permitted and which can be modified only by a subsequent norm of general international law having the same character. This could only mean that there are norms of international law that can be changed and indeed, can be derogated from. Called jus dispositivum, these norms can be derogated from by mutual consent between States. In this sense, principles of State sovereignty may become jus dispositivum, although the very essence of international law, and indeed air law, is based on this premise of State sovereignty. Although therefore **jus cogens** has priority over jus dispositivum, it does not make sense since the concept of State sovereignty which is the fundamental norm cannot be logically overridden by jus cogens, which arrives on the scene later.

The confusion that has been created by the various types of concepts permeating international law seriously affects the development of clear principles and functional parameters of international law. These concepts should be reconciled though a more cogent system of international law, thereby giving new meaning to the legal protection of the international community against the unlawful interference with international civil aviation.

The most fundamental principle in rulemaking is that the genesis of the rule should be authoritative. The most common form of rulemaking in air transport is the

[12] von der Dunk (1992), p. 219.

adaptation of an international treaty provision or a derivative thereof to a domestic or local regulatory regime. For example, the principles contained in the fundamental postulate of air transport law—The Convention on International Civil Aviation (Chicago Convention)[13]—being the genesis of rules and regulations on the subject, and its derivatives—mainly the 19 Annexes to the Chicago Convention—are generally transposed into the local laws of a contracting State to the Convention, firstly by recognition of its legislature and secondly by executive order or regulation.

Regrettably, this process does not always take place smoothly in air transport due to the weakness of the regulatory process at the top level—The International Civil Aviation Organization (ICAO).[14] I will discuss five current issues of critical importance—cyber terrorism in air transport; leasing and transfer of functions of aircraft; remotely piloted aircraft; climate change; and competition law in air transport, with a discussion on the nature of the issues involved with a view to illustrating where States have not been given the impetus they need to make their own domestic rules due to a watered down and weak foundation built by ICAO with respect to these issues. This will be followed by a chapter which recommends the manner in which rules can be made in air transport, starting with ICAO, followed by discussions in chapters to follow on regional and national rulemaking.

1.2 Cyber Terrorism

The Economist of 4 November 2014 speaks of "cyberjacking"—a phenomenon that refers to the equivalent of hijacking an aircraft with the use of cyber technology. This could happen from outside the aircraft or from the inside. The catalyst in this instance is the increasing popularity with passengers of internet connectivity on board for work, games, movies et.al. The article also mentions that internet signals are routed through existing communications architecture, such as the Aircraft Communications Addressing and Reporting System (ACARS), or the Automatic Dependent Surveillance-Broadcast (ADS-B), which is an anti-collision system, which, both being information communications systems can, in theory be targets of cyber-attacks. In its later edition of 21 May 2015 the same journal highlighted

[13]Convention on International Civil Aviation, signed at Chicago on 7 December 1944. See ICAO Doc. 7300/9:2008. See also, Abeyratne (2013) for a discussion and analysis of the Convention. Also, by the same author, Abeyratne (2012a), for a discussion and analysis of the Annexes to the Chicago Convention.

[14]ICAO is the specialized agency of the United Nations handling issues of international civil aviation. ICAO was established by the Convention on International Civil Aviation, signed at Chicago on 7 December 1944 (Chicago Convention). The overarching objectives of ICAO, as contained in Article 44 of the Convention is to develop the principles and techniques of international air navigation and to foster the planning and development of international air transport so as to meet the needs of the peoples for safe, regular, efficient and economical air transport. ICAO has 191 member States, who become members of ICAO by ratifying or otherwise issuing notice of adherence to the Chicago Convention.

that a hacker had identified a weakness with the in-flight entertainment (IFE) systems on Boeing 737-800, 737-900, 757-200 and Airbus A320 aircraft. He had demonstrated this fact by accessing the systems by plugging a laptop into one of the electronic boxes usually found under the seats either side of the aisle. Once connected, the hacker claims to have accessed other systems on the aircraft.

None of these claims have been validated by the scientific community nor have they been put into practice by terrorists or criminals against civil air transport. Nonetheless, this may be a sign of things to come, particularly when one considers that the National Aeronautics and Space Administration's computers have been hacked in the past and that all computer systems of SONY were hacked in the recent past, allegedly by a foreign State sponsored hacking exercise. As this article discusses, there has been at least one confirmed cyber-attack on a computer system of a commercial airline. The International Civil Aviation Organization has been active in the field of prevention of cyber terrorism, which this article will elaborate on, with some constructive suggestions.

On 21 June 2015, hackers attacked the computer system of LOT Polish Airlines, grounding several aircraft, resulting in the grounding of 10 flights and delay caused to 12 other flights. This caused severe inconvenience to nearly 1500 passengers. Cyber-attacks on facilities and infrastructure are here. They are no longer viewed as things to come. For instance, it has been reported that Chinese hackers broke into the computer networks housing the personal information of all federal US government employees in March 2015 in an apparent attempt to target people who had applied for top-secret security clearances. Cyber interference, cybercrime and cyber terrorism against air transport are all offences against civil aviation that end up in unlawful interference with civil aviation, which has been addressed on three major occasions, though the Tokyo Convention of 1963, The Hague Convention of 1970 and the Montréal Convention of 1971. Yet none of these conventions refer, directly or indirectly, to cyber terrorism. The first such Treaty to do so, the 2010 Convention on the Suppression of Unlawful Acts Relating to International Civil Aviation adopted in Beijing, provides in Article 1d) that an offence is committed when a person destroys or damages air navigation facilities or interferes with their operation, if any such act is likely to endanger the safety of aircraft in flight. This clearly refers, inter alia, to cyber terrorism, but links the offence exclusively to the safety of aircraft in flight. Regrettably the Beijing Convention—the only international attempt at hinting at cybercrime—does not seem to cover the LOT Polish situation.

At the apex of the issue is the International Civil Aviation Organization (ICAO) which has been charged by the international community with leading efforts in curbing aviation cybercrime.

1.2.1 Definitions and Issues

At the outset it becomes necessary to define the terms cybercrime and cyber terrorism. In a proposal for an international convention on cybercrimes and terrorism, a cybercrime is defined as conduct with respect to cyber systems that is classified as an offence under the draft convention.[15] Although cyber terrorism has been simplistically defined as "an assault on electronic communication networks", the proposed convention defines cyber terrorism as the intentional use or threat of use, without legally recognized authority, of violence, disruption or interference against cyber systems, when it is likely that such use would result in death or injury of a person or persons, substantial damage to physical property, civil disorder, or significant economic harm. The Federal Bureau of Investigation of the United States has given a more extensive definition: "the premeditated, politically motivated attack against information, computer systems, computer programs, and data which result in violence against non-combatant targets by sub-national groups or clandestine agents".[16]

The term "cyber terrorism" was coined in 1980 by Barry Collins who defined it as "the intimidation of civilian enterprise through the use of high technology to bring about political, religious, or ideological aims, actions that result in disabling or deleting critical infrastructure data or information".[17]

Since the author published his article on cyber security and aviation in 2011[18] the threat of cybercrimes on air transport has decidedly increased.[19] This is because the overall threat on computer security of industry has increased in general terms in

---

[15]Crime in Cyberspace – First Draft of International Convention Released for Public Discussion, European Committee on Crime Problems (cdpc) Committee of Experts on Crime in Cyber-Space (pc-cy), *Draft Convention on Cyber-crime* (Draft N° 19): 2000. See http://www.iwar.org.uk/law/resources/eu/cybercrime.htm. The Convention, in Article 3 states that if any person unlawfully and intentionally engages in any of the following conduct without legally recognized authority, permission, or consent: (a) creates, stores, alters, deletes, transmits, diverts, misroutes, manipulates, or interferes with data or programs in a cyber-system with the purpose of causing, or knowing that such activities would cause, said cyber system or another cyber system to cease functioning as intended, or to perform functions or activities not intended by its owner and considered illegal under this Convention; (b) creates, stores, alters, deletes, transmits, diverts, misroutes, manipulates, or interferes with data in a cyber-system for the purpose and with the effect of providing false information in order to cause substantial damage to persons or property; (c) enters into a cyber-system for which access is restricted in a conspicuous and unambiguous manner; (d) interferes with tamper-detection or authentication mechanisms; (e) manufactures, sells, uses, posts or otherwise distributes any device or program intended for the purpose of committing any conduct prohibited by Articles 3 and 4 of the Convention. Article 4 covers aiding and abetting the aforesaid offences. See Sofaer et al. (2000), Jointly Sponsored by: The Hoover Institution The Consortium for Research on Information Security and Policy (CRISP); The Center for International Security and Cooperation (CISAC) and Stanford University.

[16]http://defensetech.org/2011/09/12/cyber-terrorism-now-at-the-top-of-the-list-of-security-concerns/.

[17]Tafoya (2016); See also, Abeyratne (2010a), pp. 24–25.

[18]Abeyratne (2011d), pp. 337–339.

[19]President Barack Obama, in his State of the Union Address of 2013 said: "America must also face the rapidly growing threat from cyber-attacks . . . our enemies are also seeking the ability to sabotage our power grid, our financial institutions, our air traffic control systems. We cannot look back years from now and wonder why we did nothing in the face of real threats to our security and our economy." *President Obama Acknowledges Cyber Threat and Signs Executive Order for Improving Critical Infrastructure Cybersecurity*, February 13, 2013. See https://www.cigital.com/blog/president-obama-acknowledges-cyber-threat-and-signs-executive-order/.

recent years. In specific terms, as aviation digitized baggage handling systems, air traffic management information and communication technologies including flight information display systems, the digital sophistication introduced into these systems has spawned opportunity for hackers to exploit the vulnerabilities that came with such advancement. Added to this, computers, which have graduated from desktops and laptops to peoples' pockets are now found in all sorts of gadgets. This trend has prompted Cisco—a manufacturer of network equipment—to point out its concern, that there are currently as many as 15 billion connected devices in the world which could increase to 50 billion by 2020.[20] These have the potential of causing significant damage to life and limb as well as severe financial and economic damage. For example, in 2006 the US Federal Aviation Administration was forced to shut down air traffic control systems in Alaska as a precautionary measure against an attack on the internet. Two years later, in a scary scenario, accident investigators investigating the crash of *Spanair* Flight 5022 of 20 August 2008 involving an MD 82 aircraft,[21] concluded that the aircraft crashed due to the computer system monitoring technical problems on board was infected with malware.[22]

Concerns have also been expressed with regard to the disappearance in March 2014 of Malaysian Airlines Flight MH 370—that someone may have hacked into the airplane's computer system and taken control of the entire flight. One theory (in a newspaper report, which has not been subjected to any formal investigation) was that the hackers could have infiltrated the inflight entertainment system of the aircraft to gain access to the security software on board. It has been reported that a former security adviser to the Home Office of the United Kingdom had advised that the controls of the Boeing 777 (which operated Flight MH 370) could be accessed through a radio signal sent from a small device.[23] It has also been reported that the manufacturer of the Boeing 777 has since introduced modifications to the model 777-200 and -300Er series airplanes which will now have novel and unusual design features associated with the connectivity of the passenger service network systems to the critical airplanes systems and data networks.[24]

---

[20]Hacking the Planet, *The Economist*, July 18–24 2015, p. 10. In this article *The Economist* also mentions that on 9 July 2015 hackers had infiltrated the US Office of Personnel Management and stolen personal information of 22 million government employees. In another incident in January of the same year hackers had accessed the systems of *Anthem*, a large insurance firm, and purloined security information of 80 million employees. *Ibid.*

[21]Span air flight 5022, operated with a McDonnell Douglas MD82, crashed just after take-off in Madrid-Barajas Airport on 20 August 2008, killing 154 people.

[22]In July 2013 passport control at Istanbul Ataturk International Airport was shut down due to a cyber-attack and in the same year 75 airports in the United States were affected as a result of a cyber-attack and phishing. See Lim (2016) (20182-92), p. 85.4.

[23]Cyber Threats against the Aviation Industry, Posted in *SCADA* on April 8 2014. See http://resources.infosecinstitute.com/cyber-threats-aviation-industry.

[24]*Ibid.*

The disconcerting trend, although based on theoretical conjecture is that, while the industry is forging ahead with installing anti-hacker measures in their software, hackers are evolving new methodology to counter these measures by employing such techniques that could hijack virtual private networking (VPN) security and evade detection. This way, hackers continue to steal information and credentials and compromise software environments.[25] One of the profound weaknesses in aviation cyber security is that cyberspace is not so much a 'space' but a network of systems connected by multiple nodes which has an amorphous reach whereas cyber security in aviation is treated on the basis of cyber security regions, which divide the cyberspace networks into various sectors, thus isolating security controls at such sector nodes and making them vulnerable to attack.[26]

1.2.2 Air Traffic Management Systems

A particular vulnerability is seen in air traffic management systems where security challenges pose a two pronged threat. For one, if established systems are not fitted with the appropriate information and communication security measures, they could be vulnerable to attack. Just as an example, the common use of radio frequency in air traffic management for communication between air traffic control and aircraft, navigation, and surveillance could make it easy for the hacker to execute unauthorised transmissions through very high frequency transceivers. To circumvent this possibility one could encrypt radio transmission but this would seriously circumscribe the number of channels available for communication between air traffic control and aircraft. The radio transmission approach has an added vulnerability in that radio transmissions could easily be jammed, as in a reported instance when a portable transceiver was used to jam the Unicom frequency at Central Maine Airport.[27]

The other threat lies in new technology that may be introduced into the air traffic management networks which could create unsecured access points through which critical information and systems can be compromised in new and innovative ways. One such innovative air traffic management system, which is expected to become popular over the coming decade is Remote Tower Services (RTS) where air traffic at an airport is performed remotely, away from the local control tower. The European Cockpit Association (ECA) has suggested that cyber-security portends an ominous scenario where the very nature of the concept would lay it open to susceptibility and vulnerability. ECA therefore suggests precautionary measures to be put in place and procedures established so that possible attacks could be circumvented or at least minimized in their consequences. One of the measures

---

[25]M-Trends 2015: A View from the Frontlines, *Mandiant Threat Report*, info@mandiant.com at 1.

[26]Siu et al. (2014), pp. 73–81 at 74.

[27]Mark (2016).

suggested, as part of an efficient security management system in RTS, is a mandatory reporting system by air navigation service providers and aircraft operators that would alert authorities to occurrences related to illegal or questionable cyber conduct. This brings to bear the need for identification of the person who transmits the message as well as the potential recipient of the message. There is a critical need in this regard to adopt technical and legal measures that could ensure that the identity of the message transmitter can be authenticated, and their messages to selected recipients can be limited.[28]

1.2.3 The ICAO Role

The compelling importance of putting technical and legal measures in place is compounded by the fact that cybercrimes, whether they be through hacking or mere disruption to computer systems, take multifarious forms. Past instances have shown non-malicious mistakes; mischief; thrill seeking disruptions calculated to cause interference and inconvenience; and premeditated attacks to intentionally harm an air transport service.

The complexity and enormity of the threat of cybercrime and cyber terrorism has prompted a strong view that an overarching rule that ensures cyber security should be implemented 'top-down' through direction as well as 'bottom up' through technology:

> The 'top' of the Civil Aviation control system is the International Civil Aviation Organisation (ICAO). As a result, ICAO needs to have appropriate measures and management strategies to implement, support and secure civil aviation, particularly the new 'eEnabled' aircraft[29] and the future Air Traffic Management (ATM) systems, being designed by the SESAR, NextGen and Carats projects. A single cyber security architecture will be required to enable these new systems to inter-operate seamlessly, securely, and safely worldwide.[30]

The question is how far ICAO should go in collaborating with the industry and other key stakeholders in seeking a way forward towards guiding the rest in the context of its leadership role. The ICAO Twelfth Air Navigation Conference (AN-Conf/12), held from 19 to 30 November 2012, recommended that ICAO establish, as a matter of urgency, an appropriate mechanism including States and industry to evaluate the extent of the cybersecurity issues and develop a global air traffic management architecture taking care of cybersecurity issues. At the 38th Session of the ICAO Assembly, held from 24 September to 4 October 2013, the Assembly adopted Resolution A38-15 (Consolidated statement of continuing ICAO policies related to aviation security), Appendix A of which directs the ICAO

---

[28]Siu et al. (2014), p. 76.

[29]Boeing 787, Airbus A380 and A350 and similar aircraft.

[30]Cyber Security in Civil Aviation, Centre for the Protection of National Infrastructure, August 2012 at 1.

Council to continue, as an urgent priority, its work relating to measures for prevention of acts of unlawful interference, on the basis of the strategic direction provided by the ICAO Comprehensive Aviation Security Strategy (ICASS), and ensure that this work is carried out with the highest efficiency and responsiveness.

Strategic Focus Area 1 of this Strategy recognizes that global civil aviation operations are facing new and evolving threats, such as those posed by improvised explosive devices, unconventional terrorist attacks on airports and aircraft facilities, cyberattacks on aviation systems, including Air Traffic Management Systems, and threats to general aviation. ICAO has undertaken that it will adopt an approach in this regard that will employ a more proactive strategy to address such threats, working through the AVSEC Panel Working Group on Threat and Risk (WGTR), which monitors and evaluates new and existing threats on a regular basis, and identifies gaps in Annex 17 (Security) to the Chicago Convention,[31] for subsequent amendments. *Strategic Focus Area 2* of the overall ICAO strategy recognizes that an integral part of a proactive method of promoting innovative, effective and efficient security approaches entails a regular review and amendment of existing guidance material. This Focus Area goes on to say that ICAO, using the expertise of the AVSEC Panel Working Group on Technology, will assist member States and industry towards employing new and innovative security measures, including but not limited to, the use of advanced technology. In this context, ICAO is continuing the development of a web-based platform, named "*AVSECPaedia*", to encourage the exchange of information of a sensitive nature between States including, but not limited to, screening techniques and emerging security technologies. ICAO will also ensure the timely development of guidance material to reflect the most recent developments in aviation security and technology.[32]

1.2.4 The Work Of ICAO: Progress So Far

In a report detailing progress made by ICAO and industry partners up to 2015, presented to the ICAO Council at its 205th session in mid-2015, the ICAO Secretariat defined "cyber security" as "the collection of tools, policies, security concepts, security safeguards, guidelines, risk management approaches, actions, training, best practices, assurance and technologies that can be used to protect the cyber environment as well as organizations' and user's assets. It encompasses the protection of electronic systems from malicious electronic attack and the means by which to deal with the consequences of such attacks".[33] As to what "user's assets"

[31]Convention on International Civil aviation, signed at Chicago on 7 December 1944. The Convention came into force 4 April 1947. See ICAO doc 7300/8, 2006.

[32]ICAO Comprehensive Aviation Security Strategy (ICASS), presented by the Council of ICAO, *A37-WP/18EX/2, 28/6/10* at 2.

[33]Report on Civil Aviation and Cybersecurity, *C-WP/14266*, 21/04/15 at 2.

represented in this context, were not identified by ICAO, although this definition was followed up with the categorization of vulnerability that fundamental characteristics of information and communications technology systems were exposed to as follows: *confidentiality*, i.e. information can be accessed or used only by the authorized or intended recipients; *integrity*, i.e. information has not been tampered with in transit and therefore remains as foreseen by the sender/source; and *availability*, i.e. information is available within agreed, reasonable timelines without undue delays.[34]

It is noted that, arguably for the purpose of reaching consistency in international terminology and language, ICAO had copied almost verbatim (without acknowledgment) the aforementioned definition and categorization from the International Telecommunications Union.[35] Another fact worthy of note is that the WGTR—which is ICAO's main tool in addressing aviation cyber security—has concentrated so far (up to 2015)—3 years after the Air Navigation Conference requested that ICAO establish, "as a matter of urgency, an appropriate mechanism including States and industry to evaluate the extent of the cybersecurity issues and develop a global air traffic management architecture taking care of cybersecurity issues"—only on cyber terrorism *i.e.* terrorist related attacks only, leaving the entire issue of other cyber-attacks or disruption by hacktivists and other persons who indulge in crimes for personal thrill or mere disruption of air transport, totally ignored. No reason is given for this exclusion[36] although ICAO's remit is clearly to "evaluate the extent of cybersecurity issues". The fact of the matter is that currently, and over the past several years, there has been no cyber terrorist attack but several individual "hack" attacks on aviation although the cyber terrorist individual or organization will be a corollary to the individual hacker. As German insurer *Allianz* said, cyber terrorism may replace the hijacker and bomber and become the weapon of choice on attacks against the aviation community.[37]

It was reported in May 2015 that a security researcher had alerted US agents of the Federal Bureau of Investigation that he had been able to successfully hack into aircraft computer systems mid-flight numerous times through the in-flight entertainment systems, and at one point had caused a plane he was on to move sideways.[38] The process with which the hacking was accomplished is called reverse

[34]*Ibid.*

[35]See Definition of Cybersecurity referring to ITU-T X.1205, Overview of cybersecurity, http://www.itu.int/en/ITU-T/studygroups/com17/Pages/cybersecurity.aspx.

[36]Report on Civil Aviation and Cybersecurity, *supra* note 19, para. 3.3.

[37]Zolfagharifard (2016). It is curious that although the ICAO Report does not mention "hacktivists" an ICAO press release talks of them: "The five major international aviation organizations signed a new cybersecurity agreement late last week formalizing their common front against the hackers, 'hacktivists', cyber criminals and terrorists now focused on malicious intent ranging from the theft of information and general disruption to potential loss of life". See http://www.icao.int/Newsroom/Pages/aviation-unites-on-cyber-threat.aspx.

[38]Thompson (2016).

engineering.[39] Whether or not these claims can be authenticated or accepted for their credibility, the fact remains that at the present time, hacking by individuals who are not entirely impelled by terroristic intent cannot be ignored.

In February 2014 the ICAO Council adopted two Recommended Practices to Annex 17 to the Convention on International Civil Aviation which became effective on 17 November 2014 and which provide that each Contracting State should, in accordance with the risk assessment carried out by its relevant national authorities, ensure that measures are developed in order to protect critical information and communications technology systems used for civil aviation purposes from interference that may jeopardize the safety of civil aviation.[40] The new provisions also exhort States that they should encourage entities involved with or responsible for the implementation of various aspects of the national civil aviation security programme to identify their critical information and communications technology systems, including threats and vulnerabilities thereto, and develop protective measures to include, *inter alia,* security by design, supply chain security, network separation, and remote access control, as appropriate.[41]

Whilst the Assembly Resolution A 38-15 calls for ICAO to provide strategic direction according to ICASS, which involves ICAO's assisting member States and industry towards employing new and innovative security measures, including but not limited to the use of advanced technology, ICAO has instead come up with two recommendations on what States ought to be doing by themselves. This raises the question as to how States could encourage each other to adopt measures without any assistance by ICAO with regard to the introduction of new and innovative security measures. This disconnect has to be addressed, through the initial question: are Recommended Practices the answer to a problem described as the foremost threat on the security list after the events of 9/11?[42]

This conundrum involves another dimension—as to whether ICAO should employ the role it has been assigned in cyber security in a prescriptive manner. There has been a suggestion that ICAO guidance developed in this regard should be non-prescriptive and non-excessive.[43] This is a platitude as ICAO's very nature resonates the fact that it is a non-prescriptive Organization. Even the Standards of the ICAO Annexes (except for those of Annex 2 on Rules of the Air) are non-obligatory as States can file differences to any Standard if they are unwilling or unable to abide by them. However, it must be noted that at least a difference filed would provide some indication as to why a State does not agree to implement a Standard and therefore have some degree of persuasive authority.

[39]Reverse engineering is taking apart an object to see how it works in order to duplicate or enhance the object. The practice, taken from older industries, is now frequently used on computer hardware and software. See http://www.hackersonlineclub.com/reverse-engineering.

[40]14th Amendment to Annex 17, Recommendation 4.9.1.

[41]Id. Recommendation 4.9.2.

[42]Reed (2001).

[43]Cyber Security in Aviation (presented by the International Air Transport Association), *AVSECP/25-WP/34*, 28/2/14, para. 5.1.d).

On 5 December 2014, ICAO signed with four other Organizations—Airports Council International (ACI), the Civil Air Navigation Services Organisation (CANSO), the International Air Transport Association (IATA), and the International Coordinating Council of Aerospace Industries Associations (ICCAIA) an agreement to establish what is called a "Roadmap"[44] on cyber security based upon an agreement to establish an Industry High-level Group (IHLG) as a mechanism for high-level cooperation on issues of common interest and importance. The IHLG has determined that cybersecurity in civil aviation was a high priority transversal issue requiring collective alignment. The five organizations signed the Civil Aviation Cyber Security Action Plan and accompanying Roadmap. ICAO claims that this cooperation enables the participating parties to draw together all elements of the aviation industry to ensure a shared vision, strategy and set of commitments to tackle the cyber threat.

It is not enough for the five organizations to share a vision and strategy, even if there is one. Cooperation of States is essential and such cooperation must be insisted upon and seen to exist. This is where ICAO should come in as the United Nations specialized agency for aviation. As Director General of IATA Tony Tyler said: "governments have resources and access to intelligence that the private sector can never achieve". They also have a responsibility to use these resources to support industry efforts. We have an example of this approach in the decades of successful government-industry cooperation on safety. Unfortunately, we have not achieved that level of cooperation in security. As the threat of malicious cyber-attacks increases, the need for consultation, coordination and cooperation built on trust—among governments, between governments and industry, and within industry—becomes more critical.[45]

The key to a cybersecurity strategy is cooperation achieved through standardization and harmonization, and this is yet to be achieved in aviation security. As the author pointed out in an earlier publication, this glaring lack of sharing of information created a serious lacuna in aviation security in 2014.[46]

---

[44]ICAO claims that the Roadmap is a dynamic document containing a number of tasks and deliverables that will evolve over time to address key issues of cybersecurity. Its purpose is manifold: to support the development and promotion of a robust cybersecurity culture; to promote the use of information security and cyber protection best practices in the industry; and to share information on cyber threats and risks. It is also claimed that the Roadmap recognizes the best practices and standards on cybersecurity as provided by the International Organization for Standardization (ISO) and National Institute of Standards and Technology (NIST), recognizing that the industry is making substantial progress in developing and implementing cybersecurity tools, such as CANSO's Cyber Security and Risk Assessment Guide. See Report on Civil Aviation and Cybersecurity, supra, note 19, para 5.1.

[45]Remarks of Tony Tyler at the Civil Aviation Cyber Security Conference, Singapore, 9 July 2015 at http://www.iata.org/pressroom/speeches/Pages/2015-07-09-01.aspx.

[46]In the instance of the disappearance of Malaysian Airlines Flight MH 370, where it was revealed post facto that unbeknownst to the Malaysian authorities, two passengers had forged passports. These forgeries had been recorded in an INTERPOL maintained database and the database's existence had not been brought to the notice of ICAO member States. The author pointed out that

1.2.5 *Exhortations to ICAO by Other Entities*

1.2.5.1 IATA

At the twenty-fifth ICAO AVSEC Panel Meeting held from 17 to 21 March 2014, IATA advised that there are many players in the field of cyber security taking different approaches and looking at specific issues. Frameworks are emerging from many organizations and there is little coordination of approach. Therefore, vulnerabilities will increase due to the sheer volume of parties involved in the development and supply chain of computer systems, the data used in aviation and the increasing trend to outsource.[47] IATA advised the Panel that airline and airport networks have hundreds, if not thousands of entry points, through connectivity with the internet, mobile devices, connections with other organizations and systems such as Global Distribution Systems, governments, other airlines, financial systems, remote check in systems and more. With the increases of networked technologies and automated systems, availability and integrity of those systems increases. The evolving convenience of systems and processes, their efficiency and integration brings to bear the likelihood of increasing vulnerability of the systems to potential cyber threats.[48] It is in this context that IATA exhorted ICAO to recognize the compelling need for "the development of *specific measures* (my emphasis) and best practices focusing on the aviation industry".[49] ICAO's response to this request is reflected in the Rapporteur's Report to the AVSEC Panel—submitted to the twenty-sixth meeting of the Panel held from 13 to 17 April 2015—which says that despite broad encouragement for individuals to undertake "electronic jihad", no specific examples of terrorist cyber-attacks against aircraft have been identified. There was no evidence of meaningful advances in terrorist capability in this area. The Rapporteur further said that although individuals, including hackers, commonly make claims about the vulnerabilities of aircraft information systems, there no evidence that this has influenced terrorist intentions. However, this could encourage terrorists to try to develop this capability in the future. Somewhat flippantly, the Rapporteur's Report says that: "simply connecting or interacting with aircraft systems does not constitute the capability to manipulate the function of a safety critical system so as to endanger the aircraft. In some scenarios, the uncertainty around the likely impact of exploiting a particular vulnerability may mean they have limited appeal to a terrorist. As ever, the possibilities offered by a skilled insider need to be considered.

---

both ICAO and the International Criminal Police Organization (INTERPOL) failed to advise States and airlines of the existence of a database at INTERPOL on forged or fraudulent passports, and that ICAO and other key players concerned would have to adopt a more serious approach to the problem. Information sharing is a central process through which team members collectively utilize their available informational resources. See Abeyratne (2015), p. 18.

[47]CYBER SECURITY IN AVIATION, *AVSECP/25 -WP/34*, 28/2/14 at 3.

[48]*Id*. 1.

[49]*Ibid*.

But overall the current threat likelihood is expected to be LOW".[50] This statement is somewhat puzzling, particularly since the vulnerability of air transport was placed before ICAO by the ICCAIA[51] which, at the Twelfth Air Navigation Conference of ICAO held in Montreal in November 2012, stated that there are already a number of examples of cyber security and vulnerabilities and detailed them in a working paper to the Conference.[52]

It is noteworthy to consider IATA's three pronged approach in this regard: *risk management*—the objective being to help the industry understand the risks and put a framework in place to enable stakeholders to manage those risks consistently and effectively; *advocacy*—the objective being to work with airlines, airports, suppliers, manufacturers and regulators to ensure that standards are developed and implemented where they need to be, and to advocate for emerging regulation to be risk-based and globally coordinated; *reporting and communication*—the objective being to raise awareness of cyber issues and look for mechanisms to allow better sharing of threat information, incidents and mitigation strategies, across the industry.[53] If ICAO were to adopt this approach towards States, both ICAO and IATA would be in sync and collective work in addressing the cyber threat in aviation would be much easier. One of the conclusions of IATA is that the AVSEC Panel recommend that Member States be encouraged to consider the regulation of cyber security for aviation as part of a comprehensive and holistic national plan which covers all enterprise activities within a State, taking into account the vulnerabilities of the larger IT ecosystem.[54]

1.2.5.2 CANSO

On the subject of cybersecurity in air traffic management CANSO advised the AVSEC Panel its fivefold approach to aviation cyber security: *enterprise-wide approach*—as cyber-attacks grow in intensity and become increasingly sophisticated, changing constantly in response to the defensive systems they encounter, it will become necessary to adopt an approach to cybersecurity that is proactive, dynamic, and adaptive, evolving beyond the realm of traditional IT management

---

[50]INITIAL REPORT ON THE RISK OF CYBER ATTACK ON AIRCRAFT SYSTEMS, *AVSECP/26-WP/27*, 20/2/15 at 3.

[51]The International Coordinating Council of Aerospace Industries Associations (ICCAIA) is the international organization of aerospace industry associations. Their members are engaged in the design, development, manufacture and in-service support of aeronautical and space products and technologies, including related ground-based systems.

[52]CYBER SECURITY FOR CIVIL AVIATION, *AN-Conf/12-WP/122*, 9/10/12 at 2–3.

[53]CYBER SECURITY IN AVIATION, *supra*, note 33 at 2.

[54]*Id.* 4.

security culture; *cybersecurity culture*—the commitment of people to protecting their organisation is an essential component of a strong cyber defence. This means a critical part of the cybersecurity programme must be to focus on the human aspects of the organisation—on developing a positive security culture that is grounded in employees' attitudes, evident in the behaviours people exhibit and which is reinforced by the actions of the leadership; *training and awareness*—training is a critical element of security as employees need to understand the value of sensitive information and their role in keeping it safe. Employees need to know the policies and practices they are expected to follow in the workplace regarding cyber security; *monitoring and reporting*—to enable post-incident investigations and support disciplinary action and/or prosecution in the event of a security breach, measures should be taken to ensure that logging of security incidents is enabled for key operational and business systems; and *information-sharing and industry collaboration*—the sharing of information between Air Navigation Service Providers and with industry stakeholders of known or potential cyber threats and vulnerabilities can play a vital part in strengthening the overall response to incidents and their prevention. Information sharing protocols and trust networks provide a means by which information can be shared, analysed, managed and acted upon.[55]

CANSO requested the Panel to consider, *inter alia, encouraging* air traffic management entities follow the *international standards* (my emphasis) and industry best practices that exist for cybersecurity. There is no room for doubt that with this request, CANSO is implying that ICAO should introduce international standards in aviation cyber security.[56] This is consistent with statement of the Rapporteur of the Twenty Fifth ICAO AVSEC Panel who said in his Report that ICAO, through its relevant technical panels, should continue its work on helping to improve the resilience of aviation to the disruption of GNSS signals, including around authentication, encryption, and the use of alternative and multiple surveillance techniques. Based on issues that have been brought to the WGTR's attention, areas to consider could include, inter alia: retention of back-up facilities and redundancy; mitigations against spoofing of ADS-B data; the wider use of multilateration; built in cross-checks of surveillance data; encryption and integration of data; use of public networks for datalinks; and handling of 24-bit aircraft codes.[57] Both CANSO and the Rapporteur seem to be demanding specific standards from ICAO that would assist States in including compelling measures in their national policies.

---

[55]CYBER SECURITY IN ATM, *AVSECP/26-WP/44*, 2/4/15 at 2–3.

[56]*Id.* 4.

[57]REPORT ON THE RISK OF CYBER ATTACK THROUGH AIR TRAFFIC MANAGEMENT SYSTEMS, *AVSECP/25 – WP/4*, 7/2/14 at 4.

1.3 Leasing and Transfer of Functions

1.3.1 Introduction

At the 36th Session of the LC (LC) of the International Civil Aviation Organization (ICAO) the ICAO Secretariat presented a working paper[58] to the Committee, stating, *inter alia* that Article 83 *bis* (of the Chicago Convention[59]), which entered into force on 20 June 1997,[60] provided for the "transfer" of certain functions and duties usually incumbent on the State of Registry of a civil aircraft (the State on whose Registry the aircraft is registered) to the State of that aircraft's operator (the state in which the Operator's principle place of business is located or, if there is no such place, the operator's permanent residence). Article 83 *bis* makes this transfer applicable in cases of lease,[61] charter[62] and interchange[63] of aircraft. *Ex facie* the use of the word "transfer" by the ICAO Secretariat is correct, as the original English version of Article 83 *bis* in the Chicago Convention uses the word "transfer".[64]

The problem, however, arises when one examines related text emanating from ICAO. For instance, ICAO Assembly Resolution A23-13 (Lease, charter and interchange of aircraft in international operations) adopted at the 23rd Assembly in Montreal (16 September–7 October 1980) in Resolving Clause 3 urges *inter alia*

---

[58]Safety Aspects of Economic Liberalization and Article 83 *bis*, LC/36-WP/2-3, 27/10/15.

[59]Convention on International Civil Aviation, signed at Chicago on 7 December 1944. See ICAO Doc 7300/8, Eighth Edition, 2006.

[60]The Protocol which amended the Chicago Convention with the introduction of Article 83 *bis* entered into force on 20 June 1997. By April 2008, 153 parties had deposited their instruments of ratification of Article 83 *bis* with the depository, ICAO.

[61]A lease occurs when an aircraft is used under a contractual leasing agreement. The term has not been defined by ICAO for the reason that various jurisdictions could have differing definitions of a lease according to their applicable legal regimes. See Guidance on the Implementation of Article 83 *bis* of the Convention on International Civil Aviation, *ICAO Cir. 295*, LE/2, Definitions.

[62]In the charter of an aircraft the entire capacity is hired or purchased privately by one or more entities, which may re-sell it to the public (occurring mostly in the case of non-scheduled passenger air operations). See, ICAO Cir. 295, LE/2, *Ibid.*

[63]An interchange is regularly scheduled single plane through service linking a route of one air carrier at the interchange point to a route of a second air carrier, with the same aircraft being crewed by and under the operational control of the respective authorized carrier on each route. See Manual on the Regulation of International Air Transport, *ICAO Doc 9626,* Definitions.

[64]Article 83 *bis* provides *inter alia*: Notwithstanding the provisions of Articles 12, 30, 31 and 32 (a), when an aircraft registered in a contracting State is operated pursuant to an agreement for the lease, charter or interchange of the aircraft or any similar arrangement by an Operator who has his principal place of business or, if he has no such place of business, his permanent residence in another contracting State, the State of Registry may, by agreement with such other State, transfer to it all or part of its functions and duties as State of Registry in respect of that aircraft under Articles 12, 30, 31, and 32(a). The State of Registry shall be relieved of responsibility in respect of the functions and duties transferred. Article 12 pertains to rules of the air; Article 30 relates to the issuance of licences to aircraft and radio equipment; Article 31 pertains to certificates of airworthiness; and Article 32 relates to licensing of personnel.

that in the instance of lease, charter and interchange of aircraft, the State of the Operator change, if necessary, its national regulations to the extent required to empower it both to accept such "delegation" (my emphasis) of functions and to oblige the Operator to fulfil the obligations imposed by Annex 6. To make confusion worse confounded, The ICAO guidance material contained in Circular 295[65] speaks of the "transfer of supervisory functions" from the State of Registry to the State of the Operator of the aircraft, adding a "supervisory" layer to the transfer of functions.

At law, there is a distinct difference between the terms "transfer" and "delegation.[66] Although this is of academic interest in the context of Article 83 *bis* as the terms of the Chicago Convention are clear—that what is addressed is a transfer of functions[67]—this dichotomy which has seemingly been created by ICAO brings to bear the larger issue of liability and accountability of a State for the transfer of certain functions within the parameters of Article 83 *bis*. The main issue would be the determination of State responsibility and accountability. Would the State of Registry be retained as the supervisory State in the context of Circular 295 and therefore be held accountable for liability arising out of functions that are transferred?

The ICAO Circular speaks of supervisory responsibility being transferred from the State of Registry to the State of the Operator[68] which is calculated to make aviation safer on the ground that the State of the Operator would be the closest to the Operator to exercise supervisory authority and ensure safety oversight. The Circular goes on to say that such transfer will impose international responsibilities on the State of the Operator, who will be liable for these functions and implement them in accordance with its own laws and regulations. However, the Circular confuses the issue by first saying, correctly, that the liability of the State of the Operator would be to the extent of the functions transferred, and then going on to say that the laws of both the State of registration and the State of the Operator could apply to an aircraft, depending on the "extent of the transfer". It is not the extent of the transfer that is the key element in this context but the specific functions transferred and the extent of their scope.

When one considers this confusion alongside ICAO's Universal Safety Oversight Audit Programme (USOAP) and its Continuous Monitoring Approach (CMA), the ICAO Safety Oversight Manual poses another challenge, where it is said that Member States shall sign a Memorandum of Understanding (MOU) with ICAO to confirm their full support of the USOAP CMA process and to commit to

[65]*Supra*, n. 51.

[66]Delegation is a process of transferring powers and authority under a contract. A transfer is an assignment of rights and duties.

[67]The Vienna Convention on the Law of Treaties, in Article 31.1 provides that a treaty shall be interpreted in good faith in accordance with the ordinary meaning to be given to the terms of the treaty in their context and in the light of its object and purpose. See Vienna Convention on the Law of Treaties, Concluded at Vienna on 23 May 1969, UN Treaty Series No 18232.

[68]ICAO Cir. 295, *supra*, n. 51, para. 2.4.1.

actively participating in all USOAP CMA activities, including the provision of information through the CMA online framework. Each Member State is required to facilitate USOAP CMA on-site activities by making appropriate staff from its CAA, or other relevant entities, available for interview by the USOAP CMA mission team, as required. Furthermore, each State is obligated to facilitate the work of the USOAP CMA mission team by providing all necessary resources, documents, information, administrative and support functions.[69] The question would be, what is the position of the State of Registry and the State of the Operator in the face of this provision? Would the mere fact that Circular 295 speaks of supervisory jurisdiction of the State of Registry preclude the State of the Operator from this requirement?

Circular 295, although not legally binding on States, implicitly recognizes that one of the main purposes of Article 83 *bis* is to facilitate safety oversight, and that there will be liability of the State of the Operator in relation to the functions that are transferred to it by the State of Registry. The issue is, to what extent would the State of the Operator be liable? For that matter, is there such a thing as State liability?

1.3.2 Transfer of Functions

1.3.2.1 The Process and Its Effects

The original responsibility with regard to the elements necessary for the safety of air navigation, such as airworthiness and qualified and properly licenced technical crew lies with the State of Registry. In other words, the State of Registry has responsibility to issue the certificate of airworthiness, which establishes two requirements: the aircraft conforms to the appropriate airworthiness requirements; and the aircraft is maintained airworthy. The State of Registry has therefore the responsibility to ensure that the aircraft is airworthy even when it is operated by an operator certified by another State. The certificate of airworthiness should be kept valid through proper maintenance. The State of Registry is responsible for the oversight of maintenance organizations, modifications, repairs and other aspects of maintenance of the aircraft. The State of the Operator is responsible for ensuring that the aircraft operator meets its maintenance management responsibilities.

In accordance with established principles of international law, when some functions—such as licensing and ensuring airworthiness of the aircraft—are transferred to the State of the Operator the process of transfer must follow established rules and procedures. Firstly, such functions cannot be transferred from one State to another without a formal agreement between the two States, where both parties must have ratified the Protocol that gives legal legitimacy to Article 83 *bis*.

[69]See Universal Safety Oversight Programme Continuous Monitoring Manual, *Doc 9735*, AN/960, Third Edition: 2011 Para. 4.3.1.

Secondly, the State of the Operator must accept the transfer of functions. Therefore, Article 83 *bis* carries with it two fundamental requisites for the two States concerned: the first being that both States must fully comprehend and recognize the obligations imposed on them by Article 83 *bis*; and secondly both States must admit that Article 83 *bis* would impose those obligations and the State of the Operator must have expressly accepted those obligations in writing. Mere conduct indicating acceptance of obligations is not sufficient.[70]

As discussed earlier, the transfer of functions pertain to obligations of States arising from Articles 12, 30, 31 and 32 (a) of the Chicago Convention. In an agreement of transfer, aircraft subject to the transfer must be clearly identified and specified. The transfer must correspond to the period of operations of the aircraft from and to the State of the Operator. The State of Registry as well as the State of the Operator must enact local legislation that would admit of the transfer of functions and make rules accordingly. The State of Registry bears the responsibility of endorsing certificates issued by the State of the Operator and such endorsement must be evidenced and visible in the documents carried in the aircraft concerned. The authorities of both States must be completely briefed and informed of the conditions pertaining to the transfer of functions. Wherever the aircraft is flown into a contracting State in which the aircraft lands that State has the right to ensure that the aircraft carries adequate evidence in the documents carried in the aircraft[71] by searching the aircraft, as prescribed in Article 16 of the Chicago Convention.[72]

1.3.2.2 ICAO Requirements

The Chicago Convention, in Article 19 provides that the registration or transfer of registration of aircraft in any contracting State is required to be made in accordance with its law and regulations. Furthermore, in Article 21 the Convention requires each contracting State to provide any other contracting State or ICAO, on demand, with information concerning the registration and ownership of any particular

---

[70]This principle is an extension of Article 35 of the *Vienna Convention on the Law of Treaties* which provides that an obligation arises for a third State from a provision of a treaty if the parties to the treaty intend the provision to be the means of establishing the obligation and the third State expressly accepts that obligation in writing. See Vienna Convention, supra, note 11. Also, Aust (2000), p. 208. Although Aust refers to obligations of a third State, such obligations would also apply to a second State, as in the case of Article 83 *bis*.

[71]Article 29 of the Chicago Convention requires that every aircraft of a contracting State, engaged in international navigation, carry, in conformity with the conditions prescribed in the Convention: its certificate of registration; its certificate of airworthiness; the appropriate licenses for each member of the crew; its journey log book; if it is equipped with radio apparatus, the aircraft radio station license; if it carries passengers, a list of their names and places of embarkation and destination; and, If it carries cargo, a manifest and detailed declarations of the cargo.

[72]Article 16 stipulates that the appropriate authorities of each of the contracting States have the right, without unreasonable delay, to search aircraft of the other contracting States on landing or departure, and to inspect the certificates and other documents prescribed by the Convention.

aircraft registered in that State. In addition, each contracting State is required to furnish reports to ICAO, under such regulations as the latter may prescribe, giving such pertinent data as can be made available concerning the ownership and control of aircraft registered in that State and habitually engaged in international air navigation. The data thus obtained by ICAO is to be made available by it on request to the other contracting States.

Article Annex 6 to the Chicago Convention[73] pertaining to operations of aircraft provides *in limine* that an operator is required to ensure that all employees when abroad know that they must comply with the laws, regulations and procedures of those States in which operations are conducted, and that the operator is further required to ensure that all pilots are familiar with the laws, regulations and procedures, pertinent to the performance of their duties, prescribed for the areas to be traversed; the aerodromes to be used and the air navigation facilities relating thereto. The operator has also to ensure that other members of the flight crew are familiar with these laws, regulations and procedures as are pertinent to the performance of their respective duties in the operation of the aeroplane.[74] However, The State also bears responsibility in this regard, as Article 12 of the Convention pertaining to rules of the air provides that it is the contracting State flown over that has to ensure that measures are adopted to insure that every aircraft flying over or maneuvering within its territory and that every aircraft carrying its nationality mark, wherever such aircraft may be, comply with the rules and regulations relating to the flight and maneuver of aircraft there in force. For this objective to be achieved, each contracting State has to keep its own regulations uniform, to the greatest possible extent, with those established from time to time under the Convention.

The responsibility of a third State, as discussed above, is addressed in Annex 6 in the context of a State identifying an instance of non-compliance or suspected non-compliance by a foreign operator with laws, regulations and procedures applicable within that State's territory, or a similar serious safety issue with that operator, where that State is required to immediately notify the operator and, if the issue warrants it, the State of the Operator. Where the State of the Operator and the State of Registry are different, such notification has also to be conveyed to the State of Registry, if the issue falls within the responsibilities of that State and warrants a notification.[75] ICAO Assembly Resolution A38-12, adopted at the 38th session of the Assembly in 2013, provides that certificates of airworthiness and certificates of competency and licences of the flight crew of an aircraft issued or rendered valid by the Member State in which the aircraft is registered shall be recognized as valid by other Member States for the purpose of flight over their territories, including landings and take-offs, subject to the provisions of Articles

---

[73]Annex 6 to the Convention on International Civil Aviation (Operations of Aircraft, Part 1 International Commercial Air Transport—Aeroplanes), 9th Edition, July 2010.

[74]*Id*, 3.1.1 and 3.1.2.

[75]*Id*. 3.2.1.

32 (b) and 33 of the Convention, and pending the coming into force of international Standards respecting particular categories of aircraft or flight crew and certificates issued or rendered valid, under national regulations, by the Member State in which the aircraft is registered are also required to be recognized by other Member States for the purpose of flight over their territories, including landings and take-offs.[76]

An important ICAO requirement with regard to State responsibility for ensuring airworthiness is rulemaking. As a preliminary requisite, States are required to promulgate primary aviation legislation, such as a national civil aviation code or a civil aviation act that establishes a State's civil aviation organization. The Chicago Convention in most of its Articles refers to national laws and regulations relating to departure from a State's territory of civil aircraft engaged in international air commerce. The Convention also refers to State regulations in respect to operation, airworthiness and registration of such aircraft within its territory.[77] The airworthiness regulations developed, adopted or accepted by the State should include provisions for: mandatory registration of all aircraft; and implementation of the airworthiness provisions meeting the requirements of the Chicago Convention and the Annexes. Furthermore, all aircraft on the State's aircraft register are required to meet relevant airworthiness criteria approved or adopted by the State. The issuance, validation or acceptance of the type certificate[78] for aircraft intended to be entered on the State's aircraft register must be ensured.

Other airworthiness responsibilities of the State issuing documents for aircraft are: the issuance of production certificates or approvals of manufacturing organizations when applicable; issuance, renewal, validation or acceptance of aircraft certificates of airworthiness; issuance of export certificates of airworthiness; issuance or acceptance of ADs, bulletins and orders; issuance, amendment, cancellation and suspension of airworthiness approvals, licences and certificates; authorization of persons or organizations, on behalf of the CAA, to perform particular tasks in

[76]Resolution A38-12, Consolidated statement of continuing ICAO policies and associated practices related specifically to air navigation, *Appendix C*, p. II-8. See Assembly Resolutions in Force (as of 4 October 2014), *Doc 10022* at 24. It must be mentioned that Assembly Resolutions are considered by experts in international law as mere results of political compromises with no legal effect. See Shaw (2003), p. 110. *Brownlie* has expressed the view that decisions by international conferences and organizations can in principle only bind those States accepting them. See Brownlie (1990), p. 691.

[77]Airworthiness Manual, ICAO *Doc 9760*, AN/967, Third Edition, 2014 at 2.1.2. The Manual also provides, *inter alia* that primary aviation legislation should contain provisions to establish a civil aviation administration that proactively supervises and regulates civil aviation activities. The legislation should contain provisions for the approval and safety oversight of air operators, aircraft maintenance organizations, and maintenance training organizations for the safe operation of aircraft. It should also establish requirements for the qualification and licensing of maintenance personnel. *Id.* 2.2.1.

[78]The State of Design, upon receipt of satisfactory evidence that the aircraft type is in compliance with the design aspects of the appropriate airworthiness requirements, is required to issue a type certificate to define the design and to signify approval of the design of the aircraft type. See Annex 8 to the Chicago Convention, Airworthiness of Aircraft, 11th Edition, July 2010 at 1.4.1.

relation to the design, manufacture and maintenance of aircraft, components and parts for the issuance of State approvals, licences and certificates, as appropriate; and authorization of persons and organizations, on behalf of the CAA, to inspect and test aircraft, aircraft components, standard parts, materials or processes and systems for the purpose of ascertaining whether the processes and activities covered by an approval, licence or certificate have been carried out in a satisfactory manner, as appropriate.[79]

The ICAO requirements discussed above are translated by States through the making of rules. A rule has been defined in the United States as the whole or part of an agency statement of general or particular applicability and future effect designed to implement, interpret, or prescribe law or policy.[80] In the aviation context, The Aviation Rulemaking Advisory Committee was created by authority from the Federal Aviation Administration, which was charged with developing FAA regulations on the basis of consensual decision making.[81]

Both the State of Registry and the State of the Operator must be in sync in their rulemaking with regard to the transfer of functions under Article 83 *bis*. They should exchange rulemaking intentions and priorities of the participants to align as much as possible their respective rulemaking programmes by; identifying rulemaking initiatives of common interest that through regulatory collaboration would allow the agencies of the two States to obviate unnecessary divergence and duplication of work; and maximize resource use and mobilization and harmonize rules as much as possible for consistency.

1.4 State Liability at International Law

A typical instance where liability might arise in respect of a State in the context of Article 83 *bis* is where a State organ or agency, charged with certification of aircraft or airworthiness or the licencing of crew would negligently be in breach of that duty. In the 1927 *Massey* case[82] the decision of which can be analogically applied to

[79]*Id.* 3.2.

[80]5 U.S.C. §551(4). The APA itself is 5 U.S.C. §§551 et seq. There are three types of rules: The first category is *Legislative* or *Substantive Rules* which essentially implement a Statute or which may be derived from a bilateral treaty. In either case *Legislative Rules* have the binding force of law, obligating those who are charged with implementing such rules to strict adherence; For example, such a rule might say: "you must not operate your aircraft without a valid certificate of airworthiness issued by the State of the Operator"; The second category is *Non-legislative Rules*, which are essentially guidance rules; The third category is *Interpretive Rules* which advise the public as to what the rulemaking agency intends the statute and the rules the agency administers to convey. For example, the agency might tell you how it defines "volcanic eruption".

[81]Kerwin (2003), p. 199.

[82]*Gertrude Parker Massey (U.S.A.)* v. *United Mexican States,* Reports of International Arbitral Awards, 15 April 1927, Volume IV pp. 155–164.

a breach of an obligation under Article 83 *bis,* the Mexican Government was held liable for its servants not taking proper care in effectively retaining and apprehending a Mexican national who had killed a US citizen working in a Mexican workplace. Courts awarded damages to the wife of the deceased for the negligence. *Massey* involved the killing of an American subject by a Mexican, who was thereafter arrested and imprisoned. The assistant jail-keeper unlawfully permitted the accused to escape. There was no evidence adduced by the defence to show that the appropriate authorities look effective action to apprehend the accused. The court held the respondent Mexican government liable for the omission of one of its workers—the jail-keeper—who allowed the escape of the accused. The reasoning of the court was that there was responsibility on the part of respondent Government without regard to whether the jail-keeper was subsequently punished. The court concluded that when misconduct of any official, whatever his status or rank, results in the failure of a State to perform its international obligations, it is responsible. The circumstance that deceased American subject may have been guilty of misconduct held no bar to claim.[83] Commissioner Nielson who delivered the judgment opined that it was a sound principle to recognize that when negligence or misconduct of a State official or worker resulted in the breach of an obligation under international law, it was just and equitable to hold the State responsible. It was also held that the position of the State officer or worker, whether high or low, was immaterial.

Similarly, in the *Rainbow Warrior* incident of 1985, where a ship belonging to the Greenpeace Movement—The Rainbow Warrior—was blasted by explosives on 10 July on New Zealand waters, which killed a Portuguese crew member . A Portuguese crew member, Fernando Pereira, was killed in the explosions. The Rainbow Warrior had been involved in protests over French nuclear testing in the Pacific. The crime was imputed to the French Secret Service (DGSE) agents who were sent to prevent the Rainbow Warrior from leaving for another protest campaign elsewhere. As a consequence, two French officers were imprisoned. Although the act was committed against Greenpeace—an international organization—the New Zealand government pursued its prosecution of the French government, resulting in threats and intimidation from the French aimed at New Zealand, particularly on the international trade front.. On 8 July 1986, United Nations Secretary-General Javier Perez de Cuellar announced, in a binding decision, that New Zealand would receive an apology and compensation of $13 million from France, where the latter was also ordered not to interfere with New Zealand's trade negotiations.[84]

The *Corfu Channel* case[85] The International Court of Justice was of the view that the legal possibility of imposing liability upon a State wherever an official could be linked to that State encourages a State to be more cautious of its responsibility in

---

[83]*Id*, at 155.

[84]See New Zealand History at http://www.nzhistory.net.nz/politics/nuclear-free-new-zealand/rain bow-warrior.

[85]ICJ Reports, 1949.

controlling those responsible for carrying out tasks for which the State could be ultimately held responsible. In the same context, the responsibility of placing mines was attributed to Albania since the court attributed to Albania the responsibility, as Albania was known to have knowledge of the placement of mines although it did not know who exactly carried out the act.

When, on 4 December 2001, Israeli military forces attacked Gaza International airport, destroyed air navigation facilities and bombarded runways and taxiways until the airport became unserviceable, the Palestinian Authority claimed that the destroyed airport and air navigation facilities were used for the transportation of civilian passengers, search and rescue operations in case of emergencies, transportation of rescue material, including medical equipment, medicines and survival kits for safeguarding human lives. When the dispute was brought before the ICAO Council, it adopted a resolution strongly urging Israel to take the necessary measures to restore Gaza International Airport so as to allow its reopening as soon as possible, presumably under the notion that Israel was accountable and therefore had to make reparation to Palestine. The International Court of Justice concluded that Israel was accountable in this instance to individuals as well, who suffered injury or damage as a result of the Israeli attack.[86]

An interesting development in State accountability is a relatively recent shift from the top-down approach of State accountability—where States brought actions against individuals or other legal persons—to the bottom-up approach where individuals could bring an action against a State seeking its accountability.[87] In an interesting case[88] where the responsibility of the United Nations was brought into question, it was held by the European Court of Human Rights (ECtHR) that "the United Nations Security Council [(SC)] had neither effective control nor ultimate authority and control over the acts and omissions of troops within the Multi-National Force and that the applicant's detention was not, therefore, attributable to the United Nations", but the internment of the applicant was attributable to the United Kingdom as it was British troops that had committed the wrongful act in Iraq.[89] The court, on this basis, ascribed responsibility to the United Kingdom. When there is involvement by both a State or States and an international Organization (comprised of member states) such as NATO, Courts are inclined to ascribe joint and several liability to both.[90] This approach to liability is based on the theory of authority and control where the servants of a State perpetrating an act are under the control of both the international organization and the State concerned.

---

[86]Legal Consequences of the Construction of a Wall in the Occupied Palestinian Territory, Advisory Opinion, *ICJ Reports 2004*, p. 136 at 198, para. 153.

[87]See Brown Weiss (2007), p. 259.

[88]*Al-Jedda* v *The United Kingdom, Judgement of 7 July 2011*, [2011] ECtHR (Ser 1092), para. 84.

[89]*Id.*, para. 86.

[90]Boon (2011), p. 2.

The right of individuals to hold States accountable for injuries or damage suffered is also supported by the International Law Commission.[91] So it is with the United Nations Compensation Commission which was established in 1991 to go into claims of those who suffered from the Iraqi invasion of Kuwait. The claims that the Commission handled amounted to more than 2.6 million and compensation sought under these claims was about $352 billion. Similarly another Commission—the Eritrea-Ethiopia Claims Commission—which was established in 2000 to compensate entities and individuals who claimed that they had suffered from violations of international humanitarian law, addressed issues of State accountability and reparation. The Iran-US claims tribunal is another example where an individual successfully argued that Iran was liable for the acts of intimidation and harassment he suffered under the hands of Iranian citizens which prompted the former to leave Iran, which resulted in significant property loss.[92] However, this decision lost its force when, in a subsequent case the Tribunal required evidence of directives of the Iranian authorities—the Revolutionary Guard—that caused such intimidation to individuals.[93]

One commentator is of the view that: "imposing upon the State absolute liability wherever an official is involved encourages that State to exercise greater control over its departments and representatives.[94] However, there is an unwritten rule that the State cannot ipso *facto* be held liable for each and every act of its servants and liability could be imposed only for acts that can be imputed or attributed to the State.[95] The concept of attribution is contained in Article IV of the International Law Commission's Draft Rules of State Responsibility which state that the act of any organ of State, if it exercises legislative, judicial or executive powers, can be attributed to the State, whatever that organ's position in the State is and wherever in the hierarchy of that it is located.

One commentator comes to the conclusion that State accountability is not strictly legal although it may have legal, political and moral characteristics. She argues that this is because State accountability is a concept and not a legal principle where Kelsen's *pure theory of law*[96] can be applied as in other purely legal

[91] *Draft Articles on Responsibility of States for Internationally Wrongful Acts, Adopted by the International Law Commission* (53rd Session, 2001), Text adopted by the International Law Commission at its 53rd session, in 2001, and submitted to the General Assembly as a part of the Commission's report covering the work of that session (A/56/10), Article 33 (2).

[92] *Short* v. *Islamic Republic of Iran*, (1987) 16 Iran-US Cl Trib Rep 76.

[93] *Rankin* v. *Islamic Republic of Iran*, (1987) 17 Iran –US Cl Trib Rep 245.

[94] Shaw (2003), p. 700.

[95] In the *Corfu Channel Case*, The International Court of Justice held: "It cannot be concluded from the mere fact of the control exercised by the State over its territory and waters that that State necessarily knew, or ought to have known, of any unlawful act perpetrated therein, nor yet that it necessarily knew, or should have known, the authors. This fact, by itself, and apart from other circumstances, neither involves *prima facie* responsibility nor shifts the burden of proof". See *supra*, note 29, pp. 4 and 18.

[96] The Austrian jurist and philosopher Hans Kelsen (1881–1973) propounded his pure theory of law on the basis that the law existed for the pristine purpose of providing an explanation of legality and the normativity of law, and that therefore law was pure and unmixed with other disciplines relating to politics, sociology and morality. Therefore, according to Kelsen the law is a scheme of interpretation, based purely on its legal meaning. See Stanford Encyclopedia of Philosophy at http://plato.stanford.edu/entries/lawphil-theory/.

applications.[97] This is purely a jurisprudential argument that has to be tested against the various judicial decisions that have been discussed in this article.[98]

1.5 Remotely Piloted Aircraft Systems

1.5.1 Introduction

The 36th Session of the Legal Committee (LC) of the International Civil Aviation Organization (ICAO) was held from 30 November to 3 December 2015. One of the items under discussion was on legal issues pertaining to remotely piloted aircraft systems (RPAS) as a new component of the civil aviation system. The item had been placed on the agenda by the Council of ICAO—the governing body of the LC—pursuant to a discussion that emanated from the 38th Session of the ICAO Assembly held in 2013, whereby the Assembly had recommended that the Council further study the subject of RPAS. At the LC discussion, The ICAO Secretariat presented the LC with a paper which discussed the current regulatory position of RPAS under various existing instruments and offered various interpretations of terminology as background information for the LC. The Secretariat paper was purely informative and analytical in nature, presumably intended as a catalyst for discussion. Although the paper was acknowledged to be of high quality (as it well deserved) and endorsed as such by the majority of members of the LC, the Committee also noted that certain issues relating to the liability regime remained unaddressed. Consensually, the LC was of the view that the legal study on RPAS should remain in the agenda of the LC for some time, until all relevant legal issues on the subject were thoroughly studied and examined. Some of the issues identified by the LC as requiring attention were: the definition of aircraft in flight in the context of RPAS against the backdrop of existing legal instruments; operations over the high seas; cross border operations; and the responses of member States to a questionnaire that should be sent by ICAO.

At the 38th Session of the ICAO Assembly in 2013, the Republic of Korea submitted a working paper[99] on RPAS,[100] claiming that between the first official

[97]See Yarwood (2011), p. 159.

[98]It is interesting to debate this point against the backdrop of the judicial pronouncement in the *Charzow Factory Case* where the Permanent Court of International Justice said that: "it is a principle of international law that any breach of an engagement involves an obligation to make reparation". See *PCIJ Series A, No. 17, 1928,* p. 29.

[99]Legal Framework of Remotely Piloted Aircraft—Liability Matters, *A38-WP/262, LE/7*, 10/9/13.

[100]RPAS were originally identified as unmanned aerial vehicles (UAV). An Unmanned Aircraft System (UAS) was an aircraft and its associated elements which are operated with no pilot on board. UAS was an overarching term for the entire system comprising a UAV which is applied to describe a self-piloted or remotely piloted aircraft that can carry cameras, sensors, communications equipment or other payloads, as well those which support unmanned flights such as air traffic

instance of discussion of RPAS in ICAO—which was at the first meeting of the 169th session of ICAO Council on April 12th, 2005—to discussions in 2011, liability for RPAS accidents had not been discussed.[101] In this context, it must be noted that in early 2011, as a result of sustained work carried out on RPAS by ICAO, the Organization released a Manual[102] the purposes of which was to: apprise States of the emerging ICAO perspective on the integration of RPAS into non-segregated airspace and at aerodromes; consider the fundamental differences from manned aviation that such integration will involve; and encourage States to help with the development of ICAO policy on RPAS by providing information on their own experiences associated with RPAS. The fundamental premise that ICAO follows in this regard is that, since unmanned aircraft fall within the definition of "aircraft" all SARPs of the Annexes to the Chicago Convention applicable to aircraft would apply to RPAS as well.

The Korean paper went on to discuss various regimes of liability that might impact the operations of RPAS—in particular the Montreal Convention of 1999[103] and the modernized Rome Conventions of 2009[104]—and requested the ICAO Assembly to review the information and assessment presented in the paper; organize a study group, as the case of Unmanned Aircraft System Study Group (RPASSG), to discuss under the LC; and establish a data collection and sharing system for the issues of RPAS accidents and incidents and associated liability which may be led by ICAO.[105] The working paper exclusively addressed liability issues regarding RPAS.

Accordingly, the ICAO Council confirmed and approved the General Work Programme of the LC, including the subject of a RPAS liability study as priority number 4 in the work programme of the LC.[106] In compliance with the action of the

management and remote controllers of such aircraft. The first recorded use of a UAV in its most incipient form has been traced to 8 March 1918. See Weibel and Hansman (2009), p. 19. See also generally Newcome (2004). In World War I the US Navy used an "aerial torpedo to confront German U boats, as a result of which the "speed Scout" was developed by a private US company which was controlled by auto pilot and could be launched from warships carrying a payload of 1000 lbs.1001'9.

[101]For a discussion on ICAO's work on RPAS see Abeyratne (2011a), pp. 239–260. Also Abeyratne and Khan (2016).

[102]Unmanned Aircraft Systems (UAS), Manual *328-AN/190*.

[103]*Convention for the Unification of Certain rules for International Carriage by Air* done at Montreal on 28 May 1999. The Convention entered into force on 4 November 2003 109 States Parties have ratified the Convention.

[104]Convention on Compensation for Damage Caused by Aircraft to Third Parties, ICAO DCCD Doc No. 42 [General Risk Convention], and Convention on Compensation for Damage to Third Parties, Resulting from Acts of Unlawful Interference Involving Aircraft, ICAO DCCD Doc No. 43 [Unlawful Interference Convention].

[105]*Supra*, note 2, p. 1.

[106]C-DEC 203/5.

38th Session of the Assembly and in compliance with the Council's decision, the ICAO Secretariat undertook a study of the issue of liability as it relates to RPAS. One of the interesting points here, which neither the ICAO Secretariat nor the LC had seemingly considered is that, while the Korean initiative at the ICAO Assembly was to seek a study on liabilities per se by ICAO, which the Council mandated the LC to pursue, the overall ICAO goal is—according to The ICAO Manual on Remotely Piloted Aircraft Systems (Doc 11019)—to provide an international regulatory framework through Standards and Recommended Practices (SARPs) with supporting Procedures from Air Navigations Services (PANS) and guidance material so that RPAS could operate under the same philosophy followed by other aircraft.[107] The ICAO Remotely Controlled Aircraft Systems (RPAS) Panel is pursuing the goal enunciated in the Manual.

Doc 10019 quotes the Secretariat paper eight times, merely to say that the document states that civil aviation has, to this point, been based on the notion of a pilot operating the aircraft from within the aircraft itself and more often than not with passengers on board. The study also alluded to aspects of airworthiness and certification. One might have expected the ICAO Secretariat study to have based the examination of liabilities under the various chapters of the Manual, as such chapters would form future SARPs and liabilities that would have emerged from such provisions would have tied the legal and technical aspects well. Some of the chapters in the Manual that would have been relevant in the context of liabilities are on: responsibilities of the RPAS operator; safety management; licencing and competencies; operations-detection and avoidance; air traffic control communications; remote pilot stations; and use of aerodromes. The Secretariat had two whole years to examine liabilities in these areas.

1.5.2 *The ICAO Secretariat Study*

Discussions at the 36th session of the LC on the subject of RPAS centred entirely on the Secretariat working paper.[108] *In limine*, the LC noted the ICAO Secretariat comment that Annex 7 to the Chicago Convention[109] made it unequivocal that remotely piloted aircraft (RPAS) are simply one type of unmanned aircraft.[110]

---

[107]See Manual on Remotely Piloted Aircraft Systems, *ICAO Doc 11019, AN/507*, First Edition: 2015, FORWORD at (V).

[108]Study of Legal Issues Relating to Remotely Piloted Aircraft, *LC/36-WP/2-4*, 26/10/15.

[109]Convention on International Civil Aviation, signed at Chicago on 7 December 1944. See *ICAO Doc 7300/8* Eighth Edition: 2006.

[110]The original definition of aircraft in Annex stated that an "aircraft" is "any machine that can derive support in the atmosphere from the reactions of the air." Amendments to Annex 7 adopted in 1967 included a new definition of "aircraft" as "any machine that can derive support in the atmosphere from the reactions of the air other than the reactions of the air against the earth's surface," seemingly to exclude hovercraft from its scope.

It was also noted that a provision existed in the Chicago Convention itself pertaining to "pilotless aircraft."[111] The Convention provides that a pilotless aircraft cannot be flown over the territory of a State without "special authorization". The ICAO Secretariat has focused on the words "special authorization" and concluded that the authorization required for a pilotless aircraft to fly over a State's territory required an authorization that was specially granted, as against authorization granted generally to commercial aircraft on the basis of bilateral air services agreements entered into between States. Article 6 of the Chicago Convention, which is the applicable provision for bilateral air services agreements, provides that "no scheduled international air service may be operated over or into the territory of a contracting State, except with the special permission or other authorization of that State". It must be noted that this provision calls for "special permission or other authorization". The argument of the Secretariat on the one hand effectively precludes a regular and sustained scheduled air service under a bilateral air services agreement operating aircraft without a pilot—which could be a regular feature in commercial air transport in the future—and on the other, quibbles on a distinction between "special authorization" and "other authorization". The fact that Article 6 requires "special permission" for scheduled airlines to fly over a State's territory has not influenced the ICAO Secretariat sufficient to ascribe to the draftsmen of the Convention the thought that it would not have been elegant to repeat the word "special" in Article 6 and that authorization is authorization, special or otherwise. In this context it is also worthy of note that in another instance, in Article 3c), the Chicago Convention uses the words "without authorization by special agreement or otherwise".

The above notwithstanding, it is submitted that the Secretariat study makes a correct interpretation of Article 8 on the subject of the words "no aircraft capable of being flown without a pilot" with further focus on the words "without a pilot", concluding that Article 8 applies only to remotely controlled aircraft (from the ground, via radio signals). However, the study does not go into specifics to elucidate further. For instance, an RPAS is not an aircraft capable of being flown without a pilot. The ICAO Manual on RPAS[112] clearly defines an RPAS as "an unmanned aircraft which is piloted from a remote pilot station" and goes on to define a remote pilot as "a person charged by the operator with duties essential to the operation of a remotely piloted aircraft and who manipulates the flight controls as appropriate".[113] Therefore, clearly Article 8 of the Chicago Convention would not apply to an RPAS.

---

[111]Article 8 of the Chicago Convention, *supra*, n. 13, provides that: "no aircraft capable of being flown without a pilot shall be flown without a pilot over the territory of a contracting State without special authorization by that State and in accordance with the terms of such authorization. Each contracting State undertakes to insure that the flight of such aircraft without a pilot in regions open to civil aircraft shall be so controlled as to obviate danger to civil aircraft".

[112]*Doc 10019, supra*, n. 107.

[113]*Id.* Definitions.

The Secretariat study then goes on to quote Article 32 of the Chicago Convention and concludes that the provision refers to a pilot "on board an aircraft". However, Article 32 which provides that the pilot of every aircraft and the other members of the operating crew of every aircraft engaged in international navigation will be provided with certificates of competency and licenses issued or rendered valid by the State in which the aircraft is registered. One cannot comprehend how the Secretariat concluded that Article 32 refers only to a pilot "on board" an aircraft. On the contrary, a remote pilot, as defined above, would be a pilot operating an aircraft engaged in air navigation (one does not have to be in the aircraft to navigate it) and could well come within Article 32 of the Chicago Convention. After this intriguing conclusion, the Secretariat study correctly observes that Amendment No. 43 of Annex 2 to the Chicago Convention (Rules of the Air) which was adopted in 2012 has included a Standard requiring remote pilots to be licensed in a manner consistent with Annex 1 (Personnel Licensing).

This is followed by another inscrutable statement in the study that since Article 33 of the Convention provides that certificates of airworthiness and certificates of competency and licenses issued or rendered valid by the contracting State in which the aircraft is registered will be recognized as valid by the other contracting States, provided that the requirements under which such certificates or licenses were issued or rendered valid are equal to or above the minimum standards which may be established from time to time pursuant to this Convention, and because "certificates of competency and licenses" as alluded to in Article 33 specifically refers to the certificates and licenses mandated for pilots and crew members on board aircraft under Article 32, a "remote pilot" is not considered a "pilot" within the meaning of Article 32, and the requirement for mutual recognition of certificates and licenses under Article 33 does not extend to certificates and licenses for remote pilots.

The rest of the Secretariat study is a simple explanation of the provisions of the Montreal Convention of 1999 and the Compensation and Liability Conventions of 2009, with the statement that all three treaties would apply to RPAS and that ICAO has found a "myriad" issues arising out of the removal of the pilot from the aircraft.[114] None of these issues has either been identified or analyzed and it is hoped that a further study would attempt this task.

Since the Republic of Korea initially requested the Secretariat Study in 2013 at the ICAO Assembly, and the LC examined the issue of RPAS on the basis of liability, it is surprising that the legal issues that might arise from the liability of a carrier (not just that of RPAS) when an RPAS causes an accident to a regular commercial carrier (with a pilot on board) was not discussed. One of the major issues that the operation of RPAS raises is the danger they cause to other scheduled commercial carriers.[115] In such instances, what would be the liability of the operator of the RPAS? Would it raise different issues if the RPAS was operated

[114]Secretariat Study, *supra*, n. 108 at A-14.

[115]The Washington Post recorded in August 2015 that on a given day 12 episodes—including other incidents in New Mexico, Texas, Illinois, Florida and North Carolina—were recorded on of

internationally and came from a foreign country? Could the commercial carrier whose flight was adversely affected plead the exceptions of liability under the Warsaw Convention of 1929 or Montreal Convention of 1999 as the case may be?

Would the issue of State accountability be a consideration if an RPAS was operated internationally and caused an accident? It is submitted that, even at a later stage of the inquiry of the LC, the issue of State accountability must be on the agenda. Although such instances would commonly involve military RPAS, and the Chicago Convention does not apply to State aircraft, it is a fact that Article 3c) of the Convention has a peremptory requirement that no State aircraft shall fly over the territory of another State or land thereon without authorization or special agreement or otherwise, and in accordance with such terms of the authorization or special agreement. There is also Article 9 which stipulates *inter alia* that each contracting State may, for reasons of military necessity or public safety, restrict or prohibit uniformly the aircraft of other States from flying over certain areas of its territory, provided that no distinction in this respect is made between the aircraft of the State whose territory is involved, engaged in international scheduled airline services, and the aircraft of the other contracting States likewise engaged. Article 9 goes on to say that such prohibited areas shall be of reasonable extent and location so as not to interfere unnecessarily with air navigation.

Accountability is the natural progression of responsibility. However, holding States accountable for a breach of responsibility is a difficult task in the face of the dichotomy between State sovereignty and the perceived impotence of international law as a punitive mechanism. This reason has so far precluded State accountability from being accepted as *jus cogens*—a peremptory norm of international law. The word "accountability" has not been used often as the word "responsibility" for State actions.[116] However, there is a distinct link between enforcing accountability and the prevention of States from shirking accountability that flows from responsibility. In UN General Assembly Resolution 64/10 of 2010 which dealt with the Report on the Gaza Conflict between Israel and Palestine, one *Whereas* clause stresses "the need to ensure accountability for all violations of international humanitarian law and international human rights law in order to prevent impunity, ensure justice, deter further violations and promote peace" and *inter alia* calls upon the Government of Israel to take all appropriate steps, within a period of 3 months, to undertake investigations that are independent, credible and in conformity with international standards into the serious violations of international humanitarian and international

small drones interfering with airplanes or coming too close to airports, according to previously undisclosed reports filed with the Federal Aviation Administration. See Whitlock (2015).

[116]For example, in the aftermath of the downing of Malaysian Airlines Flight MH 17 over Ukrainian airspace in July 2014, US Secretary of State John Kerry demanded that Moscow take responsibility for actions of pro-Russian rebels in eastern Ukraine whom Washington suspects of downing the jet with a missile, and expressed disgust at their "grotesque" mishandling of the bodies. See http://www.cnbc.com/2014/07/20/us-presses-case-against-russia-on-mh17.html. For a discussion on Flight MH 17 see also Abeyratne (2014a). Published on line 2 October 2014.

human rights law reported by the Fact-Finding Mission, towards ensuring accountability and justice.[117]

Tied in with Article 3c) of the Chicago Convention is a State's accountability to an individual for damage caused by that State's RPAS. The right of individuals to hold States accountable for injuries or damage suffered is also supported by the International Law Commission.[118] So it is with the United Nations Compensation Commission which was established in 1991 to go into claims of those who suffered from the Iraqi invasion of Kuwait. The claims that the Commission handled amounted to more than 2.6 million and compensation sought under these claims was about $352 billion. Similarly another Commission—the Eritrea-Ethiopia Claims Commission—which was established in 2000 to compensate entities and individuals who claimed that they had suffered from violations of international humanitarian law, addressed issues of State accountability and reparation. The Iran-US claims tribunal is another example where an individual successfully argued that Iran was liable for the acts of intimidation and harassment he suffered under the hands of Iranian citizens which prompted the former to leave Iran, which resulted in significant property loss.

1.5.3 Safety as an Unexplored Issue

The threat faced by military drones (in particular) to civil aircraft could be ominous. It is an incontrovertible fact that those responsible for operating RPAS such as the remotely-piloted Predator MQ-1 or Reaper MQ-9 aircraft do not usually seek nor receive such permission as is prescribed by Article 3c). These RPAS which patrol the skies in some regions of the world carry sophisticated weapons such as Hellfire missiles and laser-guided bombs, and are programmed to launch lethally accurate strikes against terrorists in conflict areas of the world. There may not be a pilot in the cockpit, but each Reaper, a bigger, deadlier version of the Predator, requires more than 180 people to keep it flying. A pilot is always at the controls (albeit from a base that might be 7500 miles, or 12,000 km, away); and another officer operates its sensors and camera.[119]

The ICAO RPAS Manual recognizes a State in which hazards and risks to safety are reduced and alludes to safety management systems as systematic approaches to managing safety, including the necessary organizational structures infrastructure,

---

[117]Resolution 64/10, Follow-up to the report of the United Nations Fact-Finding Mission on the Gaza Conflict, 1 December 2009.

[118]Draft Articles on Responsibility of States for Internationally Wrongful Acts, Adopted by the International Law Commission (53rd Session, 2001), Text adopted by the International Law Commission at its fifty-third session, in 2001, and submitted to the General Assembly as a part of the Commission's report covering the work of that session (A/56/10), Article 33 (2).

[119]See Drones And The Law: America's Attacks on Suspected Terrorists Should Be More Closely Monitored, *The Economist*, 8th October 2011 at http://www.economist.com/node/21531477.

formalities and procedures.[120] It also goes on to define safety performance, safety risk and performance indicators. In mid-2015 the National Aeronautical and Space Administration (NASA) of the United States planned the first tests of an air traffic control system for RPAS, with cellular operator Verizon scheduled to introduce a concept for using cell coverage for data, navigation, surveillance and tracking of drones by 2017. The phone company hopes to finalize its technology by 2019.[121] It must be underscored that the preliminary aim of the guidance material in the ICAO Manual 10019 is to ensure aviation safety based on the fact that the risk of mid-air collisions between RPAS and aircraft manned by pilots on board is a critical safety concern for RPAS operations worldwide. Accident investigation therefore becomes crucial both in cases where accidents cause death or injury to persons and damage to property and in instances where no collision occurs between RPAS and manned aircraft, in order to determine what aspect of the operation failed, whether additional, previously unanticipated hazards were contributory, and what deficiencies need to be corrected to prevent such an event from progressing to a more serious outcome in the future.

Safety has many aspects in aviation, which are addressed below. To begin with, the Manual makes explicit mention of Article 8 of the Chicago Convention, which, as earlier discussed, requires special authorization by the State flown over by an aircraft capable of being flown without a pilot which is in fact flown without a pilot. In this context the Manual clarifies any obfuscation that may arise as to what a "pilotless aircraft" is by quoting another ICAO document which states that Article 8 refers to an aircraft which is flown without a pilot in command on board the aircraft but which is either remotely or fully controlled from another place (ground, another aircraft or space).

1.5.3.1 Pilotless Aircraft

One of the main issues addressed by the Manual is that aircraft operating without a pilot on board present a wide array of hazards to the civil aviation system. These hazards must be identified and the safety risks mitigated, just as with introduction of an airspace redesign, new equipment or procedures. In this regard, States are required to establish a State Security Programme (SSP) to include safety rulemaking, policy development and oversight. The operation of RPAS in desegregated airspace would not only affect operations carried by commercial air

---

[120] At the Directors General of Civil Aviation Conference on a Global Strategy for Aviation Safety, convened by the International Civil Aviation Organization in Montreal from 20 to 22 March 2006, Canada defined a Safety Management System as a businesslike approach to safety. An SMS is a systematic, explicit and comprehensive process for the management of safety risks that integrates operations and technical systems with financial and human resource management, for all activities related to an air operator as an approved maintenance organization's certificate holder.

[121] *First Steps Toward Drone Traffic Management*, Nasa Ames, November 19, 2015 at https://www.nasa.gov/feature/ames/first-steps-toward-drone-traffic-management.

carriers but would also affect general aviation. The International Council of Aircraft Owner and Pilot Association (IAOPA) has commented on the issue of RPAS that operating rules for RPAS must take into account their potential impact on general aviation aircraft operating in un-segregated airspace. IAOPA added that while segregated airspace contains operations subject to air traffic control, un-segregated airspace depends almost entirely on certain Annex 2 (to the Chicago Convention) cruising altitude conventions and mutual self-separation methods. Because self-separation methods for RPAS are still in the conceptual stage and will likely require some time to perfect, there will be a temptation to impose un-segregated airspace restrictions on manned aircraft to accommodate RPAS. Since un-segregated airspace is almost entirely the domain of general aviation, we do not want this to occur.

The second point raised by IAOPA is that State or military RPAS must abide by whatever RPAS operating rules are devised to ensure safe, hazard-free operations. Because non-civil RPAS operations may wish to use lower altitude un-segregated airspace, there could be a tendency for States and the military to pre-empt conventional flight rules in these areas, either on a temporary or permanent basis.

1.5.3.2 Compliance with ICAO Standards

The answer to the two points raised by IAOPA seemingly rests with the fact that RPAS will operate in accordance with ICAO Standards that exist for manned aircraft as well as any special and specific standards that address the operational, legal and safety differences between manned and unmanned aircraft operations. This includes applicable environmental rules and guidelines as well. In order for RPAS to integrate into non-segregated airspace and at non-segregated aerodromes, there will be a pilot responsible for the RPAS operation. Pilots may utilize equipment such as an autopilot to assist in the performance of their duties; however, under no circumstances will the pilot responsibility be replaced by technologies in the foreseeable future. For greater fluidity in identifying who the pilot is, the Manual has introduced the concept of "remotely-piloted aircraft" (RPAS)—which is a subset of unmanned aircraft—into the lexicon. An RPAS is an aircraft piloted by a licensed "remote pilot" situated at a "remote pilot station" located external to the aircraft (i.e. ground, ship, another aircraft, space) who monitors the aircraft at all times and can respond to instructions issued by ATC, communicates via voice or data link as appropriate to the airspace or operation, and has direct responsibility for the safe conduct of the aircraft throughout its flight. An RPAS may possess various types of auto-pilot technology but at any time the remote pilot can intervene in the management of the flight. This equates to the ability of the pilot of a manned aircraft being flown by its auto flight system to take prompt control of the aircraft.

1.5.3.3 Collision Avoidance

In terms of collision avoidance, a fundamental principle is that the pilot in command of a RPAS is as responsible as a pilot of a manned aircraft for detecting and avoiding potential collisions and other hazards. Furthermore, technology to provide the remote pilot with sufficient knowledge of the aircraft's environment to fulfil the responsibility must be incorporated into the aircraft with RPAS components located at the remote pilot station. Also, remote pilots, despite not being on board the aircraft, will be subject to the same requirements as aircraft pilots who are required to observe, interpret and heed a diverse range of visual signals intended to attract their attention and/or convey information. Such signals can range from lights and pyrotechnic signals for aerodrome traffic to signals used by intercepting aircraft. This would necessitate development and approval of alternate means of compliance with this requirement.

1.5.3.4 Air Traffic Management

With regard to air traffic management (ATM) it must be an established rule that whether the aircraft is piloted from on board or remotely, the provision of air traffic services (ATS) should, to the greatest practicable extent, be one and the same. It should further be that the introduction of RPAS must not increase the risk to other aircraft or third parties and should not prevent or restrict access to airspace. ATM procedures for handling RPAS should mirror those for manned aircraft whenever possible. There will be some instances where the remote pilot cannot respond in the same manner as could an on-board pilot and the Manual calls for ATM procedures to be able to take account of these differences. For this purpose, ATS/remote pilot communication requirements must be assessed in the context of an ATM function, taking into account human interactions, procedures and environmental characteristics. A safety management system (SMS) approach should be employed to determine the adequacy of any communications solutions. The information exchange between ATC and the remote pilot will likely require the same levels of reliability, continuity and integrity, referred to as QOS that are required to support operations with manned aircraft in the airspace in which a UA is intended to operate.

The exchange of control information between the aircraft and its remote pilot station will require an extremely high level of availability, reliability, continuity and integrity. The determination of required communication performance and associated QOS levels will be based on functionality considering the level of ATS being provided.

Annex 11 to the Chicago Convention, which deals with the subject of air traffic services, lays down requirements for coordination of activities that are potentially hazardous to civil aircraft. The International Standards and Recommended Practices (SARPS) in the Annex, Chapter 2 (2.17 and 2.18 in particular), contain provisions for co-ordination between military authorities and air traffic services and co-ordination of activities potentially hazardous to civil aircraft. These provisions specify that air traffic services authorities are required to establish and maintain close co-operation with military authorities responsible for activities that may affect flights of civil aircraft. The provisions also prescribe that the arrangements for activities potentially hazardous to civil aircraft shall be co-ordinated with the appropriate air traffic services authorities and that the objective of this co-ordination shall be to achieve the best arrangements which will avoid hazards to civil aircraft and minimize interference with the normal operations of such aircraft. Standard 2.17.1 stipulates that arrangements for activities potentially hazardous to civil aircraft, whether over the territory of a State or over the high seas, shall be coordinated with the appropriate air traffic services authorities, such coordination to be effected early enough to permit timely promulgation of information regarding the activities in accordance with the provisions of Annex 15 to the Chicago Convention. Standard 2.17.2 of Annex 11 explains that the objective of the coordination referred to in the earlier provision shall be to achieve the best arrangements that are calculated to avoid hazards to civil aircraft and minimize interference with the normal operations of aircraft. One must of course hasten to add that Article 89 of the Convention stipulates that in case of war, the provisions of the Convention (and, by implication its Annexes) shall not affect the freedom of action of any of ICAO's member States affected, whether as belligerents or as neutrals The same principle would apply in the case of any member State which declares a state of national emergency and notifies the fact to the ICAO Council.

1.5.3.5 Aerodrome Operations

In terms of aerodrome operations and RPAS, the integration of RPAS into aerodrome operations will prove to be among the greatest challenges. At issue are provisions for the remote pilot to identify, in real-time, the physical layout of the aerodrome and associated equipment such as aerodrome lighting and markings so as to manoeuvre the aircraft safely and correctly. The Manual provides that RPAS must be able to work within existing aerodrome parameters. Aerodrome standards should not be significantly changed, and the equipment developed for RPAS must be able to comply with existing provisions to the greatest extent practicable. Moreover, where RPAS are operated alongside manned aircraft, there needs to be harmonization in the provision of ATS.

1.5.3.6 Meteorology

Meteorology is another important element that needs to be properly coordinated in the operation of RPAS. Meteorological information plays a role in the safety, regularity and efficiency of international air navigation and is provided to users as required for the performance of their respective functions. Meteorological information supplied to operators and flight/remote crew members covers the flight in respect of time, altitude, and geographical area. Accordingly, the information relates to appropriate fixed times, or periods of time, and extends to the aerodrome of intended landing. It also covers meteorological conditions expected between the aerodrome of intended landing and alternate aerodromes designated by the operator.

Meteorological services are critical for the planning, execution and safe operation of international aviation. Since the remote pilot is not on board the aircraft and may not be able to determine meteorological conditions and their real-time effects on the aircraft, obtaining meteorological information from appropriate sources prior to and during flight will be especially critical for the safe operation of these aircraft.

It must also be recognized that Annex 3 to the Chicago Convention—Meteorological Service for International Air Navigation—has a requirement for aircraft on its registry operating on international air routes to make automated routine observations, if so equipped. RPAS may not be so equipped. Likewise, there is a requirement for all aircraft to make special observations whenever severe turbulence, severe icing, severe mountain wave, thunderstorms, hail, dust, stone and volcanic ash are encountered during a flight. However, RPAS may not be able to comply with these provisions as the pilot is remote from the aircraft, and the aircraft may not have the sensors to detect these phenomena.

It is also recognized that conversely, the RPAS specifically equipped for such purposes may in fact be used to monitor meteorological conditions, relaying information back to ground sensors. These aircraft could potentially be used in conditions and locations where manned aircraft cannot safely operate such as in hurricanes, convective weather or in the vicinity of volcanic ash/gases.

1.5.3.7 Flights Over the High Seas

Cross border operations and flights over the high seas are two areas identified by the LC for further discussion. Whether a military RPAS or a Civilian RPAS operates air services across borders, the three fundamental provisions that would guide them are Articles 3c), 8, and 9 as already discussed. As for flights over the high seas, Article 12[122] of the Chicago Convention governs fundamental principles. Annex 2 to the Chicago Convention, detailing the rules of the air referred to in Article 12, states *inter alia* that the rules of the air shall apply to aircraft bearing the nationality and

[122]Article 12 obligates each Contracting State to adopt measures to insure that every aircraft flying over or maneuvering within its territory and that every aircraft carrying its nationality mark, wherever such aircraft may be, will comply with the rules and regulations relating to the flight and maneuver of aircraft there in force. Article 12 obligates each contracting State to keep its own regulations in these respects uniform, to the greatest possible extent, with those established from time to time under the Chicago Convention. Over the high seas, the rules in force are those established under the Convention. Furthermore, each contracting State undertakes to insure the prosecution of all persons violating the regulations applicable.

registration marks of a Contracting State. These rules applicable to RPAS as well. Two main categories of rules of the air exist: visual flight rules and instrument flight rules. The note to article 2.2 of Annex 2 states *inter alia* that a pilot may elect to fly in accordance with instrument flight rules in visual meteorological conditions. The rules of the air adhered to are thus distinct and separate from the metrological conditions prevailing in the area of operation, except for instrument metrological conditions, requiring instrument flight rules to be applied. Chapter 3.1 of Annex 2, contains a provision on unmanned free balloons, stating that they shall be operated in such a manner as to minimize hazards to persons, property or other aircraft and in accordance with the conditions specified in Appendix 4. Appendix 4 states *inter alia* that heavy balloons need to comply with similar provisions like normal aeroplanes, inter alia minimum height over "congested areas of cities, towns or settlements or an open-air assembly of persons not associated with the operation", SSR equipment, and lightening.

Article 3.3 of Appendix 4 to the Annex 2 to the Chicago Convention contains a remarkable requirement to unmanned balloons. Such vehicles are required to be equipped with at least two payload flight termination devices or systems. It may well be argued that such devises or systems are required for RPAS as well. An analogy to the operation of RPAS exists in Annex 2 which obliges pilots-in-command to take action as will best avert collision. The Annex also requires that vigilance for the purpose of detecting potential collisions be exercised on board an aircraft, regardless of the type of flight or the class of airspace in which the aircraft is operating. Therefore, it can be concluded that pilots flying according to instrument flight rules are required to scan the environment visually in order to detect potentially conflicting traffic. This task may prove difficult in the case of RPAS in that although many RPAS are equipped with video cameras, it would be difficult for RPAS operators to detect vehicles nearby, to assess the potential for conflict and to initiate appropriate actions. This inability might result in infringement of article 3.2.1 of Annex 2, which provides that an aircraft shall not be operated in such proximity to other aircraft as to create a collision hazard. A potential solution to this problem could be that movement sensors, based on radar or ultrasound devices, similar to parking assistants for cars, are built into RPAS. The drawback of such a measure would be the cost involved and the additional weight that has to be carried by the RPAS.

Article 12 of the Convention on flights over the high seas brings to bear a singular aspect of ICAO rulemaking. There are three facets to Article 12. The first reflects that aircraft flying over or manoeuvring within the territory of a State are required to comply with the rules and regulations relating to the flight and manoeuvre of aircraft there in force. The second is that each ICAO member State undertakes to keep its own regulations in these respects uniform, to the greatest possible extent, with those established from time to time under this Convention. The third is that over the high seas, the rules in force shall be those established under this Convention. Each Contracting State undertakes to insure the prosecution of all persons violating the regulations applicable. All these three aspects inextricably link themselves to the action of the Council in pursuance of the Chicago

Convention with regard to rules of the air and this means that this provision is heavily reliant upon the Annex that would address the subject. This is Annex 2 (Rules of the Air), a discussion on which follows.

The ICAO Council on 20 June 1947 suggested that, pending the formal adoption of Standards and Recommended Practices under the terms of the Chicago Convention ICAO member States should continue to apply in their national civil aviation practices the recommendations for Standards and Recommended Practices which had been endorsed by the Interim Council of the Provisional International Civil Aviation Organization (PICAO). The Interim Council of PICAO had, on 25 February 1946 adopted "Recommendations for Standards, Practices and Procedures – rules of the Air and Air Traffic Control "of which Part 1 contained Rules of the Air." These Recommendations were developed during the first session of the RAC Division and submitted with a number of amendments to the Interim Council by the Air Navigation Committee in it twelfth Interim Report. The Council requested that States also introduce into their national practices, in so far as they individually consider it advisable and appropriate, the Recommendations presented by Divisions in the Reports not yet formally acted upon by the Council. The Council, on 15 April 1948 at the 22nd meeting of its third session considered the draft Standards and Recommended Practices for Rules of the Air and decided that "Rules of the Air" and "Air Traffic Control" were sufficiently distinctive to be issued as separate Annexes, and adopted Standards and Recommended Practices for Rules of the Air and designated them as "Annex 2 – Rules of the Air" to the Chicago Convention.

Another resolution of the Council was to the effect that States should, in complying with ICAO Standards which re of a regulatory character, to introduce the text of such standards into their national regulations, as nearly as possible, in the wording and arrangement employed by ICAO and that States be notified that "the Rules of the Air Annex constitutes rules relating to the flight and manoeuvre of aircraft within the meaning of Article 12 of the Convention and deviations from these rules may not be made in so far as they relate to flight over the high seas".

1.6 Climate Change

On 1 December 2015, at the 43rd session of the Subsidiary Body for Scientific and Technological Advice (SBSTA—a group meeting on the fringes of the Conference of the Parties (COP 21) which met in Paris under the auspices of the United Nations Framework Convention on Climate Change (UNFCCC)[123]—which was running

[123]The United Nations Framework Convention on Climate Change (UNFCCC) is an international environmental treaty negotiated at the Earth Summit in Rio de Janeiro from 3 to 14 June 1992, then entered into force on 21 March 1994. The UNFCCC objective is to "stabilize greenhouse gas concentrations in the atmosphere at a level that would prevent dangerous anthropogenic interference with the climate system". The framework set no binding limits on greenhouse gas emissions

alongside the main climate negotiations at COP21, China expressed its grave concern over the approach adopted by the International Civil Aviation Organization (ICAO)[124] on a key element of the global market-based measure (GMBM) currently being developed by ICAO. The displeasure of the Chinese delegation concerned the *Strawman* proposal[125] being progressed in ICAO with a view to developing a potential framework for the main structure of the GMBM. The main contention of the Chinese was that the approach followed by ICAO was inconsistent and incompatible with the UN principle of Common but Differentiated Responsibilities (CBDR) of States which ICAO is obligated to follow and was the cornerstone of the COP21 Agreement adopted in early December.[126] The CBDR principle is enshrined in Principle 7 of the Rio Declaration on Environment and Development which was a result of the United Nations Conference on the Environment and Development (UNCED)[127] which states:

> States shall cooperate in a spirit of global partnership to conserve, protect and restore the health and integrity of the Earth's ecosystem. In view of the different contributions to global environmental degradation, States have common but differentiated responsibilities. The developed countries acknowledge the responsibility they bear in the international pursuit of sustainable development in view of the pressures their societies place on the global environment and of the technologies and financial resources they command.

China claimed, *inter alia* that the Strawman proposal of ICAO did not take into consideration the CBDR principle, expressly identified as a key consideration in ICAO Assembly Resolution A38-18 and reaffirmed by the new UN global Sustainable Development Goals.

---

for individual countries and contains no enforcement mechanisms. Instead, the framework outlines how specific international treaties (called "protocols") may be negotiated to set binding limits on greenhouse gases.

[124]ICAO is a specialized agency of the United Nations addressing international civil aviation. It derives its origin and functions from the Convention on International Civil Aviation (Chicago Convention) signed at Chicago on 7 December 1944, Articles 43 and 44 of which details ICAO's composition and aims and objectives respectively. See ICAO Doc 7300/8: 2006.

[125]For a discussion on the Strawman Proposal see Abeyratne (2015), pp. 102–107.

[126]See COP21: China expresses "serious concerns" over ICAO global measure to limit growth of aviation emissions, See *Green Air Online* at http://www.greenaironline.com/news.php?viewStory=2165. Another statement by Argentina on behalf of a number of developing States, including China, Brazil and India, plus groups of African and Arab countries, said the CBDR principle had to be fully respected by ICAO on climate issues and measures should not constitute hidden restrictions on international trade. *Ibid.*

[127]The United Nations Conference on Environment and Development met, at Rio de Janeiro from 3 to 14 June 1992. It reaffirmed the Declaration of the United Nations Conference on the Human Environment, adopted at Stockholm on 16 June 1972, and sought to build upon it with the goal of establishing a new and equitable global partnership through the creation of new levels of cooperation among States, key sectors of societies and people. The conference also had the aim of working towards international agreements which respect the interests of all and protect the integrity of the global environmental and developmental system. See http://www.unep.org/Documents.Multilingual/Default.asp?documentID=78&articleID=1163.

At the 38th Session of the ICAO Assembly held from 24 September to 4 October 2013 the Assembly adopted Resolution A38-18 wherein the Assembly decided to develop a global MBM scheme for international aviation and in this context requested the ICAO Council *inter alia* to finalize the work on the technical aspects, environmental and economic impacts and modalities of the possible options for a global MBM scheme, including on its feasibility and practicability, taking into account the need for development of international aviation, the proposal of the aviation industry and other international developments, as appropriate,[128] and without prejudice to the negotiations under the United Nations Framework Convention on Climate Change (UNFCCC).

A key requirement of the Assembly was that ICAO study the feasibility and practicability of the possible options of global MBM scheme, including its technical aspects, environmental and financial impacts to both developed and developing countries; match possible MBM options including study of other options such as taxes, fuel or carbon charges, etc. that could also attain the objectives of MBMs for established selection criteria; integrate the concept of CBDR and Special Circumstances and Respective Capabilities (SCRC) into the global MBM scheme that would enable assistance to the developing States.

A few days after the conclusion of the COP 21 meeting, the President of the ICO Council issued a statement to the effect that "[T]he fact that international aviation was not covered by the Paris Agreement reached at COP21 last Saturday (Dec 12) is a vote of confidence in the progress ICAO and the aviation community have made towards ambitious climate goals".[129] This statement was seemingly a response to the protestations of China and an attempt at vindicating the many courageous but ineffective attempts made over the past 10 years by ICAO at presenting to the world a viable economic instrument that adequately responds to aircraft engine emissions.

Quite apart from the fact that this statement is both tendentious and blatantly misleading, it is also fundamentally flawed in that COP 21 was held to discuss climate alleviation at a generally high level on the basis of climate justice and overall goals and that neither aviation nor maritime transport were individually examined by the general meeting, as they are mere subsets of the overall policy discussed, which did not constitute discussions on individual economic instruments

[128]This requirement was influenced by the 37th Session of the ICAO Assembly, held in Montreal from 28 September to 8 October 2010, which noted that, if the global community were to stabilize greenhouse gas emissions in the atmosphere and maintain it at a level that would prevent dangerous anthropogenic interference with the climate, the increase in global temperature would have to be maintained below 2 °C. In order to achieve this target, deep cuts in global emissions would be needed, and all sectors of the economy were being looked to for their contribution—including international aviation, which is well known as representing a significant and growing source of emissions.

[129]See Omission of international aviation from Paris climate agreement a vote of confidence, says ICAO President, *Green Air on Line* at http://www.greenaironline.com/news.php?viewStory=2173.

coming under various aspects of sectoral pollution. This article will discuss climate justice, the achievements of COP 21 and their effects on aviation.

1.6.1 Climate Justice and COP 21

1.6.1.1 Climate Justice

Climate justice, broadly speaking is: "the fair treatment of all people and freedom from discrimination with the creation of policies and projects that address climate change and the systems that create climate change and perpetuate discrimination."[130] In this sense, both the Agreement of COP21 and ICAO Assembly Resolution A38-18 inevitably involve climate justice in that both speak of CBDR which affords developing countries fair and equal opportunities to develop without having to pay the same price for the dangerous levels of global warming that industrialized countries helped to create in the nineteenth and twentieth centuries. Climate justice also recognizes the factors that made rich countries become richer while some countries became poor, and the fallacy behind the misconception that the environment should be considered in its simplistic sense—and that it is the overall summation of all things natural. In this context, as Nobel laureate Amartya Sen observes, the pervasive common view is that this "state of nature" will remain without change as long as we interfere with it as little as possible.[131] Sen further states that this misconception can be rejected on two counts, the first being that the value of the environment does not lie in its existing state but in the opportunities it offers humankind, and the second being that it is not sufficient to ensure that the environment is passively preserved by us but there needs to be active initiatives in educating the populace of the world on the environment and the benefits that would accrue to it by our actions such as reducing the population of the world and creating employment opportunities.[132]

Another compelling need for global climate justice is the available scientific and empirical evidence that climate change is causing a global glacier melt resulting in the irreversible collapse of a vast portion of the West Antarctic ice sheet at *Thwaites Glacier*[133] that would, *inter alia* result in the rise in sea levels, gravely endangering the survival of small island developing States such as the Maldives which has little or no responsibility for causing climate change through greenhouse gas emissions. Arguably, the most compelling justification for CBDR and SCRC is in the fact that some countries developed while others stayed poor owing to the exponential

[130]https://www.google.ca/?gfe_rd=cr&ei=O2V5VsvLKMaC8QeZhaNw&gws_rd=ssl#q=climate+justice.

[131]Sen (2009), p. 248.

[132]*Id.* 248–249.

[133]Taillant (2015), p. 151.

industrialization of the former caused by the prolific use of coal—the largest polluter and producer of greenhouse gases.[134]

ICAO's initial work in 2010, following the findings of COP 15 held in Copenhagen in December 2009 were deeply rooted in climate justice through aviation. An ICAO working group (Group on International Civil Aviation and Climate Change, GIACC) adopted global aspirational goals of reaching an annual fuel efficiency improvement until 2012 of 2 % for the short-term, an annual fuel efficiency improvement of 2 % until 2020 or 2025 for the medium-term (GIACC agreed 2020) and an annual fuel efficiency improvement of 2 % from 2021 to 2050 for the long-term. This compares to the goals expressed by IATA[135], which are the equivalent of a short-term goal in 2012 of about 2.1 % annual fuel efficiency improvement, about 1.9 % per annum in the medium-term of 2020 and about 1.1 % per annum in the long-term of 2050.

With regard to market based measures, GIACC recommended that the process to develop a framework for MBMs for international aviation should properly address major issues related to their implementation, in particular: (a) the principles of non-discrimination and equal and fair opportunities set forth in the Chicago Convention are fully taken into account; (b) the specific circumstances and different capabilities of each Contracting State and Region are fully taken into account; (c) only the most effective and efficient measures are chosen; (d) industry compliance is facilitated; (e) market-based measures can be coordinated and are not duplicative; and, (f) the geographical scope issues are considered.

The goals agreed by GIACC were not calculated to attribute specific obligations to individual States. It was believed that the different circumstances, respective capabilities and contribution of developing and developed States to the concentration of aviation GHG emissions in the atmosphere would determine how each State may contribute to achieving global aspirational goals. GIACC expressed support for the development of a CO2 standard for new aircraft types. GIACC also agreed to a basket of measures that can be selected by States to apply to their international aviation sector in line with their circumstances and capabilities and, which include measures to facilitate access to assistance, particularly for developing countries.

---

[134]See Sachs (2015), pp. 101–138.

[135]The International Air Transport Association, an association of air carriers, was formed in 1919 as the International Air Traffic Association. IATA's priorities are in safety and efficiency of air transport. In the safety area, IATA conducts Operational Safety Audits (IOSA) which use internationally recognised quality audit principles and are designed so that audits are conducted in a standardised and consistent manner. It is envisioned that, as a result of these audits, the industry will be in a position to achieve the benefits of cost-efficiency through a significant reduction in audit redundancy. On the efficiency side, IATA has introduced its Simplified Passenger Travel (SPT) Programme which introduces paperless passenger tickets and air way bills. The SPT has its genesis in an IATA project, launched in December 2004, that is designed to remove all the paper for all stakeholders from passenger and air cargo transportation by 2010, with a "fast-track" programme to accommodate those parties that are able to free their supply chain processes from paper by 2007.

1.6.1.2 The COP 21 Agreement

As many as 195 States were parties to the discussions in Paris on the COP 21 Agreement which was accepted in general by consensus. The Agreement will be deposited at the UN in New York and opened for 1 year for signature on 22 April 2016—Mother Earth Day.

The Agreement will enter into force after 55 countries that account for at least 55 % of global emissions have deposited their instruments of ratification. The overall aim of the Agreement is to maintain a global temperature rise in the twenty-first century to well below 2 °C and to strive to limit the temperature increase even further to 1.5 °C above pre-industrial levels, the lower level recognized as a buffer against worst case scenario impacts of climate change. Another important goal of the Agreement is to strengthen the capacity of States to effectively address and mitigate the impacts of climate change.

Article 2 of the Agreement stipulates that the Agreement aims to strengthen the global response to the threat of climate change, in the context of sustainable development and efforts to eradicate poverty, including by: holding the increase in the global average temperature to well below 2 °C above pre-industrial levels and to pursue efforts to limit the temperature increase to 1.5 °C above pre-industrial levels, recognizing that this would significantly reduce the risks and impacts of climate change; increasing the ability to adapt to the adverse impacts of climate change and foster climate resilience and low greenhouse gas emissions development, in a manner that does not threaten food production; and making finance flows consistent with a pathway towards low greenhouse gas emissions and climate-resilient development. Article 2.2. is explicit in stating that the Agreement will be implemented to reflect equity and the principle of common but differentiated responsibilities and respective capabilities, in the light of different national circumstances.[136]

The Agreement also recognizes the need to put in place appropriate financial tools in order to achieve the aforementioned ambitious goals with a view to enabling developing states to face the challenges of mitigating climate change at their own pace and in accordance with their own national objectives.

There was considerable hope that the agreement would truly promote sustainable development. UN Secretary General Ban Ki-moon said: "We have entered a new era of global cooperation on one of the most complex issues ever to confront humanity. For the first time, every country in the world has pledged to curb emissions, strengthen resilience and join in common cause to take common climate action. This is a resounding success for multilateralism."

The critical areas covered by the COP 21 Agreement are: *mitigation*—reducing emissions fast enough to achieve the temperature goal; *a transparency system and global stock-take*—accounting for climate action; *adaptation*—strengthening

[136]Conference of the Parties, Twenty-first session, Paris, 30 November to 11 December 2015, FCCC/CP/2015/L.9/Rev.1, 12 December 2015.

ability of countries to deal with climate impacts; *loss and damage*—strengthening ability to recover from climate impacts; and *support*—including finance, for nations to build clean, resilient futures The Agreement espouses a long term direction that would enable States to reach a peak in their emissions as soon as possible and continue to submit national climate action plans that detail their future objectives to address climate change.

A UNFCCC Secretariat statement claims that, in the spirit of the Agreement, 188 countries have undertaken to contribute climate action plans in accordance with the new agreement, which is calculated to dramatically slow the pace of global greenhouse gas emissions. The basic philosophy of the Agreement is that future national plans will be no less ambitious than existing ones, which means these 188 climate action plans provide a firm floor and foundation for higher ambition. It has also introduced nationally determined contributions (NDCs)—updated plans for reducing greenhouse gas emissions—once every 5 years, which will regularly and consistently improve their strategy towards achieving their overall goals in the long-term.

The Agreement also provides for action to be taken even before 2020 where States are required to continue to engage in a process on mitigation opportunities and will put added focus on adaptation opportunities. Furthermore, since reaching the ambitious target of 1.5 % below industrial levels would mean keeping at least 75 % of the current flow of fossil fuels on the ground, and using renewable energy instead, States will raise climate finance up to $ 100 billion by 2020 that would assist developing countries to develop such energy resources. States will, in this regard, work towards defining a clear roadmap on ratcheting up climate finance to USD 100 billion by 2020 while also before 2025 setting a new goal on the provision of finance from the USD 100 billion floor. A roadmap in this regard will be developed by States. There will also be put in place a robust transparency and accounting system that would allow for special circumstances and respective capabilities of States to be recognized and taken as part of the equation. Support and cooperation are the main themes of this philosophy. The Agreement also strengthens international cooperation on climate-safe technologies and building capacity in the developing world to address climate change.

All States are required to submit adaptation communications, in which they may detail their adaptation priorities, support needs and plans. There is also provision for developing countries to receive increased support for adaptation actions, for which there will be an assessment of the adequacy of this support that will be given. As already mentioned, the Agreement has incorporated a robust transparency framework for both action and support. The framework will provide clarity on countries' mitigation and adaptation actions, as well as the provision of support. At the same time, it recognizes that Least Developed Countries and Small Island Developing States have special circumstances.

According to the UNFCCC Secretariat, the agreement includes a global stocktake starting in 2023 to assess the collective progress towards the goals of the agreement. The stocktake will be done every 5 years and the agreement includes a compliance mechanism, overseen by a committee of experts that operates in a non-punitive way. From a technical standpoint, COP 21 addressed a number of issues which go to say that under the Kyoto Protocol[137]; there is now a clear and transparent accounting method for carry-over credits for the second commitment period, creating a clear set of rules; and the first round of international assessment and review process (IAR) that was launched in 2014 was successfully completed. A number of technical and implementation issues related to the existing arrangements on technology, adaptation, action for climate empowerment and capacity building were also successfully concluded.

All the above mentioned features of the Agreement stand as a precursor to the upcoming ICAO MBM scheme, at least in principle, and should be considered as analogical influences when ICAO develops its proposal to the 39th Session of the Assembly.

1.6.2 ICAO'S Work

In earlier publications,[138] the author has discussed in detail the current work being conducted by ICAO in preparation for the 39th Session of the ICAO Assembly to be held in late 2016 and therefore such work needs no further discussion in this article. However, it is necessary to discuss the philosophy of ICAO's work, particularly in the context of COP 21 and its agreement, since both involve principles of CBDR and SCRC as integral elements.

Firstly, ICAO will have to go on the fundamental basis that Article 2.2. of the Kyoto Protocol merely gives impetus to ICAO's work in addressing greenhouse gas emissions and places a certain responsibility upon ICAO but does not constitute ICAO's "mandate". Besides, the Protocol became extinct in 2012. ICAO derives its legal legitimacy from the Convention on International Civil Aviation (Chicago Convention), Annex 16 of which addresses aviation and the environment. It is on the basis of these documents that ICAO achieves its aims and objectives, based on the doctrine of empowerment which stems from the Organizations' member States.

---

[137]The Kyoto Protocol to UNFCCC was adopted in Kyoto, Japan, on 11 December 1997. Due to a complex ratification process, it entered into force on 16 February 2005. The Kyoto Protocol is what "operationalizes" the Convention. It commits industrialized countries to stabilize greenhouse gas emissions based on the principles of the Convention. The Convention itself only encourages countries to do so. The Protocol sets binding emission reduction targets for 37 industrialized countries and the European community in its first commitment period. Overall, these targets add up to an average 5 % emissions reduction compared to 1990 levels over the 5-year period 2008 to 2012 (the first commitment period). It was structured on the principles of the Convention. It only binds developed countries because it recognizes that they are largely responsible for the current high levels of GHG emissions in the atmosphere, which are the result of more than 150 years of industrial activity. The Kyoto Protocol places a heavier burden on developed nations under its central CBDR principle.

[138]See Global Market-Based Measures for Aviation Emissions, *supra*. Also, Abeyratne (2014b), ISBN: 978-3-319-08442-8 (Print) 978-3-319-08443-5 (Online).

Therefore, irrespective of any other agreement (including the COP 21 Agreement) ICAO can, and indeed will carry on its work on aviation and the environment. Furthermore, ICAO is obligated by its Assembly Resolution A38-18 adopted by its 38th Assembly in 2013 that, at the 39th Assembly in 2016 it should come up with a global market based measure to counter engine emissions that would take effect in 2020.

Another factor for consideration is that, in a way, ICAO's task is more daunting than the skeletal framework of the COP 21 Agreement, which, on the one hand introduced an ambitious goal of emissions reduction by 1.5 % of pre industrial levels, on the other hand did not develop an implementation mechanism to ensure the achievement of the goal, nor did it introduce and agree upon a monitoring mechanism. The Agreement also did not offer any way that States could prevent a rise in CO2 emissions. ICAO, on the other hand, has to present to the 39th Session of the Assembly an MBM scheme which should have follow up recommendations and justifications in terms of utilization of resources collected and implementation of the scheme.

ICAO would also be aware that the COP 21 Agreement is a glorified "pledge" by States who cannot force each other to honour their commitments. As against this approach, ICAO has to introduce an emissions trading mechanism based on markets and economic principles. In other words, ICAO has to come up with a viable alternative to the proposed Emissions Trading Scheme (ETS) of the European Union which caused much consternation in the ICAO Council between 2010 and 2013.[139]

A major factor in looking at the COP 21 Agreement analogically to the proposed ICAO MBM scheme lies in Article 4 of the Agreement which establishes a mechanism to contribute to the mitigation of greenhouse gas emissions and support sustainable development under the authority and guidance of the Conference of the Parties serving as the meeting of the Parties to the Paris Agreement for use by Parties on a voluntary basis. The mechanism will be supervised by a body designated by the Conference of the Parties serving as the meeting of the Parties to the Paris Agreement, and will aim: to promote the mitigation of greenhouse gas emissions while fostering sustainable development; to incentivize and facilitate participation in the mitigation of greenhouse gas emissions by public and private entities authorized by a Party; to contribute to the reduction of emission levels in the host Party, which will benefit from mitigation activities resulting in emission reductions that can also be used by another Party to fulfil its nationally determined contribution; and to deliver an overall mitigation in global emissions.

The 39th ICAO Assembly may have to develop similar wording in the establishment of the MBM mechanism under the auspices of the Assembly. As to whether such a scheme would be voluntary or be vested with some degree of compulsion would be left for the Assembly to decide.

---

[139]See Abeyratne (2011b), pp. 855–889. Also by the same author, Abeyratne (2011c), pp. 143–157. Abeyratne (2010b), pp. 319–328.

Notwithstanding the above differences, there are a few principles of the COP 21 Agreement that ICAO may wish to emulate in the development of the MBM scheme. For instance, Article 4.19 of the Agreement states that all Parties should strive to formulate and communicate long-term low greenhouse gas emission development strategies, taking into account their common but differentiated responsibilities and respective capabilities, in the light of different national circumstance. In this regard the Agreement requests Parties to communicate, by 2020, to the Secretariat, mid-century, long-term low greenhouse gas emission development strategies in accordance with Article 4, paragraph 19, of the Agreement, and requests the Secretariat to publish on the UNFCCC website Parties' low greenhouse gas emission development strategies as communicated.

Another feature of the Agreement is the establishment of a Committee on Capacity Building whose aim will be to address gaps and needs, both current and emerging, in implementing capacity-building in developing country Parties and further enhancing capacity-building efforts, including with regard to coherence and coordination in capacity-building activities under the Convention. Analogically, the ICAO scheme could have a mechanism for capacity building and training of personnel and increasing synergies through cooperation and avoidance of duplication among existing bodies facilitating implementation in member States who could ensure the overall implementation of the MBM mechanism in the scheme.

A good example for the ICAO scheme lies in Article 7 of the Agreement which recognizes the need for sharing information, good practices, experiences and lessons learned, including, as appropriate, as these relate to science, planning, policies and implementation in relation to adaptation actions; strengthening institutional arrangements, including those under the Convention that serve the Agreement, to support the synthesis of relevant information and knowledge, and the provision of technical support and guidance to Parties; strengthening scientific knowledge on climate, including research, systematic observation of the climate system and early warning systems, in a manner that informs climate services and supports decision-making; assisting developing country Parties in identifying effective adaptation practices, adaptation needs, priorities, support provided and received for adaptation actions and efforts, and challenges and gaps, in a manner consistent with encouraging good practices; improving the effectiveness and durability of adaptation.

The example of Article 7 should resonate the need for a global cooperative effort in the implementation of the ICAO MBM scheme, as against the current anomaly found in air transport economics of airlines banding together in alliances and other plurilateral and multilateral arrangements.

1.6.2.1 Regulatory Challenges for ICAO: Introduction

ICAO has been grappling for more than 6 years with the daunting task of coming up with a global market based measure for engine emissions in the midst of polarizing positions between developed States and developing States as well as issues of extra territorial application of a market based measure from Europe.[140] In late February 2016, after nearly two and a half years of diligent but difficult work on a requirement imposed on it by the 38th Assembly of the ICAO held in late 2013, the ICAO Council came up with a Draft Policy Proposal on a Global MBM Scheme (GMBM) which, at the time of writing, stood as of 17 December 2015. These draft policy proposals were incorporated into a draft Assembly Resolution which advocates, as its suggested GMBM, a single global carbon offsetting scheme. Before one examines in some detail the proposals in the draft Resolution, it is useful to delve historically into how the issue has been handled by ICAO.

It is important to note that ICAO has been given two major tasks by the 38th Assembly. Through its Resolution A38-18[141] The Council has been requested to present at the 39th Session of the Assembly finalized work on the technical aspects, environmental and economic impacts and modalities of the possible options for a Global Market Based Measures (GMBM) scheme, including on its feasibility and practicability, and also to identify the major issues and problems, including for Member States, and make a recommendation on a GMBM scheme that appropriately addresses them. These two requirements can be subsumed into a consolidated task of firstly identifying issues and secondly, based on the issues and the challenges they might present, offer possible options for a GMBM. At the time of writing there was no evidence that a study had been undertaken or carried out by ICAO on the issues that affect ICAO's 191 member States in the area of aviation and climate change. However, with the draft Resolution developed, some issues emerged in the form of comments by members of ICAO's Council voicing their concerns on the text of the draft. These were subjective to their individual interests and by no means replace the compelling need for a study to have been conducted by ICAO as a precursor to addressing the ultimate issue of a suitable GMBM.

ICAO employed an Environmental Action Group (EAG) comprised mainly of Representatives of member States in its Council to work on the tasks at hand. It is assumed that the ICAO Secretariat would have provided administrative support to this group which it usually does. The EAG in turn recommended to the Council that a High Level Group on a Global Market Based Measure Scheme (HLG-GMGM), comprising high level aviation and/or transport experts from 18 of the 36 Council members be established—narrowing the numbers that existed in the EAG. The task of the HLG-GMBM was to facilitate the convergence of views that emerged from the draft Resolution developed by the EAG.

Going back a few years, the 37th Session of the ICAO Assembly, held in 2010, adopted Resolution A37-19 which required ICAO to develop a framework for market-based measures while attaining global aspirations in the reduction of

[140]See Abeyratne (2011c), pp. 143–157. Also by the same author: Abeyratne (2011b), pp. 855–889; Abeyratne (2012b), pp. 7–46; Abeyratne (2014c), pp. 57–74; and Abeyratne (2015), pp. 102–107.

[141]A38-18, Consolidated statement of continuing ICAO policies and practices related to environmental protection—climate change, Assembly Resolutions in Force as of 4 October 2013, *ICAO Doc 10022*, 1–68.

emissions taking into consideration *inter alia* the maturity of aviation markets and the sustainable growth of the international aviation industry. Although on the one hand the Resolution only required its recommendations to be reviewed at the 38th Session in 2013, there was an explicit requirement in Resolving Clause 13 of the Resolution that the Council, with the support of member States, undertake work to develop a framework for market-based measures (MBMs) in international aviation. This was nearly 6 years ago.

At the 38th Session of the Assembly, all ICAO could come up with after 3 years of going to and fro in the Council, admittedly with the difficult polarization of tendentious political nit picking between States,[142] were three options that States could choose from, two of which were: a *global mandatory offsetting*, where participants acquire emissions units to offset emissions from international aviation above an agreed baseline; and a *global mandatory offsetting complemented by a revenue generation mechanism* which would generally function the same way as the mandatory offsetting scheme. A key difference between the two is that in the second option, in addition to offsetting, revenue would be generated by applying a fee to each tonne of carbon, for instance, through a transaction fee. The revenue would be used for agreed purposes, such as climate change mitigation or providing support to developing States to reduce GHG emissions. The third option was *a global emissions trading scheme using a cap & trade approach*, where total international aviation emissions are capped at an agreed level for a specified compliance period. Aviation allowances (one allowance is equivalent to one tonne of CO2) would be created for all the emissions under the cap. These allowances would then be distributed among, or auctioned to, participants, using an agreed method. At the end of each compliance period, participants would need to surrender sufficient aviation allowances, or other emissions units, such as offsets from other sectors, to cover all the emissions generated during that period. Revenues can be generated by auctioning aviation allowances.[143]

The Assembly resolved that, States and relevant Organizations will work through ICAO to achieve a global annual average fuel efficiency improvement efficiency of 2 % until 2020 and an aspirational global fuel efficiency improvement rate of 2 % per annum from 2021 to 2050, calculated on the basis of volume of fuel used per revenue tonne kilometre performed.[144] By implication, therefore, whatever market based "scheme" that would be developed and placed before the 39th session of the Assembly in 2016 would have to ensure that this goal, particularly from 2020 onwards was achieved. The Assembly requested The Council of ICAO to exercise continuous leadership on environmental issues relating to international civil aviation, including GHG emissions and to continue to study policy options to limit or reduce the environmental impact of aircraft engine emissions and to develop "concrete proposals" (my emphasis) *inter alia* to the Conference of the

[142]See generally, Abeyratne (2011c).

[143]A38-WP/29, EX/24, 4/09/13 at 2.

[144]Executive Committee's Report to the Plenary of the Assembly, A38-WP/430, P/44, 3/10/13.

Parties (COP) of the United Nations Framework Convention on Climate Change (UNFCCC),[145] encompassing technical solutions and market based measures, and taking into account potential implications of such measures for developing as well as developed States.

The Council settled for a *Strawman* approach[146] to achieve a GMBM which, after long and polarized deliberations, seems to have abandoned. The *Strawman* approach in this context was a non-starter for the reason that it starts off with an intellectually dishonest proposition which the opposition has to demolish until a perfect solution is reached. The Council, in view of the polarized debate that required a solution based on the *Pareto Principle*[147] of equal distribution of benefits on the principle that at least one party benefits and none loses on the deal, was confronted with the compelling need, as required by Assembly Resolution A38-15, to base an ultimate GMBM on two principles: *Common But Differentiated Responsibilities (CBDR)*; and *Special Circumstances and Respective Capabilities* (SCRC) of the 191 member States of ICAO.[148]

It must be noted that, as already mentioned, at the 38th Session of the Assembly the ICAO member States were presented with three GMBM options: global mandatory offsetting; global mandatory offsetting with revenue; and global emissions trading. The Assembly was advised, based on a Report prepared, that the results of the qualitative and quantitative analyses of the three options (global mandatory offsetting, global mandatory offsetting with revenue, and global emissions trading) showed that all three options were technically feasible and had the capacity to contribute to achieving ICAO's environmental goals. It also said that global mandatory offsetting could be less complex than global mandatory offsetting complemented by a revenue generation mechanism and global emissions trading.

---

[145]The United Nations Framework Convention on Climate Change (UNFCCC) was adopted on 9 May 1992 and the treaty entered into force on 21 March 1994. The UNFCCC or FCCC is an international environmental treaty produced at the United Nations Conference on Environment and Development (UNCED), informally known as the Earth Summit, held in Rio de Janeiro in 1992. The treaty aimed at reducing emissions of greenhouse gas in order to combat global warming. The treaty as originally framed set no mandatory limits on greenhouse gas emissions for individual nations and contained no enforcement provisions; it is therefore considered legally non-binding. Rather, the treaty included provisions for updates (called "protocols") that would set mandatory emission limits. The principal update is the Kyoto Protocol, which has become much better known than the UNFCCC itself. The stated objective of UNFCCC is "to achieve stabilization of greenhouse gas concentrations in the atmosphere at a low enough level to prevent dangerous anthropogenic interference with the climate system."

[146]See Abeyratne (2015), pp. 102–107. The main characteristic of the "Strawman" is that it is a tentative draft proposal which can be taken apart as more information becomes available. Therefore a Strawman helps one to make a start in a project and build on propositions as one goes along and gives a tangible starting tool. Often the start-up information is incomplete and is developed with the techniques of research, testing and criticism. The entire process is based on falsification of existing propositions, which is calculated to assist in reaching a final viable proposition.

[147]http://betterexplained.com/articles/understanding-the-pareto-principle-the-8020-rule/.

[148]See Abeyratne (2014b), ISBN: 978-3-319-08442-8 (Print) 978-3-319-08443-5 (Online).

At the time of writing, just six months away from the 39th Assembly, ICAO has only a draft Assembly Resolution, which was still in bits and pieces, which has to satisfy the requirement of Resolution A38-18 which are: to finalize the work on the technical aspects, environmental and economic impacts and modalities of the possible options for a GMBM scheme, including on its feasibility and practicability, taking into account the need for development of international aviation, the proposal of the aviation industry and other international developments, as appropriate, and without prejudice to the negotiations under the UNFCCC.

In essence the draft Resolution advocates that an International Aviation Global Offsetting (IAGOF)—which, as Assembly Resolution A37-19 recognized, was preferred by the aviation industry—will be implemented in two stages that are calculated to cater to: an implementation stage from 2021 to apply only to States that are classified as high income States in terms of gross national income (GNI) per capita (calculated by the World Bank method); and States whose individual share of international aviation activities in Revenue Tonnes Kilometers (RTKs) in year 2018 is above 1.0 % of total RTKs, or whose cumulative share in the list of States from the highest to the lowest amount of RTKs reaches 80 % of total RTKs. The second implementation phase would apply from 2026 to the following: States that are classified as upper medium income States in terms of GNI per capita (calculated by the World Bank method); and States whose individual share of international aviation activities in RTKs in year 2018 is above 0.5 % of total RTKs, or whose cumulative share in the list of States from the highest to the lowest amount of RTKs reaches 95 % of total RTKs.[149]

1.6.2.2 The IAGOF Mechanism

The principle of carbon offsetting requires companies that operate aircraft to compensate for their carbon footprints. Carbon offset schemes allow individuals and companies to invest in environmental projects around the world in order to balance out their own carbon footprints by investing in projects that are most commonly designed to reduce future emissions. This could involve introducing and using clean energy technologies or purchasing carbon credits from an emissions trading scheme. The IAGOF will be operated on the principle that the amount of CO2 emissions required to be offset by an aircraft operator would be calculated by multiplying its 2020 emissions with an annual growth rate of the international aviation sector's total emissions from 2021 compared to the 2020 levels. A new entrant would be exempted from the application of the IAGOF scheme for 5 years

[149]The IAGOF scheme does not apply to States which are classified as the Least Developed Countries (LDCs), Small Island Developing States (SIDS) or Landlocked Developing Countries (LLDCs), unless those States meet all criteria applicable to States falling within the two phases of implementation. Nevertheless, States that are not included in the IAGOF scheme are encouraged to voluntarily determine to participate in the scheme, in particular those States that are members of a regional economic integration organization.

or until the year in which its annual emissions exceed 0.5 % of total emissions in 2020, whichever occurs earlier. From the subsequent year, the new entrant would be included in the scheme and treated in the same way as the other operators.

Notwithstanding the above principles, the IAGOF scheme would not apply to low levels of international aviation activity—a measure recommended to avoid an administrative burden. This aviation activity covers: aircraft operators emitting less than 10,000 metric tonnes of CO2 emissions from international aviation per year; aircraft with less than 5700 kg of Maximum Takeoff Mass (MTOM); or humanitarian, medical and firefighting operations.

Emissions that are not covered by the scheme, as the results of phased implementation and exemptions, would not be recognized as obligations of any operators included in the scheme. A key element in the IAGOF is a monitoring, reporting and verification (MRV) system which is elaborated in an Annex to the draft Resolution. The Annex contains certain key elements of the monitoring, reporting and verification (MRV) system, criteria for emissions units to be purchased by aircraft operators, and registries under the IAGOF scheme, as contained in the Annex. The draft Resolution recommends a 3 year compliance cycle, starting with the first cycle from 2021 to 2023, within which aircraft operators should reconcile their obligations under the scheme, while they report the required data to a single State authority every year.

A sunset clause prescribes that the scheme would cease to apply if the total CO2 emissions from international aviation go below the 2020 levels for 3 consecutive years. The design elements of the IAGOF scheme would apply until the end of 2035, with a periodic review every 3 years, and a review for any extension of the scheme beyond 2035 is undertaken by end 2032.

1.6.2.3 Concerns of States on the Text of the Draft Resolution

To start with the sunset clause, one State was of the view that such a clause was not necessary when one takes into consideration current knowledge of the expected technological development in the aviation industry, where one could conclude with confidence that the CO2 emissions of international civil aviation sector would continue to grow in the foreseeable future. The deletion was sought on another ground—that a GMBM would slowdown technological development of the industry, which could result in a negative impact on the rate of increase in the volume of emissions.

The draft Resolution has a provision where it is averred that the GMBM scheme will play a complimentary role to other elements of a basket of measures as a temporary emissions gap filler that could enable the aviation community to achieve its aspirational goals. The same State which objected to the sunset clause was of the view that the word "temporary" should be deleted as a GMBM scheme should not be considered a stop gap measure. It was further contended that the offsetting mechanism pertaining to the IAGOF should be made compatible with the Sustainable Development Goals of the United Nations so as to apply until 2030.

One of the most relevant recommendations was that ICAO should offer possible options for a legally binding mechanism for a GMBM implementation and to supplement the draft resolution by an appropriate text; and look at the feasibility of inclusion into the draft Resolution a provision, which would obviously imply that a GMBM replaces regional or national emissions trading schemes. As for the 5 year moratorium offered to new entrant operators it was contended that this should be reduced to 1 year on the ground that as a result of the constant increasing of a financial burden of offsetting purchases, the costs of liquidation and the establishment of new airlines could be considerably lower than the costs associated with participation in a GMBM.

As for calculations of a CO2 offset, one State suggested that the calculation should be based on multiplying an operator's 2020 emissions should be multiplied by an annual growth rate of the international aviation sector's total emissions from 2021 until 2026 compared to the 2020 levels, while excluding emissions of a "new entrants" and States, which should be exempted at the first phase of a GMBM implementation, and; by multiplying its 2020 emissions with an annual growth rate of the international aviation sector's total emissions from 2021 compared to the 2020 levels, while excluding emissions of "new entrants".

The provision in the draft Assembly that states that the two implementation phases should apply to routes depending on whether they are operated by high income States of a gross national income level (a purely economic indicator) as determined by the World Bank per capita in 2018 came under criticism by one State which questioned why the World Bank standards had been singled out over criteria used by other economic institutions as World Bank standards had not been used in this context in environmental calculations. The question was also raised as to why the developed countries[150]/developing countries[151] criteria were not used by ICAO.

An interesting diversion from the CBDR and SCRC principle was seen where one State requested the use of "special needs and special circumstances of

[150]A developed country, industrialized country, or "more economically developed country" (MEDC), is a sovereign state that has a highly developed economy and advanced technological infrastructure relative to other less industrialized nations. Most commonly, the criteria for evaluating the degree of economic development are gross domestic product (GDP), gross national product (GNP), the per capita income, level of industrialization, amount of widespread infrastructure and general standard of living. See *The Least Developed Countries Report 2014*, United Nations Conference on Trade and Development Growth with structural transformation: A post-2015 development agenda, 27 November 2014, UN: New York, Geneva, Executive Summary.

[151]The list of LDCs is reviewed every 3 years by the United Nations Economic and Social Council (ECOSOC), based on recommendations of the Committee for Development Policy (CDP). The following three criteria were used by the CDP in its most recent review of the list in March 2012: (a) Per capita income, based on a 3-year average estimate of the per capita gross national income (GNI), with a threshold of $992 for candidate countries for addition to the list, and a threshold of $1190 for graduation from LDC status; (b) Human assets, involving a composite index (the Human Assets Index) based on the following indicators: (i) nutrition (percentage of the population that is undernourished); (ii) health (child mortality ratio); (iii) school enrolment (gross secondary school enrolment ratio); and (iv) literacy (adult literacy ratio); and (c) Economic vulnerability, involving a composite index (the Economic Vulnerability Index) based on certain indicators. *Ibid.*

developing States" to be mentioned the draft Resolution. Tied to this was a concern for "safeguards" that should ensure sustainable development of aviation. The draft Resolution suggests that the Carbon Offsetting Scheme for International Aviation (COSIA) should carry the protection of providing safeguards in the COSIA to ensure the sustainable development of the international aviation sector and against inappropriate economic burden on international aviation due to market failure, such as excessive pricing of emissions units or restrictions to carbon market access; where under such circumstances, the Council should intervene to review the COSIA and consider possible means to address these issues. One State has suggested that this provision should apply to the GMBM rather than to COSIA.

1.6.2.4 The Council

The ICAO Council would, under the draft Resolution, have follow up work to be carried out. It is firstly required to develop, with the technical contribution of the Council's Committee on Aviation Environmental Protection (CAEP),[152] the rules for the implementation of the MRV system by Member States from year 2018, for adoption by the Council by June 2017. The Council is also required to develop, with the technical contribution of CAEP, necessary guidance material to support implementation of the scheme by Member States, including for the development of registries by 2018; and establish necessary infrastructure for implementation of the scheme, including the establishment of a consolidated central registry under the auspices of ICAO by 2018. In terms of governance the ICAO Council is charged with tasking the Environmental Action Group (EAG)—the Council working group which was active within ICAO in developing the draft Resolution—to oversee the functioning of the IAGOF scheme, with support provided by CAEP, such as the application of an agreed Emissions Unit Criteria (EUC) to determine eligible emissions unit programmes for the scheme as well as the review of the EUC and other design elements of the scheme, and make recommendations to the Council.

Most importantly and as a matter of assistance to ICAO's 191 Member States, the Council is required to expand the provision of capacity building and assistance for the preparation and implementation on Member States' action plans, in order to accommodate capacity building and assistance for implementation of the IAGOF scheme, including organization of seminars and training in all regions for the MRV system and registry development, while encouraging Member States to build partnerships among themselves to support the implementation of the scheme, such as cooperation on the MRV system, joint-implementation of registries, and possible pilot implementation. There is also a useful clause which requests the

[152]The Committee on Aviation Environmental Protection (CAEP) is a technical committee of the ICAO Council established in 1983. CAEP assists the Council in formulating new policies and adopting new Standards and Recommended Practices (SARPs) related to aircraft noise and emissions, and more generally to aviation environmental impact. See http://www.icao.int/environmental-protection/pages/CAEP.aspx.

Council to promote the use of credits generated from the Clean Development Mechanism (CDM)[153] by the IAGOF scheme which could benefit projects involving developing States.

Finally, the Council is requested to explore further development of the CDM methodologies for aviation projects, and encourage States to use such methodologies in taking actions to reduce aviation CO2 emissions, which would further enable the use of credits generated from the CDM by the IAGOF scheme.

Aircraft Operators

It has already been said that it is the Council of ICAO that has to develop the rules for the MRV system. However, the Annex to the draft Resolution gives the Council some guidance as to the key elements of such a system. It is the aircraft operators who would have the task of preparing monitoring plans which include the operator identification information, fleet and operations data, means for calculating emissions and ways to manage data, for review and approval by a State in which the operator is registered. As an integral task within this process, an aircraft operator would report emissions information each year to a State in which the operator is registered, using a standard tool/template. Small operators would be allowed to use simplified procedures. Furthermore, aircraft operators will have to account for alternatives as generating CO2 emissions reduction pursuant to a formula, with relevant emissions factors, to be provided by ICAO. As for States, each year they would have to compile and transmit aggregated emissions information of their operators to ICAO, which would in turn calculate the total emissions from the international aviation sector based on the submissions. States have also to verify that a report is carried out by: internal pre-verification by an aircraft operator; third-party verification before reporting from the operator to a State; and post-reporting review by the State.

Criteria for Emissions Units to be Purchased by Aircraft Operators

The first criterion for purchase is the use by operators of aircraft of clear, publicly disclosed, methodologies and protocols which are driven by considerations of the scope of activities; credit issuance and retirement procedures; identification and tracking of units; appropriate legal measures and transfer of units; validation and

[153]CDM is one of the Flexible Mechanisms defined in the Kyoto Protocol (IPCC, 2007) that provides for emissions reduction projects which generate Certified Emission Reduction units which may be traded in emissions trading schemes. Defined in Article 12 of the Protocol, CDM allows a country with an emission-reduction or emission-limitation commitment under the Protocol (Annex B Party) to implement an emission-reduction project in developing countries. Such projects can earn saleable certified emission reduction (CER) credits, each equivalent to one tonne of CO2, which can be counted towards meeting Kyoto targets.

verification procedures; governance; transparency and public participation provisions; safeguarding systems to address environmental and social risks; sustainable development criteria; and the avoidance of double counting, issuance and claiming. As for delivery, the IAGOF programmes are required to deliver offset credits that represent emissions reductions, avoidance, or sequestration. In order to achieve this objective the programmes are required to be based on a realistic and credible baseline; are quantified, monitored, reported, and verified; have a clear and transparent chain of custody; represent permanent emissions reductions; safeguard against a potential increase in emissions elsewhere; are only counted once towards a mitigation obligation; and do no net harm.

The Resolution recommends that credits from aviation and other CDM projects should be preferred, however, aircraft operators can also meet obligations through credits and allowances from other sources, provided that these comply with the six key criteria: environmental integrity; voluntary participation of jurisdictions; market access; double claiming; registry of allowance units; and transparency. States will be required to establish their own registries. However, groups of States can cooperate to establish group registries, to record and track compliance data of their aircraft operators, and to communicate such data to a consolidated central registry, which is established by ICAO to ensure efficient and transparent recording of compliance data and actions under the scheme.

1.7 A Global Law on Competition in Air Transport

1.7.1 Introduction

Air transport is unlike any other mode of transportation. For that matter, it is different from any other trading activity. For one, a scheduled airline has to obtain permission from a State to land in its territory if it is bringing paying passengers for discharge in that State (the same goes for revenue freight) or take such paying passengers or revenue freight therefrom; the ownership and control of national airlines have usually to be with majority (51 % or more) of the nationals of the country in which the airline is registered; and there are severe restrictions on foreign direct investment in airlines. For instance, one could fly from Montreal in a British registered aircraft to London; stay in a hotel owned by a Dutch national; rent a car made in Italy to tour the countryside and have lunch in Yorkshire in a pub owned by a Pakistani national. In air transport, the situation is different, where one has to fly from Montreal to London in an aircraft that is majority owned by the nationals of the country in which the aircraft is registered and only if that aircraft has permission given by both Canada and the United Kingdom to fly that route on a revenue generating basis.

To circumvent this anomaly, airlines have formed strategic alliances and code sharing agreements to optimize their revenues and fly on routes they are not permitted to fly.

To make matters worse, this curious commercial anomaly has given rise among the air transport community to confusion worse confounded by misconception and misinterpretation. At the apex of this conundrum is the hapless International Civil Aviation Organization (ICAO)—a specialized agency of the United Nations for international civil aviation—which was created by a multilateral treaty—The Convention on International Civil Aviation (Chicago Convention). Academics (who have not worked at ICAO) often misquote the Chicago Convention, or demonstrate their ignorance of the meaning, purpose and functions of ICAO as happened at the ICAO Air Transport Symposium with the ambitious title "*Addressing Competition Issues: Towards a Better Operating Environment*" held at ICAO Headquarters from 30 to 31 March 2016. At this Symposium, one academic was vocal and vehement that ICAO should proclaim a global competition law on air transport. This claim is not only baseless and unfounded but is also plain wrong. Another academic (obviously ignorant of the provisions in the Chicago Convention) advocated that ICAO should establish a judicial tribunal to adjudicate on disputes between States, only to be endorsed by another academic who misquoted ICAO's dispute resolution provisions in the Chicago Convention, saying that ICAO could indeed adjudicate disputes as it was a judicial body.

Neither the United Nations nor ICAO which is a specialized agency of the UN is a world parliament that can make laws. However, both bodies can generate legally binding norms at international law. This is true of ICAO at least in the context of the principles and techniques of air navigation, but not true in terms of economic regulation. It is in the latter instance where ICAO backs down and seeks refuge under its self-imposed title of "global forum which develops policy and guidance with the collaboration of States"—a principle embodied in ICAO's mission Statement. Any policy which is so adopted by ICAO is non coercive, non-compelling and, at its strongest, discretionary on the part of States.

The Statute of The International Court of Justice[154] is explicit in recognizing that there are only four sources of international law: international conventions, whether general or particular, establishing rules expressly recognized by the contesting states; international custom, as evidence of a general practice accepted as law; the general principles of law recognized by civilized nations; judicial decisions and the teachings of the most highly qualified publicists of the various nations, as subsidiary means for the determination of rules of law.[155] In light of this basic principle, one might justifiably say that ICAO cannot adopt a global competition law for air transport.

In the context of ICAO establishing a dispute settlement tribunal on competition, Article 84 of the Chicago Convention provides that if any disagreement between

[154]http://www.icj-cij.org/documents/?p1=4&p2=2.

[155]Article 38 of The Statute of the International Court of Justice.

two or more Contracting States relating to the interpretation or application of the Convention and its Annexes cannot be settled by negotiation, it shall, on the application of any State concerned in the disagreement, be decided by the Council. No member of the Council can vote in the consideration by the Council of any dispute to which it is a party. Any Contracting State may, subject to Article 85, appeal from the decision of the Council to an ad hoc arbitral tribunal agreed upon with the other parties to the dispute or to the Permanent Court of International Justice. Any such appeal is required to be notified to the Council within 60 days of receipt of notification of the decision of the Council. This provision was blatantly misquoted at the ICAO Air Transport Symposium of March 2016 where a commentator stated that the mere fact that the Council can decide upon a disagreement between States grants the ICAO Council adjudicatory powers of a court which can impose its "judgment".

The Council takes decisions, adopts policy and resolutions and issues statements. It does not hand down judicial decisions that are enforceable. For instance, one can consider the issue between Israel and Palestine as an example, when on 4 December 2001, Israeli military forces attacked Gaza International airport, destroyed air navigation facilities and bombarded runways and taxiways until the airport became unserviceable. When the Palestinian Authority attempted a repair on 11 January 2002, the Israeli military forces bombarded once again the airport and its facilities by aircraft, artillery and tanks, thereby destroying the runway, the taxiways and all facilities.

The Palestinian Authority claimed that the destroyed airport and air navigation facilities were used for the transportation of civilian passengers, search and rescue operations in case of emergencies, transportation of rescue material, including medical equipment, medicines and survival kits for safeguarding human lives.

When the matter was brought before the Council under the dispute resolution provisions of the Chicago Convention, the Council, on 13 March 2002, adopted a resolution strongly condemning the destruction of Gaza International Airport and its air navigation facilities. In its Resolution, the Council, strongly condemned all acts of unlawful interference against civil aviation, wherever, by whomsoever and for whatever reasons they are perpetrated. It also strongly condemned the destruction of Gaza International Airport and its air navigation facilities while reaffirming the important role of ICAO in facilitating the resolution of questions which may arise between Contracting States in relation to matters affecting the safe and orderly operation of international civil aviation throughout the world. The Council urged Israel to fully comply with the aims and objectives of the Chicago Convention, while strongly urging Israel to take the necessary measures to restore Gaza International Airport so as to allow its reopening as soon as possible. Additionally, the Council requested the President of the ICAO Council to attend to the implementation of this Resolution, and to secure the full cooperation of the parties with respect to the application of the Chicago Convention and of the above-mentioned principles. Finally, the Council requested the Secretary General to inform all Contracting States of the Resolution. There was no judgment.

Nothing happened. If the Council were an adjudicatory body having the powers of a court of law, why did the Council adopt just a resolution which was a result of a political compromise between the parties? Why did the Council "urge" Israel and not "order" Israel to make reparation? And why was Israel not obligated to comply?

One commentator noted in 1979: "The Council of ICAO cannot be considered a suitable body for adjudication in the proper sense of the word—i.e. settlement of disputes by judges and solely on the basis of respect for law. The Council is composed of States (not independent individuals) and its decisions would always be based on policy and equity considerations rather than on pure legal grounds…truly legal disputes…can be settled only by a true judicial body which can bring into the procedure full judicial detachment, independence and expertise. The under-employed ICJ is the most suitable body for such types of disputes".[156]

ICAO has done much in the field of air transport within its limited role of "fostering the planning and development of air transport" as defined in the Chicago Convention.[157] It can do more provided it is not misled by the pretension of misguided and unfounded wisdom that is both misleading and dangerous.

1.7.2 Competition in Air Transport

1.7.2.1 Auctioning Air Traffic Rights

The self-imposed obstacles by States in Article 6 of the Chicago Convention[158] has led to many difficulties as discussed above, which have confused States as to what principles of competition would operate in air transport. The ambivalence of ICAO on this issue has not helped matters. The confusion has impelled both States and air carriers to find ways and means of circumventing market distortions and find convenient ways and means to protect their own air transport markets. For instance, one of the extensions of the commercial anomaly attached to competition in air transport came to a head at the time of writing in the nature of a decision seriously contemplated by the Indian authorities of auctioning air traffic rights. It was claimed by India that the measure was calculated to further liberalizing the air transport market and toward protecting domestic carriers[159] but it drew negative responses. The rationale for the Indian measure was based on an effort to curb

[156]Milde (1979), p. 88.

[157]Convention on International Civil aviation signed at Chicago on 7 December 1944, ICAO Doc 7300/9, 9th Edition: 2006, Article 44.

[158]Article 6 provides that no scheduled international air service may be operated over or into the territory of a contracting State, except with the special permission or other authorization of that State, and in accordance with the terms of such permission or authorization.

[159]Foreign carriers may not get landing rights on demand, says Civil Aviation Ministry, *Aviation Security International*, 25 December 2015 at http://www.dnaindia.com/money/report-foreign-carriers-may-not-get-landing-rights-on-demand-says-civil-aviation-ministry-2159662.

excess capacity being injected to the Indian air transport market which would eventually drive prices down, hurting Indian carriers.

The Universal Declaration of Human Rights of The United Nations in Article 13 sets forth the fundamental principle that everyone has the right to freedom of movement and residence within the borders of each state and that everyone has the right to leave any country, including his own, and to return to his country. Embodied in these principles is the right of movement without undue restrictions brought about by abuse of fair competitive practices and the rights of persons to have equal rights to travel. The right to travel by air is entrenched in the philosophy of the "common carrier" which is, as per *Burnett* v. *Riter*[160] decided in 1925 in the United States is: "[A]n individual or business that makes itself available to the world at large to transport people or property in exchange for a fee". There is a legal obligation on the part of the common carrier to carry all passengers or freight as long as there is enough space, the fee is paid, and no reasonable grounds to refuse to do so exist. A common carrier that unjustifiably refuses to carry a particular person or cargo may be sued for damages.

The right to travel by air was recognized as a specific and inherent right of the individual at the Chicago Conference held in November/December of 1944 where 52 countries assembled to draw up a global constituent treaty which culminated in the signing of the Convention on International Civil Aviation (Chicago Convention) at Chicago on 7 December 1944. At the Chicago Conference several States wielding the credibility of their global stature elaborated on how the right should be implemented by States in the context of the provision of air services by their air carriers.

At the Chicago Conference in 1944, the United States proposed a multilateral agreement calculated to guarantee commercial landing rights everywhere in the globe to all the world's airlines without restriction. The United States took the position that the use of the air and the use of the sea were both common in that they were highways given by nature to all men. They were different in that man's use of the air is subject to the sovereignty of nations over which such use is made. The United States was therefore of the opinion that nations ought to arrange among themselves for its use in such manner as would be of the greatest benefit to all humanity, wherever situated. The United Kingdom contended: "While recognizing national interests we want to encourage enterprise and efficiency which are indeed themselves a national as well as an international interest. And we want therefore to encourage the efficient and to stimulate the less efficient. . .only by common action on some such lines as indicated can we reduce and gradually eliminate subsidies, thereby putting civil aviation on an economic footing and incidentally very considerably relieving the tax payer. Unrestricted competition is their most fruitful soil".

The United Kingdom seems to have adopted a balanced approach at the Conference that supported the establishment of air services to serve the needs of the

---

[160]276S.W. 347.

travelling public, while not unduly affecting the rights of States to have a fair share of traffic for themselves.

India, while believing that it was essential for air services to develop rationally with a certain degree of freedom of the air being the inherent right of every State, went on to say: "We believe that the grant of commercial rights—that is to say, the right to carry traffic to and from another country,—is best negotiated and agreed to on a universal reciprocal basis, rather than by bilateral agreements. We think that only such an arrangement will secure to all countries the reciprocal rights which their interests require. But the grant of any such freedoms and rights must, in our opinion, necessarily be associated with the constitution of an authority which will regulate the use of such freedoms. It will be the function of such authority…to ensure that the interests of the people, both of the most powerful and of the smaller countries, are secured".[161]

India's position in 1944 at the Conference was therefore to recommend a liberal approach of universal reciprocity within the parameters of control by an authority which could ensure that the smaller nations were protected from being swamped by larger States.

The position taken by India at the Chicago Conference is seemingly at variance with the confusing reports coming out of the country—that India is considering auctioning air traffic rights. Other reports say that the Indian authorities are merely trying to put in place a mechanism for the provision of additional seats by auction to interested foreign carriers. Bidding will be introduced if domestic airlines have not fully utilised their quota. The additional rights granted through bidding will be for a 3-year period and proceeds would go to regional connectivity fund.

The International Air Transport Association (IATA)—the international association of airlines—claims that the auction pertains to air traffic rights and states: "[A] s far as IATA is aware, there is no precedent for States auctioning traffic rights among carriers. The proposal potentially raises important questions of compatibility with ICAO (International Civil Aviation Organization) policies and guidance on the subject of air service agreements, with negative consequences for the industry and consumers". IATA has quoted relevant ICAO Resolutions adopted at the 38th Session of ICAO's Assembly in 2013 and ICAO's vision recognized in 2015 on "fair and equal opportunity" and non-discrimination for all States and their stakeholders. IATA goes on to say: "A policy decision by the Indian government to auction traffic rights for certain markets – namely those under 5,000 km distance from the capital – but not for others – raises questions about whether India is pursuing a fair and equal, non-discriminatory approach. Such auctioning also could create unequal treatment between incumbent carriers and new entrant carriers and between domestic and foreign airlines".[162]

---

[161]See Proceedings of the International Civil Aviation Conference, Chicago, Illinois, November 1—December 7, 1944 United States Government Printing Office: Washington, 1948 at 76.

[162]Auctioning of air traffic rights anti-competitive, says IATA. See http://articles.economictimes.indiatimes.com/2016-03-10/news/71382311_1_traffic-rights-aviation-policy-aviation-market.

IATA's claim is that such a practice would lead to market distortions between carriers and to higher fares, thus eroding the desired connectivity in global air transport. At the time of writing, it was not clear whether the Indian authorities had taken a policy decision to auction air traffic rights.

If the debate pertains to the auctioning of air traffic rights, there are three basic issues to be considered: what is an air traffic right?; can a State indulge in an auction with airlines?; and does the practice of auctioning air traffic rights erode international legal principles applicable to competition in air transport?

Air traffic rights are freedoms granted through permissions given by one State to another for the latter's carrier/s to operate non-commercial or commercial air transport through/into and out of the former's territory (as per Articles 5 and 6 of the Chicago Convention). These rights are granted through negotiations usually between States and not between States and airlines. An auction is a sale in which goods or property are sold to the highest bidder.[163] Air traffic rights are neither goods nor property but mere permissions. Therefore air traffic rights cannot be subject to auctions.

Air traffic rights are granted through bilateral or multilateral agreements called treaties. Article 2 of the Vienna Convention on the Law of Treaties (1969) defines a Treaty as: "an international agreement concluded between States in written form and governed by international law, whether embodied in a single instrument or in two or more related instruments and whatever its particular designation. Therefore a State cannot deal direct with airlines on the issue of traffic rights or allocation of seats".

On the subject of competition, the Chicago Convention is clear that air services have to be operated soundly and economically and with *equality of opportunity* (my emphasis) for carriers. This is tied in with a premise that ICAO's aims and objectives should meet the needs of the (sic) "peoples" of the world for safe, regular, economical and efficient air services. The "equality of opportunity" principle has been interpreted by learned jurists as "equality of opportunity to compete" and not mere "equality of opportunity to operate air services".

The auctioning process will effectively preclude carriers with less resources than those that have both the superior capacity, financial resources and ability to overbid the former and dominate the market. This will bring to bear the principle of abuse of dominant position and antitrust principles that are widely recognized throughout the world and could result in market distortion, anti-competitive conduct and discriminatory practices. Such a practice would not serve the travelling public to the extent that the *travaux preparatoires* (preparatory work) and principles of the Chicago Convention intended.

In view of the aforesaid discussion, it is evident that, by their very nature, air traffic rights cannot be auctioned; States cannot deal with air carriers under

---

See also *Draft National Civil Aviation Policy 2015* (India), Feedback provided by IATA, 25 November 2015 at 9–10.

[163] *Payne* v. *Cave*, (1789) 3 TR 148.

principles applying to them under international air law and the principles contained in the Chicago Convention. Auctioning of air traffic rights could for global principles lead to anti-competitive and discriminatory conduct that would seriously jeopardize the travelling public. This example makes the need for global principles on competition in air transport all the more compelling.

1.7.2.2 What Can ICAO Do to Promote Competition and Liberalization of Air Transport?

ICAO has already done much within its limited scope. The Organization has developed and published a compendium of conclusions and decisions adopted by the ICAO Assembly and the Council. Additionally ICAO has developed guidance material for its member States with regard to the economic regulation of international air transport.[164] For the guidance of States in their interpretation or application of Articles 5 and 6 of the Chicago Convention, the Council of ICAO has, in its compendium, developed a definition for the term "scheduled international air service" which is accompanied by "Notes on the Application of the Definition and an Analysis of the Rights Conferred by Article 5 of the Convention". The Council recognized, when developing the definition, that the right of Contracting States to impose regulations, conditions and limitations on the taking on or discharging of passengers, cargo or mail by commercial non-scheduled air transport is unqualified. It has expressed the opinion, however, that it should be understood that the right would not be exercised in such a manner as to render the operation of this important form of air transport impossible or non-effective.

In its *Manual on the Regulation of International Air Transport*[165] ICAO explains what bilateral and multilateral air services agreements are and lays down the existing practices on market access, but goes no further. ICAO has not identified the principles of competition in air transport nor has it taken a position on what principles its member States should adhere to in demanding of their national carriers that they abide by the principles of safe and orderly conduct in the operation of air services that grants each player equality of opportunity.[166]

Regrettably, ICAO has, for the past 72 years of its existence, only spewed out manuals and guidance material defining various concepts of commercial practice in the operation of air services without setting out distinct and specific commercial practices that States should follow when monitoring their national carriers, and, more importantly, what practices they should avoid. The sum total of ICAO's contribution to policy has been in its general acknowledgement that it favours liberalization of air transport.

---

[164]See Policy and Guidance Material on the Economic Regulation of International Air Transport, *Doc 9587* (Third Edition – 2008).

[165]Doc 9626.

[166]For a discussion on the principles of competition see Abeyratne (2016), pp. 76–97.

A Code of Conduct

Although ICAO does not have the authority to promulgate a global law on competition in air transport, one has to take cognizance of the fact that ICAO's aim and objective in the economic field as prescribed by the Chicago Convention is to foster the planning and development of air transport. Implicit in the "planning" aspect is planning for the safe and orderly development of air transport that ensures equality of opportunity for each player to compete on a level playing field. In this context, it is suggested that ICAO should, after embarking on a detailed study of applicable competition laws, adopt a code of conduct that specifically lays down concrete principles of competition. These principles could be incorporated in the nature of Standards and Recommended Practices (SARPs) in a new Annex to the Chicago Convention. Even if States will not be not bound by the SARPs therein, the SAPRs would impel States to take more cognizance of inequalities generated by anti-competitive commercial practices of their national carriers and that if they fail to take any action, such States would be exposed to the international aviation community the same way States which have serious safety and security concerns which do not ameliorate or correct them are exposed, under ICAO's safety and security audits.[167]

Such a competition code in the new Annex should have, as its cornerstone, strict prohibitions on the restraint of trade that could erode the principle of equality of opportunity that is so prominently addressed in the *Preamble* to the Chicago Convention. The provisions should specify that any contract, trust or conspiracy that is calculated to foster restraint of trade should be considered illegal by the member States of ICAO if such involve the operation of air services between States. Each Member State should be required to adopt punitive legislative measures against such activity. It must be mentioned that the prohibition of these contracts and practices must be limited to illegal restraint of trade.[168] Applicable factors for the determination of an airline's conduct should be: the airline's existing market share and competitive ability; the competitive structure of the airline industry; the deleterious effects of the practice in question; and the duration of the practice along with its history.

Price fixing is another adverse practice that should be prohibited in the ICAO instrument. Price fixing is the raising, lowering, fixing, pegging or stabilizing the price of air transport. This practice may involve setting minimum or maximum prices or limiting the capacity of the air transport product. An example of this practice in judicial determination was seen in the collusive monopolization case in

[167]Article 54j) of the Chicago Convention prescribes that the ICAO Council, as one of its mandatory functions, is required to report to contracting States any infraction of the Convention as well as any failure to carry out recommendations or determinations of the Council.

[168]*Standard Oil Company of New Jersey* v. *United States*, 221 USI, 31 S. Ct. 502, Lexis 1725 (U.S. Sup. Ct.).

1984 involving *American Airlines* and *Braniff Airlines*[169] which invoked section 2 of the Sherman Antitrust Act of 1890[170] against the defendants, American Airlines, and its president, for his proposal to the president of *Braniff Airlines* that the two airlines control the market and set prices. Market sharing agreements which illegally divide markets between airlines could come under this head. So would arrangements between two or more airlines which enter into a contract that restraints trade.[171] If an airline unilaterally chooses not to enter into a contract on the abovementioned terms, it may exculpate itself from liability, even if it entered into preliminary discussions on the subject without collusion.[172]

Commercial monopolization is another practice that should enter into the statute books of States as an illegal competitive practice in air transport. If an airline were to monopolize, or attempt to monopolize or conspire with other airlines to monopolize international air transport, such airlines should be subject to punitive measures. Exceptions to the practice of illegal monopolizing would be: innocent acquisition caused by superior business practices; management skill and corporate foresight; and a natural monopoly practice where only one competitor can exist in a limited market. On the issue of monopolization, the famed *Microsoft* case[173] is relevant as an analogy. *Microsoft*, with over 30 years of established reputation as the world's largest software company, threatened *Apple*—a manufacturer of personal computers—that it would cancel Microsoft office software for Apple if it did not use "Explorer"—the Microsoft web browser—and kept using the Netscape web browser (a competitor of Microsoft) instead. The United States Court of Appeal upheld the District Court's judgment that Microsoft was guilty of monopolization under local law and ordered Microsoft to refrain from such coercive commercial activities.

ICAO could also inquire whether it would be acceptable for one airline to use the substitute principle. In other words, could an airline competing with another airline that offers the consumer a choice of a substitute product acquire the assets of the latter airline and thus restrain competition? These are called horizontal mergers

---

[169]*United States of America, Plaintiff-Appellant*, v. *American Airlines, Inc. and Robert L. Crandall, Defendants-Appellees*, No. 83-1831. 743 F.2d 1114, 53 USLW 2209, 1984-2 Trade Cases 66,232.

[170]Section 2 states that: "Every person who shall monopolize, or attempt to monopolize, or combine or conspire with any other person or persons, to monopolize any part of the trade or commerce among the several States, or with foreign nations, shall be deemed guilty of a felony, and, on conviction thereof, shall be punished by fine not exceeding $10,000,000 if a corporation, or, if any other person, $350,000, or by imprisonment not exceeding three years, or by both said punishments, in the discretion of the court".

[171]For analogy, see *State Oil Co*. v. *Khan*, 522 U.S., 3, 118 S. Ct. 275, 1997 U.S. Lexis 6705. See also *Arizona v. Maricopa County Medical Practices*, 457 U.S. 332. Also, *States* v. Topco *Associates Inc*, 405 U.S. 596.

[172]See *United States* v. *Colgate*, 250 U.S. 300, S. ct. 465, 1919 U.S. Lexis 1748 (U.S. S. Ct).

[173]*United States* v. *Microsoft Corporation*, 2002 U.S. Dist, Lexis 22804 (Dist. Ct, D.C.). See also, *Greyhound* v. *International Business Machine Corporation*, 559 F.2d. 488, 1977 U.S. App, Lexis 11957 (9th Case).

which have been judicially pronounced to be illegal.[174] However, exceptions to this rule prevail, such as the *Failing Company Doctrine* where a competitor may merge with a failing company if there is no way out for a failing company to survive. Additionally, two or more companies could merge or strengthen their positions and offer a better product to the consumer.

Price discrimination, where an airline would, without just cause, enforce fluctuation of prices of the same product—a practice that is calculated to restrain competition—would also be unacceptable. The exceptions to price discrimination would be cost justification where differences in price differential is due to escalating costs of production, sale or delivery of the air transport product. Changing conditions or market fluctuations of the radical nature would also constitute exceptions. Furthermore, lawful engagement of price differentiation to meet a competitor's arbitrary low pricing would also be considered a justifiable defence against an allegation of price discrimination.

Another anti-competitive activity that could be investigated by ICAO as a possible inclusion in its codification is abuse of dominant position where a carrier would use its dominant position in the market to run other carriers out of business, or uses a collective dominant position shared with another carrier in the process. The European Court said in 1978 that: "The dominant position...relates to a position of economic strength enjoyed by an undertaking which enables itself to prevent effective competition being maintained in the relevant market by affording it the power to behave to an appreciable extent of its competitors, customers and ultimately of its consumers".[175] The foremost drivers in the assessment of abuse of dominant position are the dynamics of the market and the extent to which the product is differentiated. In this context it is relevant to note an important judicial determination in 1979 that an undertaking which has "a very large market share and holds it for some time is...by virtue of that share is in a position of strength..."[176]

An extremely important consideration for ICAO in establishing an anti-competitive code is the interpretation given to the emerging concept of *Disruptive Innovation*. There is a popular misconception that business entities such as *Uber* (a global private taxi service operating in 60 countries and valued at $ 60 billion) and *Airbnb* (global hotel accommodation services) are disruptive innovators. Disruptive innovation occurs when a business entity finds a new market and caters to it or finds a neglected market and offers its services to that market. Neither *Uber* nor *Airbnb* comes within this category.[177] Nor does *Emirates Airlines* or *Etihad* in their competition with the United States carriers.[178] Disruption occurs when a smaller

---

[174]*United States* v. *Philadelphia National Bank*, 374 U.S. 321, 83 S. Ct. 171C.

[175]*Case 27/76* [1976] E. C.R., 207.

[176]*Hoffman-La Roche* v. *Commission*, Case 85/76 [1979] E.C.R. 461.

[177]See Christensen et al. (2015) *innovation* where the authors give the example of *Xerox* which targeted large corporations with their photo copying machines because these corporations could pay a high price for the product. Xerox ignored libraries, bowling league operators and other small customers who could not afford *Xerox*'s prices, until personal copier manufacturers took over the neglected market.

[178]For discussion on this subject see Abeyratne (2016), pp. 99–102.

business entity challenges with success the business model and established market of a larger business. A typical example of disruptive innovation is when a company targets an overlooked segment of a market and offers a product at a lower price than is offered by an existing product of another company. A hypothetical example would be the targeting of the growing number of ageing baby boomers and pensioners, where an airline could offer specialized services to those who have leisure time to travel, such as more comfortable seats and more attention with inflight meals, all at a price lower than those offered by legacy carriers or other low cost carriers. Another example could be the creation of a new market, which targets youth and young adults having the travel bug. It is important to note that *Disruptive Innovation* is a process and not a product *per se* as exemplified by mini computers which graduated from the fringe to the mainstream.[179]

Another important dimension for consideration is the apparent public policy conflict between freedom of contract and a contract calculated to restrain freedom of trade. Should a contract be rendered void *ab initio* n or voidable if its purpose resulted in a restraint of freedom to contract? Judicial findings lean toward the principle that while an agreement, the sole purpose of which is to restrain commercial activity is unenforceable, ancillary restraints to otherwise promote transactions are permissible at law.[180]

It goes without saying that an ICAO code that is incorporated in an Annex to the Chicago Convention or any other form of instrument would, in addition to being discretionary on the part of ICAO member States as per Article 38 of the Chicago Convention,[181] be also subject to laws enacted in States that exempt commercial entities from the anti-competitive practices discussed above.

---

[179]Harvard Business Review, *supra*, note 177, *ibid.*

[180]*Vancouver Malt and Sake Brewing Co. Ltd.*, v. *Vancouver Breweries Ltd*, [1934] 2 D.L.R. 310 (P.C.).

[181]Article 38 provides: "Any State which finds it impracticable to comply in all respects with any such international standard or procedure, or to bring its own regulations or practices into full accord with any international standard or procedure after amendment of the latter, or which deems it necessary to adopt regulations or practices differing in any particular respect from those established by an international standard, shall give immediate notification to the International Civil Aviation Organization of the differences between its own practice and that established by the international standard. In the case of amendments to international standards, any State which does not make the appropriate amendments to its own regulations or practices shall give notice to the Council within sixty days of the adoption of the amendment to the international standard, or indicate the action which it proposes to take. In any such case, the Council shall make immediate notification to all other states of the difference which exists between one or more features of an international standard and the corresponding national practice of that State".

1.8 Conclusion

It is submitted that the only way in which ICAO can vindicate itself by showing at least a semblance of credibility in the economic field is to obviate its mindset—that it exists merely to provide definitions of various concepts in the economic field—and use the relevant provisions of the Chicago Convention to introduce concrete principles of competition that could be monitored by ICAO. In view of the preceding paragraph which clearly indicates that States cannot be brought before the Council under the dispute resolution provisions of the ICAO Council in the face of Article 38 of the Chicago Convention, ICAO could, under the principles of the notification clause in the provision which impels States to advise ICAO of any deviation from the Annexes, monitor States as to whether they encourage anti-competitive conduct of their airlines or turn a blind eye to their airlines activities. ICAO could then advise States under Article 54j) of the Chicago Convention of the conduct of States which do not comply with provisions of the Annex on competition. This would at least effectively preclude the free for all that is occurring in the economic aspect of air transport and introduce some degree of clarity to the operation of air services. This measure could also provide some justification for the meaning and purpose of the founding fathers of the Convention as to what air transport should be, as discussed at the beginning of this article.

ICAO cannot do this alone. In the ultimate analysis, ICAO needs the cooperation of its member States. It is one thing for ICAO to develop SARPs on competition. Since member States are not obligated to comply with SARPs, they could well support their national carriers in their anti-competitive practices. In such an event, those States whose airlines are marginalized as a result of the anti-competitive practices of their competitors could bring the issue to the attention of their States who in turn could submit the matter to the dispute resolution mechanism of the ICAO Council. As already discussed, Article 84 of the Chicago Convention provides that if any disagreement between two or more contracting States relating to the interpretation or application of the Convention and its Annexes cannot be settled by negotiation, it is required to, on the application of any State concerned in the disagreement, be decided by the Council. As already discussed, the Council is not a tribunal nor is it arbitral body. However, if the Council were to either make a statement or adopt a resolution, and the aggrieved State is not satisfied with the outcome, it can appeal from the decision of the Council to an *ad hoc* arbitral tribunal agreed upon with the other parties to the dispute or to the International Court of Justice (ICJ).

Article 85 of the Convention follows through, saying that if any contracting State party to a dispute in which the decision of the Council is under appeal has not accepted the Statute of the Permanent Court of International Justice (now the ICJ) and the contracting States parties to the dispute cannot agree on the choice of the arbitral tribunal, each of the contracting States parties to the dispute could name a single arbitrator who shall name an umpire. If either contracting State party to the dispute fails to name an arbitrator within a period of 3 months from the date of the appeal, an arbitrator would be named on behalf of that State by the President of the Council from a list of qualified and available persons maintained by the Council. If, within 30 days, the arbitrators cannot agree on an umpire, the President of the Council can designate an umpire from the list previously referred to. The arbitrators and the umpire would then jointly constitute an arbitral tribunal. Any arbitral tribunal is entitled to settle its own procedure and give its decisions by majority vote, provided that the Council may determine procedural questions in the event of any delay which in the opinion of the Council is excessive. Article 86 stipulates that the decision of either the arbitral tribunal or the ICJ would be deemed final.

The role of the Council does not end there. While Article 85 amply demonstrates that the Council has an important role to play in the selection of the judicial and arbitral process which involves either a tribunal or the ICJ, the Council can, under Article 87 impose an obligation on member States of ICAO to be bound not to allow the operation of an airline of a member State through the airspace above its territory if the Council has decided that the airline concerned is not conforming to a final decision rendered in the adjudicatory process by the arbitral tribunal or the ICJ.

There have been instances in the past where some members of the Council have suggested an Annex to the Chicago Convention on liberalization—a concept supported by ICAO purely as a matter of principle. This suggestion pertained to the adoption of SARPs on how to liberalize and not on competition itself. It is submitted that an Annex on competition is an entirely different issue and it will be extremely difficult for any State to object to competition rules being adopted under the ICAO umbrella since such objections could be perceived as anti-competitive, self-serving and retrogressive. Therefore, it is time for ICAO to give this suggestion its active consideration.

As was stated at the outset of this book, ICAO has been given a clear task by the international community, both at the Twelfth Air Navigation Conference of 2012 and by the 38th Session of the ICAO Assembly in 2013, to urgently establish an appropriate mechanism including States and industry to evaluate the extent of the cybersecurity issues and develop a global air traffic management architecture taking care of cybersecurity issues and to continue its work on a basis of urgency in terms of introducing measures for prevention of acts of unlawful interference, on the basis of the strategic direction provided by ICASS. That strategic direction has already been discussed.

The issue is whether two Recommended Practices in an Annex to the Chicago Convention would cut it under such compelling circumstances. These two recommendations provide that States *should* (which gives them a discretion) ensure that measures are developed to protect information and communications technology systems from unlawful interference with civil aviation and encourage entities to identify critical information *et al.* that would be exposed to vulnerability. There is no mention of responsibility on the part of States or accountability including a duty to monitor the continuous protecting of information systems with a view to protecting systems of air transport. It must be mentioned that the European Civil Aviation Conference (ECAC) has done a much better job in its Guidance Material issued to its members—which was presented to the AVSEC Panel of ICAO in

2011—by being much more specific than the ICAO Annex by specifying that those responsible should ensure that measures are implemented and not just put in place.[182]

Furthermore, it is curious that ICAO is effectively precluded from determining whether the States have taken any action regarding its two Recommended Practices, as its Security Audit Process, which comes under its Universal Security Audit Programme—Continuous Monitoring Approach (USAP-CMA) has a limited scope of looking at only the Standards of Annex 17 and security-related Standards of Annex 9 (Facilitation). At a time when a previous administration of the ICAO Secretariat (which functioned until 31 July 2015) gives way to a new executive who took over in August 2015, it might be prudent for the ICAO Council and the Secretariat to re-visit the issue of aviation cyber security against the backdrop of ICAO's mandate which has been explicitly assigned to it by the aviation community.

Against the backdrop of three scenarios: State sponsored cyber terrorism; politically motivated cyber terrorism carried out by an individual or groups of individuals; and plain cybercrime carried out by individuals, ICAO might wish to place before the upcoming 39th Session of the Assembly in 2016 a scheme calculated to address the issue on a global scale based upon a sustained study to be conducted by the Aviation Security Panel in collaboration with the Legal Committee of ICAO. Given the time constraint, it could merely be a feasibility scheme along the lines of the Market Based Measures Resolution presented at the 37th Assembly (2010) under Resolution A37-19.[183] The Assembly could then direct the Council to develop an appropriate a cybersecurity regime that would be analogous to the stringent passenger screening schemes now in place that would be interoperable and globally accepted with some degree of legal binding force.

With regard to transfer of functions of aircraft and registration of aircraft, it must be noted that the First Session of the ICAO Assembly, held in Montreal from 6 to 27 May 1947, adopted Resolution A1-46 creating the LC Committee as a permanent body of the Organization. According to this Resolution, The Committee is a permanent Committee of ICAO, constituted by the Assembly and responsible to the Council. The duties and functions of the Committee are *inter alia* to advise the Council on matters relating to the interpretation and amendment of the Chicago Convention as referred to it by the Council and to study and make recommendations on such other matters relating to public international air law as may be referred to it by the Council or the Assembly. These duties were reiterated and endorsed by Resolution A7-5 adopted at the Seventh Session of the ICAO Assembly (Brighton, 16 June-6 July 1953). It is interesting that in the Report of the 35th Session of the

[182]See GUIDANCE MATERIAL ON CYBER THREATS TO AVIATION, *AVSECP/22-WP17*, 14/3/11, Appendix B.

[183]A37-19: *Consolidated statement of continuing ICAO policies and practices related to environmental protection-climate change*, Annex. See Assembly Resolutions (as of 8 October 2010), ICAO: 2011, 1–67 at 1–73.

LC, released in 2013, it is recorded that the Working Group appointed to consider progress on Article 83 *bis* and make recommendations to the ICAO Council recommended that the Secretariat could review ICAO Circular 295 to determine whether changes are necessary to address some key questions, such as the voluntary nature of these agreements; when these various aircraft lease and/or interchange agreements implicate Article 83 *bis*; whether agreements for transfer of aircraft from one State to another State on a short term basis involve (or necessitate) a transfer of State of Registry responsibilities under Article 83 *bis*; and the legal implications for each State of entering into an Article 83 *bis* Agreement, etc.

It is submitted that there is a distinct link between the mandate of the LC as charged by Assembly Resolution A1-46—to study and make recommendations to the Council on matters relating to public international air law and the recommendation of the 35th Session of the LC that the ICAO Secretariat should review Circular 295 and make recommendations pertaining to the legal implications for each State that enters into an Article 83 *bis* agreement. This clearly devolves responsibility upon the ICAO Secretariat to address issues of legal liability of both the State of Registry and the State of the Operator. Besides, Resolution A1-46 clearly lays down the fundamental requirement that the LC, must advise the Council on matters relating to the interpretation and amendment of the Chicago Convention.

However, The Secretariat, in its submission to the 36th Session of the LC avoided any reference to the legal implications for States under Article 83 *bis* as recommended by the 35th Session of the Committee and instead gave a historical account of the development of the provision and sought measures such as e-registration. It is now time for the Council of ICAO to request implementation of the recommendation which came out of the 35th session of the LC.

In the context of RPAS, At the time of writing, there was a distinct division between the work of the LC and the Remotely Controlled Aircraft Systems Panel (RPAS Panel) of ICAO, in that the LC was engaged in a theoretical exercise of sifting through statements and interpretations of treaty provisions regarding liability issues of RPAS while the RPAS Panel was seeking a practical outcome to ICAO's work on RPAS. For example, The RPAS Panel, at its meeting on 15 March 2015, clearly indicated that the overall objective of the Panel was to facilitate the safe, secure and efficient integration of RPA into non-segregated airspace and aerodromes by: maintaining existing level of safety for manned aviation; developing Standards and Recommended Practices (SARPs), procedures and guidance; and being the focal point and coordinator of all ICAO RPAS related work. To develop SARPs on RPAS, ICAO would need clear interpretive guidance on liability issues as well as procedural issues from the LC so that a Standard could be designed in a compelling manner as to lead to accountability as discussed earlier in this article.

The first step towards this goal is the sensible suggestion of the LC that a questionnaire be sent to all 191 ICAO contracting States—detailed and well thought through. Thereafter, with the information gathered, a select committee comprising some members of the RPAS and LC should work together to mesh the legal nuances with the technical considerations in an Annex to the Chicago

Convention. Although SARPs do not have the legal legitimacy of compulsion and obligation (except in the case of Annex 2) this would be a good opportunity to infuse some moral obligation on States in a growing area of concern to the aviation community.

Finally, on climate change, it must be recognized that ICAO's task in developing a global MBM scheme is by no means an easy task. *A fortiori*, the difficulties are aggravated because such a scheme is being developed in the midst of the threat of the EU ETS being reintroduced if the ICAO scheme is found not acceptable; an economy wide carbon cap being introduced by China; and market jurisdictions are being considered by Canada and the United States. Although carbon pricing may be a more efficient tool to address global warming than renewable energy, one must consider that subsidies for fossil fuels exceed those for renewables and therefore the development of renewables has an edge over any MBM.

From a global perspective, the system of placing caps on countries emissions is now considered archaic. The Kyoto Protocol, which was the United Nations sponsored treaty which brought this about, is now extinct. The new trend is for countries to take it upon themselves to curb their own emissions, and the COP 21 Agreement speaks for this voluntary approach by limiting emissions to an aspirational level of 1.5 % of pre industrial levels on a purely voluntary basis. This is based on a concept called "intended nationally determined contributions". This phenomenon is justified by the fact that many countries tend to shy away from carbon taxes and cap-and-trade- schemes which are thrust upon them, opting instead to select their own way of restricting carbon emissions in their countries. Whether this would influence the ICAO deliberations is to be seen.

A key factor in the MBM equation would be aircraft engine performance. The three major problems of aircraft are that: they are inefficient; they are big; and they run on toxic fuels. According to Rolce Royce which makes engines for the gigantic A 380 aircraft, a fully laden A380, uses as much energy as 3500 family cars, equivalent to 6 cars for each passenger. Long haul flights produce on average twice as much emissions per mile traveled per passenger than cars and short haul flights produce three times as much. When this is matched with the projections of the major aircraft manufacturers Airbus and Boeing—that there will be approximately 26,000 new aircraft introduced to the air transport market by 2030 the prospect for engine emissions become ominous.[184]

The fundamental consideration for ICAO is that, unlike in usual circumstances, it will be the Assembly that will develop an MBM scheme based on input provided by the Council. Therefore, the Council will have to explain fully the process it followed; the propositions it considered and discarded, and justify the criteria in recommending a suitable framework; process and final recommendation for a

[184] As soon as airplanes leave the gate, they begin to produce phenomenal amounts of nitrogen oxides (NOx), carbon monoxide, particulate matter, and cancer-causing toxics such as benzene and formaldehyde. This pollution travels miles downwind, contributing to asthma, lung and heart disease, and a large number of cancers. See http://www.flyingclean.com/impacts_airplane_pollution_climate_change_and_health.

global MBM. This process would need the scheduling of extra time at the Assembly, and prior notification of details of the various steps taken by the Council in the Strawman approach. Rejection of the original Strawman and acceptance of validated alternatives would have to be explained in detail to ICAO member States. This would in turn make it necessary for credible studies that the Council, and indeed the Secretariat of ICAO should carry out on critical issues involved including but not limited to CBDR and SCRC. At the end of the day, ICAO will succeed only if its MBM scheme subscribes fairly and squarely to both CBDR and SCRC, and it will be interesting to see whether ICAO will include the principles of the COP 21 Agreement discussed in this segment or relegate the Agreement to a mere *Whereas* clause in its final proposal to the Assembly.

Some may argue that what the ICAO proposal of carbon offsetting accomplishes is the award of a moratorium to certain States below a given line of national income per capita, to keep polluting without paying a penalty. The basis of the ICAO framework seemingly is that if an airline operator emitted CO2 in excess of its allocated amount it would have to purchase carbon credits. *Ex facie* this does not seem any different from the fundamental principle of emissions trading except that the ICAO model would be globally applicable, which means that the reporting, monitoring and verification of an airline's emissions activity would have to be done on a global basis. However, the moratorium on the need to purchase carbon credits would be applicable to aircraft operators of certain States until 2026, flouting the polluter pays principle that is advocated by many who are proponents of a carbon tax. Some others might argue that the proposal does nothing to bring down the rate of pollution, but merely appeases the guilty conscience of big polluters. Alarmingly, there is not one single mention of alternative fuels in the ICAO draft Resolution.

On the other hand, Christine Legarde, Director General of the International Monetary Fund advocates a carbon tax. Legarde has said: "A lot of people would rather do emissions trading systems, but we believe that carbon taxation would be a lot better"[185]... charging for the emissions of fossil fuels puts in place the needed incentives for low-carbon investments; it also provides revenues to safeguard the poor, reduce debt, and lower the burden of other taxes on households and businesses".[186] On the same page is Dr. Hoesung Lee, the Chair of the UN Intergovernmental Panel on Climate Change (IPCC), who has emphasized that there is a compelling need to price the "externalities" of carbon pollution. Lee has said: "[When] my action affects other persons' welfare, but I do not pay for these disadvantages... those are externalities. Climate change is a typical example ...

---

[185]http://www.carbontax.org/blogarchives/2015/10/08/carbon-tax-convergence-as-imf-and-ipcc-chiefs-speak-out/.

[186]Reports from IMF and French economists call for climate taxes on international aviation fuel or air travel, *GREENAIR online* 15 January 2016, http://www.greenaironline.com/news.php?viewStory=2183. A Paris School of Economics (PSE) paper by Lucas Chancel and best-selling author Thomas Piketty estimates a €180 ($200) levy on business class tickets and €20 ($22) on economy class would raise around €150 billion ($165bn) a year for climate adaptation. *Ibid.*

[T]he way to correct the externality problem is to have a price on certain activities that cause those externalities . . . a carbon tax". Lee ranks a carbon tax as his—and now, perhaps, the IPCC's—highest priority: "if you ask me to choose the most important work in climate change issues, then I'll choose carbon price. That's because it is the driver to put us into the right track".[187]

Former Secretary of State George Schultz and Gary S. Becker writing in the *Wall Street Journal* say: "energy producers . . . should bear the full costs of the use of the energy they provide. Most of these costs are included in what it takes to produce the energy in the first place, but they vary greatly in the price imposed on society by the pollution they emit and its impact on human health and well-being, the air we breathe and the climate we create. We should identify these costs and see that they are attributed to the form of energy that causes them".[188]

The tax referred to here by these leaders is a tax levied on the total quantity of greenhouse gases emitted. The European Union once considered a carbon tax as a viable economic instrument that could be effective in curbing emissions. However, it was concluded that a carbon tax provided less flexibility for member states since E.U. members have varying amounts of pollution and wealth. Since a tax would impose the same levy on all countries, rich and poor, and some members would have been paying a great deal more in taxes than others, the EU's conclusion on a carbon tax was that, using a trading scheme instead would improve flexibility, particularly if, along the lines of current practice in the EU, under a cap-and-trade system the E.U. could set one overall cap on emissions, while allocating allowances to each country based on its individual emissions. Such a trading scheme meant less pressure on industry if the allowances were initially issued for free, whereas a tax (or auctioned allowances) charges industry for all residual emissions.[189]

An interesting dimension has been presented by one commentator who says: "[A]lthough taxation is an option to address climate change, such an alternative faces numerous hurdles in the international aviation context where fuel – the common denominator for measuring emissions – has traditionally been exempted from taxes".[190] He cites, in support of his statement Article 24 of the Convention on International Civil Aviation (Chicago Convention)[191] saying: "Article 24 of the Chicago Convention exempts fuel on board aircraft upon arrival and retained on board upon leaving the territory of another ICAO Member State from taxation".[192] This statement is flawed on two counts. Firstly, Article 24 applies to an exemption on fuel carried on board the aircraft and it does not exempt a tax on carbon emitted. Secondly, and more importantly, a careful reading of the provision reveals that the

---

[187]*Ibid.*

[188]Schultz and Becker (2013).

[189]See generally, Owen and Hanley (2004), p. 115.

[190]Piera (2013).

[191]Convention on International Civil Aviation signed at Chicago on 7 December 1944. See ICAO Doc 7300 (9th Edition) 2008.

[192]*Ibid.*

exemption applies to "customs duty, inspection fees or similar national or local duties and charges".[193] The Chicago Convention was signed in 1944 where importation and exportation of goods on board aircraft was the main concern. It is also noted that duty is only levied on produce and not on individuals. The duty that is levied for goods manufactured inside the state is called an excise duty. And the duty that is levied on goods imported from a foreign country is the customs duty. It is therefore clear that the words in the Chicago Convention covering fuel does not include a fuel tax or a carbon tax.

It is submitted that, prior to submitting its proposal to the Assembly, it behoves ICAO to submit it to all its member States at least 6 months prior, with a detailed study detailing the reasons why an IAGOF is the best GMBM. Comments from States should be received which should be given detailed consideration and review by the Council prior to the Assembly and appropriate amendments made. This would ensure validation by all ICAO member States and not just the 36 members of the Council which, although on paper represents ICAO States, are not practically representative of the entirety of ICAO. If a revision or amendment to an Annex to the Chicago Convention undergoes a similar practice, there is no reason why a burning issue affecting air transport cannot have the benefit of such a practice. The Study should also explain, *inter alia*, how the IAGOF addresses the aspirational goals alluded to earlier in this article which have formed an integral part of Assembly Resolution A38-18, particularly how they can be achieved.

With regard to the issues discussed in the conclusion of this chapter, States would find it difficult to figure out what to make of ICAO's recommended practices—whether they are compelling enough to be adopted as internal rules or whether they should be treated as applicable only when convenient to do so. Can a rule come out of an Assembly Resolution which is just the outcome of political compromise? On such an important issue as aviation and climate change, should ICAO not promulgate more coercive rules and regulations?

References

Abeyratne R (2010a) Aviation security law. Springer, Heidelberg, pp 24–25

Abeyratne R (2010b) Environmental prospects for the air transport industry. Environ Policy Law 40(6):319–328

[193] Article 24 provides: "Aircraft on a flight to, from, or across the territory of another contracting State shall be admitted temporarily free of duty, subject to the customs regulations of the State. Fuel, lubricating oils, spare parts, regular equipment and aircraft stores on board an aircraft of a contracting State, on arrival in the territory of another contracting State and retained on board on leaving the territory of that State shall be exempt from customs duty, inspection fees or similar national or local duties and charges. This exemption shall not apply to any quantities or articles unloaded, except in accordance with the customs regulations of the State, which may require that they shall be kept under customs supervision".

Abeyratne R (2011a) Unmanned aircraft systems—the civil aviation (Revised) perspective. Eur Transp Law XLVI(3):239–260
Abeyratne R (2011b) Investing in mitigating the effects of aircraft engine emissions. J World Invest Trade 12(6):855–889
Abeyratne R (2011c) Carbon trading in commercial aviation. Eur Transp Law XLVI(2):143–157
Abeyratne R (2011d) Cyber terrorism and aviation – national and international responses. J Transp Secur 3:337–339. doi:10.1007/512198-011-0074-3. http://link.springer.com/article/10.1007/s12198-011-0074-3
Abeyratne R (2012a) Air navigation law. Springer, Heidelberg, ISBN: 978-3-642-25834-3
Abeyratne R (2012b) Aviation and climate change—in search of a framework for market based measures. Issues Aviat Law Policy 12(1):7–46
Abeyratne R (2013) Convention on international civil aviation – a commentary. Springer, Heidelberg. ISBN 978-3-319-00067-1
Abeyratne R (2014a) Flight MH 17 and state responsibility for ensuring safety and security of air transport. J Air Transp Secur. doi:10.1007/s12198-014-0148-0
Abeyratne R (2014b) Aviation and climate change: in search of a global market based measure. Springer. ISBN: 978-3-319-08442-8 (Print) 978-3-319-08443-5 (Online)
Abeyratne R (2014c) Aviation and climate change: a compelling legal challenge for a toothless tiger? J Int Comp Law 1:57–74
Abeyratne R (2015) Global market-based measures for aviation emissions. Environ Policy Law 45 (3–4):102–107
Abeyratne R (2016) Competition and investment in air transport: legal and economic issues. Springer, Heidelberg, pp 76–97
Abeyratne R, Khan A (2016) State use of unmanned military aircraft – a new international order? J Transp Secur. doi:10.1007/s12198-013-0131-1
Akehurst M (1974–1975) The hierarchy of the sources of international law. British Yearbook International Law. Clarendon Press, Oxford, p 273
Aust A (2000) Modern treaty law and practice. Cambridge University Press, p 208
Bodin J (1955) Six books of the commonwealth. Blackwell, Oxford, pp 25–36
Boon KE (2011) New directions in responsibility: assessing the international law commission's draft articles on the responsibility of international organisation. Yale J Int Law 37:2
Brown Weiss E (2007) Bottom up accountability. Environ Policy Law 37:259
Brownlie I (1990) Principles of Public International Law, 4th ed. Clarendon Press, Oxford, p 1
Christensen CM, Raynor ME. McDonald R. (2015) What is disruptive innovation? Harv Bus Rev. https://hbr.org/2015/12/what-is-disruptive
Fawcett JES (1971) The United Nations and International Law. In: Twitchett KJ (ed) The evolving United Nations: a prospect for peace. Europa Publications, London, pp 57, 65–66
Kerwin CM (2003) Rulemaking: how government agencies write law and make policy. CQ Press, Washington, p 199
Lim B (2016) Emerging threats from cyber security in aviation—challenges and mitigations. J Aviat Manag Singap 20182-92:85.4
Mark RP (2016) Radio Jamming at Maine Airport Continues. http://www.ainonline.com/aviation-news/ainsafety/2013-09-02/radio-jamming-maine-airport-continues
Milde M (1979) Dispute settlement in the framework of the international civil aviation organization (ICAO). In: Settlement of Space Law Disputes, vol 87. p 88
Newcome LR (2004) Unmanned aviation: a brief history of unmanned aerial vehicles. American Institute of Aeronautics and Astronautics
Owen AD, Hanley N (eds) (2004) The economics of climate change. Routledge, New York, p 115
Piera A (2013) Why taxes are not an option in addressing international civil aviation's carbon footprint. GREENAIR online, 26 March 2013. http://www.greenaironline.com/news.php?viewStory=2065
Rajan S (1958) United Nations and Domestic Jurisdiction. Orient Longmans, Bombay, p 3

Reed J (2001) Cyber terrorism now at the top of the list of security concerns. Defensetec, 12 September 2001. http://defensetech.org/2011/09/12/cyber-terrorism-now-at-the-top-of-the-list-of-security-concerns/

Sachs JD (2015) The age of sustainable development. Columbia University Press, New York, pp 101–138

Schultz G, Becker GS (2013) Why we support a revenue-neutral carbon tax. Wall Street J. April 7 2013, at http://www.wsj.com/articles/SB10001424127887323611604578396401965799658

Sen A (2009) The idea of justice. Harvard University Press, Cambridge, p 248

Shaw MN (2003) International Law, 5th ed. Cambridge University Press, p 110

Siu M, Goh D, Lim C (2014) Aviation cyber security: a new security landscape. J Aviat Manage Singap 73–81 at 74

Sofaer AD, Goodman SE, Cuéllar M-F, Drozdova EA, Elliott DD, Grove GD, Lukasik SJ, Putnam TL, Wilson GD (2000) A Proposal for an International Convention on Cyber Crime and Terrorism

Sztucki J (1974) Jus Cogens and the Vienna convention on the law of treaties – a critical appraisal. Springer, Wien, p 69

Tafoya WL (2016) Cyber Terror, FBI Law Enforcement Bulletin. https://leb.fbi.gov/2011/november/cyber-terror

Taillant JD (2015) Glaciers: the politics of ice. Oxford University Press, p 151

Thompson C (2016) Researcher claims he hacked into aircraft systems mid-flight through entertainment system. http://globalnews.ca/news/2005345/researcher-claims-he-hacked-into-aircraft-systems-mid-flight-through-entertainment-system/

von der Dunk FG (1992) Jus Cogens Sive Lege Ferenda: Jus Cogendum? Air and Space Law: De Lege Ferenda. Essays in Honour of Henri A. Wassenbergh. Martinus Nijhoff, Netherlands, p 219

Weibel RE, Hansman JR (2009) Safety Considerations for Operations of Unmanned Aerial Vehicles in the National Airspace System. MIT International Centre for Air Transportation, Report No. ICAT -2005 -1, p 19

Whiteman MM (1977) Jus Cogens in International Law, with a projected list. J Int Comput Law 7:609–613

Whitlock C (2015) FAA records detail hundreds of close calls between airplanes and drones. The Washington Post, 20 August 2015. https://www.washingtonpost.com/world/national-security/faa-records-detail-hundreds-of-close-calls-between-airplanes-and-drones/2015/08/20/5ef812ae-4737-11e5-846d-02792f854297_story.html

Yarwood L (2011) State accountability under international law: holding states accountable for a breach of Jus Cogens norms. Routledge, London, p 159

Zolfagharifard E (2016) 'Hackers are a serious threat to aircraft safety': aviation chiefs warn of the devastating consequences of a cyber-attack. Mail on line, http://www.dailymail.co.uk/sciencetech/article-2869827/Hackers-threat-aircraft-safety-Aviation-chiefs-warn-devastating-consequences-cyber-attack.html

Chapter 2
Can ICAO Make Laws or Deliver Judgments?

The answer is an emphatic "NO" as demonstrated in ICAO's Mission Statement which is: "[T]o serve as the global forum of States for international civil aviation. ICAO develops policies and Standards, undertakes compliance audits, performs studies and analyses, provides assistance and builds aviation capacity through many other activities and the cooperation of its Member States and stakeholders". No one will be able to detect even a hint of law making authority of ICAO in this statement. However, this having been said, no one could deny ICAO some credibility and persuasive effect in its adoption of Standards and Recommended Practices (SARPs) and policy guidance, which have stood the test of time as sage guidance for States in their rulemaking process.

ICAO's empowerment by the Chicago Convention is clear in Article 44 of the Convention which restricts ICAO to "aims and objectives" (not a mandate as some would argue) in developing the principles and techniques of air navigation and fostering the planning and development of air transport. These words are unequivocal in denying ICAO any law making power. If one takes other examples of United Nations specialized agencies the World Health Organization (WHO) says of its mission: "Our primary role is to direct and coordinate international health within the United Nations' system" giving the word "direct" a sense of authority that ICAO does not profess to have. The International Telecommunications Union (ITU) states: "[W]e allocate global radio spectrum and satellite orbits, develop the technical standards that ensure networks and technologies seamlessly interconnect, and strive to improve access to ICTs to underserved communities worldwide". The word "allocate" gives the ITU authority to dictate what radio spectrum and satellite orbits to prescribe. The Food and Agriculture Organization states its objective to be: "[T]o meet the demands posed by major global trends in agricultural development and challenges faced by member nations, FAO has identified key priorities on which it is best placed to intervene… our mandate is to support members in their efforts to ensure that people have regular access to enough high-quality food. We can help by supporting policies and political commitments that promote food security and good nutrition and by making sure that up-to-date

R. Abeyratne, *Rulemaking in Air Transport*, DOI 10.1007/978-3-319-44657-8_2

information about hunger and malnutrition challenges and solutions is available and accessible". FAO talks of a mandate of, *inter alia* making sure that up-to-date information is available. There are no such words used by ICAO.

Neither the United Nations nor ICAO which a specialized agency of the UN is a world parliament that can make laws. However, both bodies can generate legally binding norms at international law. This is true of ICAO at least in the context of the principles and techniques of air navigation, but not true in terms of economic regulation. This is where ICAO backs down and seeks refuge under its self-imposed title of "global forum which develops policy with the collaboration of States. The policy which is so adopted is non coercive, non-compelling and, at its strongest, discretionary.

2.1 Legislative Power of ICAO

The words "legislative power" have been legally defined as "power to prescribe rules of civil conduct",[1] while identifying law as a "rule of civil conduct". The word "quasi" is essentially a term that makes a resemblance to another and classifies it. It is suggestive of comparative analogy and is accepted as the conception to which it serves as an index and its connection with the conception with which the comparison is instituted by strong superficial analogy or resemblance.[2]

The question *stricto sensu* according to the above definition is therefore whether the ICAO Council now has power to prescribe rules of civil conduct (legislative power) or in the least a power that resembles by analogy the ability to prescribe rules of conduct (quasi-legislative power). Since legislative power is usually attributed to a State, it would be prudent to inquire, on a general basis, whether the ICAO Council has law making powers (in a quasi-legislative sense). Therefore, all references hereafter that may refer to legislative powers would be reflective of the Council's law making powers in a quasi-legislative sense.

Article 54(l) of the Chicago Convention prescribes the adoption of SARPS and their designation in Annexes to the Convention, while notifying all Contracting States of the action taken. The adoption of SARPS was considered a priority by the ICAO Council in its Second Session (2 September-12 December 1947)[3] which attempted to obviate any delays to the adoption of SARPS on air navigation as required by the First Assembly of ICAO.[4] SARPS inevitably take two forms: a

---

[1]*Schaake* v. *Dolly* 85 Kan. 590., 118 Pac. 80.

[2]*People* v. *Bradley* 60 Ill. 402, at 405. Also, *Bouviers Law Dictionary and Concise Encyclopedia* 3 ed. Vol 11, Vernon Law Book Co., New York 1914.

[3]Proceedings of the Council 2nd Session 2 September-12 December 1947, Doc 7248 - C/839 at 44–45.

[4]ICAO Resolutions A - 13 and A - 33 which resolved that SARPS relating to the efficient and safe regulation of international air navigation be adopted.

negative form e.g. that States shall not impose more than certain maximum requirements; and a positive form e.g. that States shall take certain steps as prescribed by the ICAO Annexes.[5]

Article 37 of the Convention obtains the undertaking of each Contracting State to collaborate in securing the highest practical degree of uniformity in regulations, standards, procedures and organization in relation to international civil aviation in all matters in which such uniformity will facilitate and improve air navigation. Article 38 obligates all Contracting States to the Convention to inform ICAO immediately if they are unable to comply with any such international standard or procedure and notify differences between their own practices and those prescribed by ICAO. In the case of amendments to international Standards, any State which does not make the appropriate amendment to its own regulations or practices shall give notice to the Council of ICAO within 60 days of the adoption of the said amendment to the international Standard or indicate the action which it proposes to take.

The element of compulsion that has been infused by the drafters of the Convention is compatible with the "power to prescribe rules of civil conduct" on a *stricto sensu* legal definition of the words "legislative power" as discussed above. There is no room for doubt that the 18 Annexes to the Convention or parts thereof lay down rules of conduct both directly and analogically. In fact, although there is a conception based on a foundation of practicality that ICAO's international Standards that are identified by the words "Contracting States shall" have a mandatory flavour (infused by the word "shall") while Recommended Practices identified by the words "Contracting States may have only an advisory and" recommendatory connotation (infused by the word "may") , it is interesting that at least one ICAO document requires States under Article 38 of the Convention, to notify ICAO of all significant differences from both Standards and Recommended Practices, thus making all SARPS regulatory in nature.[6]

Another strong factor that reflects the overall ability and power of the Council to prescribe civil rules of conduct (and therefore legislate) on a strict interpretation of the word is that in Article 22 of the Convention each Contracting State agrees to adopt all practical measures through the issuance of special regulations or otherwise, to facilitate and expedite air navigation… It is clear that this provision can be regarded as an incontrovertible rule of conduct that responds to the requirement in Article 54(l) of the Convention. Furthermore, the mandatory nature of Article 90 of the Convention—that an Annex or amendment thereto shall become effective within 3 months after it is submitted by the ICAO Council to Contracting States

[5]ICAO Annex 9, Facilitation, Foreword.

[6]*Aeronautical Information Services Manual*, ICAO Doc 8126 -0 AN/872/3. ICAO Resolution A 1-31 defines a Standard as any specification for physical characteristics…the uniform application of which is recognised as *necessary*… and one that States *will conform to*. The same resolution describes a Recommended Practice as any specification for physical characteristics… which is recognised as *desirable* …and one that member States *will endeavour to conform to*…Buergenthal (1969), p. 10 also cites the definitions given in ICAO's Annex 9 of SARPS.

is yet another pronouncement on the power of the Council to prescribe rules of State conduct in matters of international civil aviation. *A fortiori*, it is arguable that the Council is seen not only to possess the attribute of the term "jurisfaction"(the power to make rules of conduct) but also the term "jurisaction" (the power to enforce its own rules of conduct). The latter attribute can be seen where the Convention obtains the undertaking of Contracting States not to allow airlines to operate through their air space if the Council decides that the airline concerned is not conforming to a final decision rendered by the Council on a matter that concerns the operation of an international airline.[7]

This is particularly applicable when such airline is found not to conform to the provisions of Annex 2 to the Convention that derives its validity from Article 12 of the Convention relating to rules of the air.[8] In fact, it is very relevant that Annex 2, the responsibility for the promulgation of which devolves upon the Council by virtue of Article 54(l), sets mandatory rules of the air, making the existence of the legislative powers of the Council an unequivocal and irrefutable fact. Academic and professional opinion also favours the view that in a practical sense, the ICAO Council does have legislative powers.

Milde concludes that ICAO has regulatory and quasi-legislative functions in the technical field and plays a consultative and advisory role in the economic sphere.[9] A similar view had earlier been expressed by Buergenthal who states:

> the manner in which the International Civil Aviation organization has exercised its regulatory functions in matters relating to the safety of international air navigation and the facilitation of international air transport provides a fascinating example of international law making... the Organization has consequently not had to contend with any of the post war ideological differences that have impeded international law making on politically sensitive issues.[10]

Dempsey endorses in a somewhat conservative manner, the view that ICAO has the ability to make regulations when he states:

> In addition to the comprehensive, but largely dormant adjudicative enforcement held by ICAO under Articles 84-88 of the Chicago Convention, the Agency also has a solid foundation for enhanced participation in economic regulatory aspects of international aviation in Article 44, as well as the Convention's Preamble.[11]

A significant attribute of the legislative capabilities of the ICAO Council is its ability to adopt technical standards as Annexes to the Convention without going through a lengthy process of ratification.[12] Eugene Sochor refers to the Council as a

---

[7]Article 86 of the Convention.

[8]Article 12 stipulates that over the high seas, the rules in force shall be those established under the Convention, and each contracting State undertakes to insure the prosecution of all persons violating the applicable regulations.

[9]Milde (1994), pp. 401–452, 422.

[10]Buergenthal (1969), p. 9.

[11]Dempsey (1987), p. 302.

[12]Sochor (1991), p. 58.

powerful and visible body in international aviation.[13] It is interesting however to note that although by definition, the ICAO Council has been considered by some as unable to deal with strictly legal matters, since other important matters come within its purview,[14] this does not derogate the compelling facts that reflect the distinct law making abilities of ICAO. Should this not be true, the functions that the Convention assigns to ICAO in Article 44—that ICAO's aims and objectives are to "develop the principles and techniques of international air navigation and to foster the planning and development of international air transport"—would be rendered destitute of effect.

Under the Interim Agreement the PICAO Council was required to act as an arbitral body on any differences arising among member States relating to matters of international civil aviation which may be submitted to it, wherein the Interim Council of PICAO was empowered to render an advisory report or if the parties involved so wished, give a decision on the matter before it.[15] The Interim Council, which was the precursor to the ICAO Council, set the stage therefore for providing the Council with unusual arbitral powers which are not attributed to similar organs of the specialised agencies of the United Nations system.[16]*A fortiori*, since the ICAO Council is permanent and is almost in constant session, Contracting States could expect any matter of dispute brought by them before the Council to be dealt with, without unreasonable delay.[17]

Most Contracting States have, on their own initiative, enacted dispute-settlement clauses in their bilateral air services agreements wherein provision is usually made to refer inter-State disputes relating to international civil aviation to the ICAO Council, in accordance with Chapter XV111 of the Convention. In this context, it is also relevant to note that the President of the Council is empowered by the Convention to appoint an arbitrator and an umpire in certain circumstances leading to an appeal from a decision of the Council.[18]

A most interesting aspect of the ICAO Council remains to be that one of its mandatory functions is to consider any subject referred to it by a Contracting State for its consideration.[19] or any subject which the President of the Council or the Secretary General of the ICAO Secretariat desires to bring before the Council.[20]

[13]*Ibid.*

[14]Tobolewski (1979), pp. 349, 359.

[15]Interim Agreement, Article 111, Section 6(i).

[16]Schenkman (1955), p. 160.

[17]See statement of R. Kidron, Israeli Head Delegate, Statement of the Second Plenary Meeting of the Seventh Assembly on June 17, 1953, reported in *ICAO Monthly Bulletin*, August-October 1953, at 8.

[18]Article 85.

[19]Rules of Procedure for the Council Fifth Edition 1980, Section 1 V, Rule 24 (e). Also, Article 54 (n) stipulates that one of the mandatory functions of the Council is to consider any matter relating to the Convention which any contracting State refers to it.

[20]Rules of Procedure for the Council, *Id.* Rule 24 (f). The two additional multilateral agreements stemming from the Convention and providing for the exchange of traffic rights—the Air Services

Although the Council is bound to consider a matter submitted to it by a Contracting State it can refrain from giving a decision as the Council is only obligated to consider a matter before it.

2.2 Judicial Power of ICAO

As for the judicial power of ICAO with regard to settling disputes, Article 84 of the Chicago Convention provides that if any disagreement between two or more Contracting States relating to the interpretation or application of this Convention and its Annexes cannot be settled by negotiation, it shall, on the application of any State concerned in the disagreement, be decided by the Council. No member of the Council shall vote in the consideration by the Council of any dispute to which it is a party. Any Contracting State may, subject to Article 85, appeal from the decision of the Council to an ad hoc arbitral tribunal agreed upon with the other parties to the dispute or to the Permanent Court of International Justice. Any such appeal shall be notified to the Council within sixty days of receipt of notification of the decision of the Council. This provision was blatantly misquoted at the ICAO Air Transport Symposium of March 2016 where a person claiming to be from a reputed university stated that the mere fact that the Council can decide upon a disagreement between States grants the ICAO Council adjudicatory powers of a court which can impose its "judgment". The Council takes decisions, adopts policy and resolutions and issues statements. It does not hand down judicial decisions that are enforceable. For instance, one can consider the consideration of the issue between Israel and Palestine when on 4 December 2001, Israeli military forces attacked Gaza International airport, destroyed air navigation facilities and bombarded runways and taxiways until the airport became unserviceable and the Palestinian Authority attempted a repair on 11 January 2002, the Israeli military forces bombarded once again the airport and its facilities by aircraft, artillery and tanks, thereby destroying the runway, the taxiways and all facilities.

The Palestinian Authority claimed that the destroyed airport and air navigation facilities were used for the transportation of civilian passengers, search and rescue operations in case of emergencies, transportation of rescue material, including medical equipment, medicines and survival kits for safeguarding human lives.

It was noted by the Council that the airport was developed with voluntary contributions from a number of European countries, which recognized beyond doubt the urgent need for the airport. Nevertheless, the airport was destroyed without paying attention to any humanitarian consideration. This led the

---

Transit Agreement and the Air Transport Agreement, also contain provisions that empower the ICAO Council to hear disputes and make appropriate findings and recommendations... see Air Services Transit Agreement Article 11 Section 1, and the Air Transport Agreement Article 1 V Section 2.

European Union to condemn the Israeli actions and reserve the right to demand compensation for the damages. The Council was further advised that the destruction of the civil airport in Gaza was an act deliberately perpetrated by a Contracting State. It was claimed that such destruction took place under the watchful eyes of the international community and was widely covered by local and international media reports and the Council was requested to consider the ramifications of the act, i.e. contempt of respect for human life, the disrespect of international laws, including the relevant conventions on civil aviation security.

Among the considerations of the Council were relevant provisions of the Chicago Convention, the first being Article 4 which stipulates that *each Contracting state agrees not to use civil aviation for any purpose inconsistent with the aims of this Convention*. Also considered was Article 44 which lays down the objectives of ICAO, particularly to *meet the needs of the peoples of the world for safe, regular, efficient and economical air transport.* [21] Another Convention, the Montreal Convention (1971)[22] was also considered by the Council, particularly the views of the State parties to the Convention, to the effect that:

> Unlawful acts against the safety of civil aviation jeopardize the safety of persons and property, seriously affect the operation of air services, and undermine the confidence of the peoples of the world in the safety of civil aviation", that "the occurrence of such acts is a matter of grave concern" and that "for the purpose of deterring such acts, there is an urgent need to provide appropriate measures for punishment of offenders.[23]

The Council was reminded of Resolution A20-1, adopted at the 20th Session of the Assembly (Rome, 28 August, 21 September 1973), in particular Resolving Clause (3), where the Assembly solemnly warned Israel that if it continued committing such acts the Assembly will take further measures against Israel to protect international civil aviation. Also recalled was Resolution A33-2, adopted by the 33rd Session of the Assembly (Montreal, 25 September-5 October 2001) where the Assembly stated that *Whereas* acts of unlawful interference against civil aviation have become the main threat to its safe and orderly development; and *Recognizing* that all acts of unlawful interference against international civil aviation constitute a grave offence in violation of International law; the Assembly *Strongly condemned* all acts of unlawful interference against civil aviation wherever and by whomever and for whatever reason they are perpetrated. It was noted that the challenge facing this High-Level, Ministerial Conference is to take effective measures in order to help States in responding to unlawful interference against civil aviation security and to reject and condemn the use of civil aviation as weapon of destruction against human lives and properties.

Based on its considerations of the issue, the Council, on 13 March 2002, adopted a resolution strongly condemning the destruction of Gaza International Airport and

---

[21] Chicago Convention, *supra,* Article 44(d).

[22] *Convention for the Suppression of Unlawful Acts Against Civil Aviation*, Signed at Montreal on 23 September 1971. ICAO Doc. 8966.

[23] *Id.* Preamble.

its air navigation facilities. In its Resolution, the Council, strongly condemned all acts of unlawful interference against civil aviation, wherever, by whomsoever and for whatever reasons they are perpetrated. It also strongly condemned the destruction of Gaza International Airport and its air navigation facilities while reaffirming the important role of ICAO in facilitating the resolution of questions which may arise between Contracting States in relation to matters affecting the safe and orderly operation of international civil aviation throughout the world. The Council urged Israel to fully comply with the aims and objectives of the Chicago Convention, while strongly urging Israel to take the necessary measures to restore Gaza International Airport so as to allow its reopening as soon as possible. Additionally, the Council requested the President of the ICAO Council to attend to the implementation of this Resolution, and to secure the full cooperation of the parties with respect to the application of the Chicago Convention and of the above-mentioned principles. Finally, the Council requested the Secretary General to inform all Contracting States of the Resolution.[24]

Nothing happened. If the Council were an adjudicatory body having the powers of a court of law, why did the Council adopt just a resolution which was a result of a political compromise between the parties? Why did the Council "urge" Israel and not "order" Israel to make reparation?

2.3 The WTO Example of Adjudication

In stark contrast to ICAO's dispute settlement mechanism is the dispute resolution mechanism of the World Trade Organization (WTO) which is well explained in the Boeing/Airbus dispute which was brought before the WTO dispute settlement mechanism. On 31 May 2005, it was reported that United States Trade Representative Rob Portman had issued a statement calling for the World Trade Organization (WTO) to appoint a panel of judges to go into the claim of the United States that European governments were illegally subsidizing *Airbus Industrie*, the Toulouse based manufacturing consortium which builds the Airbus range of aircraft.[25] The US case, which had been earlier initiated, had been suspended for some time pending an attempt at negotiation and a possible settlement with Europe, where governments of the United States and Europe agreed in January 2005 to desist from subsidizing the Boeing Co. and Airbus for the next 3 months while they tried to resolve a decades-old dispute over billions in subsidies to the aircraft makers. The European Union has reportedly filed its own case against Boeing, the Chicago based

[24]By State Letter E 5/61-02/42 dated 26 April 2002, the Secretary General of ICAO advised all ICAO Contracting States of the Council Resolution. See also, ICAO official press release PIO 03/02 (ICAO Council Adopts Resolution Strongly Condemning the Destruction of Gaza International Airport.

[25]Paul Blustein, Aircraft-subsidy Battle is Going Back to WTO, *Washington Post*, Tuesday, May 31, 2005 (electronic version) at e-1.

US manufacturer, counter claiming that Boeing is benefitting from illegal subsidies including those provided indirectly through military contracts.[26] According to a monitoring study carried out on behalf of the European Commission in 1998, it was estimated that the amount of US Government indirect support to its Large Civil Aircraft (LCA) industry reached almost $ 2 billion in 1997, i.e. around 7 % of its commercial turnover. This is well above the 3 % limit set by the 1992 Agreement[27] which was concluded with the signature of the EC-US Agreement on Trade in Large Civil Aircraft which focuses on the limitation of both direct and indirect government support, and which, in terms of State aid and subsidies, was acceptable to both the European Union and the United States.

The Airbus/Boeing subsidies issue came under the *Agreement on Subsidies and Countervailing Measures of the WTO* (SCM) which is enforced through the WTO dispute settlement system. The Agreement deals with two subjects closely related to each other. The first is concerned with issues of multilateral disciplines regulating the provision of subsidies and the second provides rules for the use of countervailing measures to offset injury caused by subsidized imports. Of these, the first will be applicable to the dispute between the two aircraft manufacturers in the determination of whether subsidies have in fact passed between the governmental authority and manufacturer concerned. The second would apply in determining what countervailing measures have to be taken by the WTO Dispute Settlement Body. Of primary concern would be Part 1 of the Agreement which specifies that the SCM would apply exclusively to subsidies that are specifically given to an enterprise or a group of enterprises or industries. The SCM goes on to define a subsidy as a provision which is composed of three fundamental elements: it has to be a financial contribution; it has to be made by a government or any public body within the territory of a WTO member; and it has to confer a benefit to the recipient. It must be noted that according to the SCM, subsidies, as defined, have to be specific. In other words, the subsidy has to be specifically provided to an enterprise or industry or group of enterprises or industries, resulting in the distortion of the allocation of resources within the economy.

The SCM recognizes four types of specificity: *enterprise specificity*, where a government identifies and provides a subsidy to a particular business entity; *industry specificity*, where a government targets a particular industrial sector; *regional specificity*, where a government targets business entities in a region or part of its territory; and *prohibited subsidies*, where a government subsidizes export goods or goods using domestic resources and inputs. Of these, clearly, the Airbus/Boeing dispute would be considered under the enterprise specificity. The next step would be to slot the dispute into one of two categories: prohibited category, and actionable category. The prohibited category is composed of two sub categories, the first being contingent upon export performance and the second being applicable to the use of

[26]Edward Alden, EU Retaliates Against US over Airline Subsidies, Financial Times (electronic version), May 31, 2005 at e-1.

[27]1992 EC/US Agreement on Trade in Large Civil Aircraft.

domestic over imported goods. These two categories are prohibited on the ground that they are directly calculated to adversely affect trade, impacting the interests of other members. Actionable subsidies, on the other hand, are not prohibited, but nonetheless subject to challenge either through a multilateral dispute settlement system or through the imposition of countervailing actions. If adjudicated by the Dispute Settlement Body, the Airbus Boeing dispute would clearly become an actionable issue under the latter category, on the basic assumption that the issue at stake is injury to a domestic industry.

The next issue was to look at the dispute resolution process, which, in the WTO system essentially concerns inconsistencies in a commercial activity. Trade in civil aircraft and related services is a much evolved commercial process which stands today as one of the most prolific financial activities of the commercial world. It comes within the purview of the General Agreement for Tariffs and Trade (GATT) and is therefore now governed by the Marrakesh Declaration of 15 April 1994, which heralded the conclusion of the Uruguay Round of Multilateral Trade Negotiations and established the WTO.[28] The Marrakesh Agreement (hereafter sometimes referred to as the Agreement) ushered in a new era of global economic co-operation, reflecting the widespread desire to operate in a fairer and more open multilateral trading system for the benefit and welfare of its member States.[29] A critical issue that emerged from this legal instrument was the function of the WTO as a forum for negotiations among its Members concerning their multilateral trade relations in matters which are dealt with under the agreements in the Annexes to the Agreement. The WTO may also provide a forum for further negotiations among its members concerning their multilateral trade relations, and a framework for the implementation of the results of such negotiations, as may be decided by the Ministerial Conference.[30] The WTO also administers the Understanding on Rules and Procedures Governing the Settlement of Disputes (hereafter referred to as the

[28]The WTO comprises a Ministerial Conference composed of representatives of all Member countries and meets at least once every 2 years. The Ministerial Conference carries out the functions of the WTO and takes necessary action to this effect. There is also within the WTO structure, a General Council composed of representatives of all Member countries and this Council meets as deemed appropriate. As necessary, the General Council conducts the functions of the Ministerial Conference when the latter does not meet. It also carries out its functions as assigned by the Agreement. Furthermore, the General Council also discharges the responsibilities of the Dispute Settlement Body (DSB) under the Dispute Settlement Understanding (DSU). The Dispute Settlement Body may have its own Chairman and shall establish such rules of procedure as it deems necessary for the fulfilment of those responsibilities. See *Marrakesh Agreement infra*, note 3, Article IV 1, 2 and 3.

[29]Marrakesh Declaration of 15 April 1994, para. 2. The Marrakesh Agreement came into being with the Marrakesh Declaration and is an integral part therefore of the Marrakesh Declaration. See *The Results of the Uruguay Round of Multilateral Trade Negotiations, The Legal Texts*. GATT Secretariat: Geneva 1994, for the text of the Declaration.

[30]Marrakesh Declaration, *id*. Article III.2. The Ministerial Conference is composed of representatives of all Members, which meets at least once every 2 years. The Conference carries out the functions of the WTO and takes action necessary to this effect. The Ministerial Conference also has the authority to take decisions on all matters under any multilateral trade agreements if so

Dispute Settlement Understanding or DSU) in Annex 2 to the Agreement.[31] Annex 2 to the Agreement, which addresses issues on dispute settlement and contains an Understanding on Rules and Procedures Governing the Settlement of Disputes, underscores the philosophy of dispute settlement reflected in the Agreement as being to strengthen the multilateral system of trade relations that the WTO represents. Article 23 of Annex 2 provides that when Members seek the redress of a violation of obligations or other nullification or impairment of benefits under the covered agreements or an impediment to the attainment of any objective of the covered agreements, they shall have recourse to, and abide by, the rules and procedures of the Understanding. In such cases, members are required to abstain from making a determination to the effect that a violation has occurred, that benefits have been nullified or impaired or that the attainment of any objective of the covered agreements has been impeded, except through recourse to dispute settlement in accordance with the rules and procedures of the Understanding.[32]

Members are also required to follow the procedures set forth in Article 21—which call for prompt compliance with recommendations of the dispute settlement body, with particular attention being given to developing country Members with respect to measures which are subject to dispute settlement. This measure has been taken to determine the reasonable period of time for the Member concerned to implement the recommendations and rulings,[33] and follow the procedures set forth in Article 22. Article 22 provides for international conditions for compensation and the suspension of concessions, in order to determine the level of suspension of concessions or other obligations and obtain authorization from the dispute resolution body before suspending concessions or other obligations in response to the failure of the Member concerned to implement the recommendations and rulings within that reasonable period of time.

The Dispute Settlement Body (DSB) which is established under the Council for Trade in Services, which are in turn established under the General Council of the WTO, was established to administer the rules and procedures in the Annex and, except as otherwise provided in a covered agreement, the consultation and dispute settlement provisions of the covered agreements. Accordingly, the DSB has the authority to establish panels, adopt panel and Appellate Body reports, maintain surveillance of implementation of rulings and recommendations, and authorise suspension of concessions and other obligations under the covered agreements.[34] The DSB is required to inform the relevant WTO Councils and Committees of any

requested by a Member, in accordance with the specific requirements for decision making in the Marrakesh Agreement and in the relevant multilateral trade agreement. See Article IV. 1. *Id.*

[31] *Id.* Article III. 3.

[32] Annex 2, Article 23(a).

[33] Annex 2, Article 23(b).

[34] Annex 2, Article 2.1.

developments in disputes related to provisions of the respective covered agreements.[35] Under Article 3 of the Annex, Members affirm their adherence to the principles of the management of disputes heretofore applied under Articles XXII and XXIII of GATT 1947, and the rules and procedures as further elaborated and modified in the Annex.[36] This means that effectively, trade in civil aircraft and services related thereto would be governed by the initial structural format of the 1947 rules as amended. Emphasis is placed on the prompt settlement of situations in which a Member considers that any benefits accruing to it directly or indirectly under the covered agreements are being impaired by measures taken by another Member. The effective functioning of the WTO and the maintenance of a proper balance between the rights and obligations of Members has been identified as critical in the dispute settlement process, which is required to be expedient.[37] Recommendations or rulings made by the DSB are calculated to aim at achieving a satisfactory settlement of the matter in accordance with the rights and obligations under the Understanding and under the covered agreements.[38]

One of the fundamental principles of the Understanding is that requests for conciliation and the use of the dispute resolution procedures should not be intended or considered as contentious acts. If a dispute arises, all Members are required to be involved in the procedures in good faith in an effort to resolve the dispute. Furthermore, complaints and counter- complaints in regard to distinct matters should not be linked.[39]

In the Airbus/Boeing dispute, as in any other, the WTO dispute settlement structure encouraged conciliation and mediation under procedures that are undertaken voluntarily if the parties to the dispute so agree.[40] Any party to a dispute may, at any time, request good offices, conciliation and mediation. They may begin at any time and be terminated at any time. Once procedures for good offices, conciliation or mediation are terminated, a complaining party may then proceed toward the establishment of a panel. At the request of the complaining party, a panel is established under the Agreement latest at the DSB meeting following that at which the request first appears as an item on the agenda of the DSB, unless of course, the DSB decides not to establish a panel at its meeting.[41] A Panel is composed of well-qualified governmental and/or non-governmental individuals, including persons who have served on or presented a case to a panel; served as a representative of a Member or if a contracting party to GATT 1947; or, as a representative to the Council or committee of any covered agreement or its predecessor agreement, or in the Secretariat; has taught or published on international trade law or policy; or,

[35] Annex 2, Article 2.2.

[36] Annex 2, Article 3.2.

[37] Annex 2, Article 3.3.

[38] Annex 2, Article 3.4.

[39] Annex 2, Article 3.10.

[40] Annex 2, Article 5.1.

[41] Annex 2, Article 6.1.

served as a senior trade policy official or member[42] and they are selected in such as way as to ensure the independence of the members and to give the panel a diverse selection of individuals with a wide spectrum of experience and exposure.[43] To this end, the WTO Secretariat maintains an indicative list of governmental and non-governmental individuals possessing the qualifications to assist in the selection of panellists as required.

Could this issue have been settled by the ICAO Council? Although the Airbus/Boeing subsidies dispute might be considered as a dispute between aircraft manufactures, it is incontrovertible that this is a dispute between governments pertaining to a trade issue and is not a spat between the two manufacturers. Aviation and governmental activity regarding aviation are essentially the business of the International Civil Aviation Organization (ICAO). Therefore, technically, it is arguable that the United States and the European Union could refer the dispute to the Council of ICAO, which, according to the Convention on Civil Aviation, (Chicago Convention) of 1944[44] can hear disputes between two or more Contracting States relating to the interpretation or application of the Convention or its Annexes. One of the objectives of ICAO is to prevent economic waste by unreasonable competition.[45] The Convention, in its Preamble, provides that States Parties have agreed that international civil aviation be developed in a manner that would ensure equality of opportunity, which might well form the point at issue if the subsidy dispute were to be brought before the ICAO Council, which, by virtue of Article 54 n) of the Chicago Convention is empowered to consider any matter relating to the Convention which any Contracting State refers to it.

The above notwithstanding, there is an unfortunate dichotomy in terminology in the Convention since on the one hand, Article 54(n) makes it mandatory that the Council shall merely *consider* any matter relating to the Convention which any contracting State refers to it, while on the other, Article 84 categorically states that any disagreement between two or more States relating to the interpretation or application of the Convention and its Annexes, that cannot be settled by negotiation shall. . .be decided by the Council. The difficulty arises on a strict interpretation of Article 54(n) where even a disagreement between two States as envisaged under Article 84 could well be considered as 'any matter' under Article 54(n). In such an instance, the Council could well be faced with the dilemma of choosing between the two provisions. It would not be incorrect for the Council to merely consider a matter placed before it, although a decision is requested by the Applicant State, since,

[42]Annex 2, Article 8.1.

[43]Annex 2, Article 8.2.

[44]Convention on International Civil Aviation, signed at Chicago on 7 December 1944 (Chicago Convention), ICAO Doc 7300 8ed., 2000, Article 84. The International Civil Aviation Organization (ICAO) was created to promote the safe and orderly development of civil aviation in the world. A specialised agency of the United Nations, it sets international standards and regulations necessary for the safety, security, efficiency and regularity of air transport and serves as the medium for cooperation in all fields of civil aviation among its 183 Contracting States.

[45]*Id.* Article 44(e).

Article 54(n) is perceived to be comprehensive as the operative and controlling provision that lays down mandatory functions of the Council. It is indeed unfortunate that these two provisions obfuscate the issue which otherwise would have given a clear picture of the decision making powers of the Council. A further thread in the fabric of adjudicatory powers of the Council is found in Article 14 of the Rules of Settlement promulgated by the Council in 1957[46] which allows the Council to request the parties in dispute to engage in direct negotiations at any time.[47] This emphasis on conciliation has prompted the view that the Council, under article 84 would favour the settling of disputes rather than adjudicating them. This view seems compatible with the proposition that the consideration of a matter under Article 54(n) would be a more attractive approach *in limine* in a matter of dispute between two States.

In the four decades since the promulgation of Chapter XV111, only three disputes had been submitted to the Council for formal resolution: the first involved a dispute between India and Pakistan (1952), where India complained that Pakistan was in breach of the Convention by not permitting Indian aircraft to overfly Pakistani airspace on their way to Afghanistan; the second was a complaint filed by the United Kingdom against Spain (1969), alleging the violation by Spain of the Convention by the establishment of a prohibited zone over Gibraltar; and the third was a complaint by Pakistan against India (1971), concerning a hijacking of Indian aircraft which landed in Pakistan. India unilaterally suspended Pakistan's overflying privileges, five days after the hijacking. The first complaint was amicably resolved by the parties, the second was differed by the parties *sine die*, and the third was suspended with the formation of the State of Bangladesh in 1972, even though the matter had been processed as an appeal from the Council to the International Court of Justice. Unfortunately, none of these instances was taken to its conclusion so that the World could have had the opportunity to evaluate clearly, ICAO's decision making process.

One commentator noted in 1979:

> The Council of ICAO cannot be considered a suitable body for adjudication in the proper sense of the word - *i.e.* settlement of disputes by judges and solely on the basis of respect for law. The Council is composed of States (not independent individuals) and its decisions would always be based on policy and equity considerations rather than on pure legal grounds…truly legal disputes…can be settled only by a true judicial body which can bring into the procedure full judicial detachment, independence and expertise. The under-employed ICJ is the most suitable body for such types of disputes.[48]

The perceived inadequacies of the ICAO Council in being ethically unsuitable to decide on disputes between States can only be alleviated by the thought that the members of the Council are presumed to be well versed in matters of international civil aviation and therefore would be deemed to be better equipped to comprehend

[46]Rules for the Settlement of Differences, ICAO Doc 7782/2 (2ed. 1975).

[47]*Id.* Article 14(a).

[48]Milde (1979), pp. 87, 88.

economic issues pertaining to aviation placed before them than say the distinguished members of the International Court of Justice, some of whom may not be experts of international air law as applicable through principles of the Chicago Convention. Nonetheless, there is no doubt that the ICAO Council possess juridical powers[49] and that as one commentator said if ICAO did not exist, it would have to be invented; otherwise, international civil aviation would not function with the safety, efficiency and regularity that it has achieved today.[50]

Although it is arguable that the Boeing-Airbus subsidies dispute could be also considered under the ICAO umbrella, the proper forum would indubitably be the WTO, particularly as the Organization has its own rules on subsidies and is more active in international trade law than its aviation counterpart. It is quite clear that when one considers the roles of WTO and ICAO on dispute resolution of two different areas of aviation, their different characters and personalities bring to bear their individual ability to accomplish dispute resolution. For example, while WTO provides the common institutional framework for the conduct of trade relations among its members, who may enter into covered agreements based on such a framework, ICAO prescribes uniform rules of conduct which are contained in 18 Annexes to the Chicago Convention. As discussed, these rules—although not constituting law in the sense of carrying with them penal functions - do have the persuasive force necessary for compliance by ICAO's contracting States and are inflexible. The WTO provides the forum for negotiations among its Members concerning their multilateral trade relations in matters dealt with under the agreements in the Annexes to the Agreement. ICAO's functions do not require the establishment of such a forum and the ICAO Council acts as a body which determines regulation in international civil aviation and usually submits such regulations for the approval of the Assembly. In this sense, WTO is more aligned towards adopting a negotiatory and conciliatory stance and gearing itself to constant mediation between Member States in their trade relations whereas the ICAO Council would attempt a settlement of a dispute only when States require mediation in instances where the provisions of the Chicago Convention or Standards and Recommended Practices of the Annexes to the Convention, or any other norm of customary or written international air law is allegedly breached.

The WTO dispute settlement rules, in keeping with the scope and functions of the organization, are set out in greater detail than those that pertain to ICAO. In the context of the nature of the work of the two organizations, this seems quite understandable.

---

[49]For an in-depth study of the dispute resolution abilities and powers of the ICAO Council, see, see Abeyratne (1992), pp. 387–394 See also, Sampayo de Lacerda (1978), p. 219.

[50]Fitzgerald (1976), pp. 47, 50.

References

Abeyratne RIR (1992) Law making and decision making powers of the ICAO council - a critical analysis. Zeitschrift Fur Luft-und Weltraumrecht 41(4):387–394

Buergenthal T (1969) Law making in the international civil aviation organization. Syracuse University Press, Syracuse, p 9

Dempsey PS (1987) Law and foreign policy in international aviation. Transnational, New York, p 302

Fitzgerald GF (1976) ICAO now and in the coming decades. In: Matte NM (ed) International air transport law, organization and politics for the future. McGill, Montreal, pp 47–50

Milde M (1979) Dispute settlement in the framework of the international civil aviation organization (ICAO). Settlement of Space Law Disputes 2(1):87

Milde M (1994) The Chicago convention- are major amendments necessary or desirable 50 years later? Ann Air Space Law XIX-I:401–452

Sampayo de Lacerda JC (1978) A study about the decisions of the ICAO council. Ann Air Space Law 111:219

Schenkman J (1955) International civil aviation organization. Librairie E. Dross, Geneve, p 160

Sochor E (1991) The politics of international aviation. Macmillan, London, p 58

Tobolewski A (1979) ICAO's legal syndrome. Ann Air Space Law 1:349–359

Chapter 3
How to Make Rules

Rulemaking by the ICAO Council comports with three provisions of the Chicago Convention. The first is in the mandatory functions of the Council where in Article 54l)—The Council may adopt international standards and recommended practices; for convenience, designate them as Annexes to the Convention; and notify all contracting States of the action taken. It is on the basis of this Article that the Council has so far adopted 19 Annexes to the Convention, which goes on to say in Article 37 that each contracting State undertakes to collaborate in securing the highest practicable degree of uniformity in regulations, standards, procedures, and organization in relation to aircraft, personnel, airways and auxiliary services in all matters which such uniformity will facilitate and improve air navigation. To this end ICAO is required to adopt and amend from time to time, as may be necessary international standards and recommended practices and procedures dealing with the subject matter covered by each Annex.

So far, so good. The problem starts with the following provision—Article 38—which stipulates that any State which finds it impracticable to comply in all respects with any such international standard or procedure, or to bring its own regulations or practices into full accord with any international standard or procedure after amendment of the latter, or which deems it necessary to adopt regulations or practices differing in any particular respect from those established by an international standard, is required to give immediate notification to ICAO of the differences between its own practice and that established by the international standard. In the case of amendments to international standards, any State which does not make the appropriate amendments to its own regulations or practices is obligated to give notice to the Council within 60 days of the adoption of the amendment to the international standard, or indicate the action which it proposes to take. In any such case, the Council has to make immediate notification to all other states of the difference which exists between one or more features of an international standard and the corresponding national practice of that State.

A careful reading of this provision reveals that by the words *bring its own regulations or practices into full accord with any international standard or*

R. Abeyratne, *Rulemaking in Air Transport*, DOI 10.1007/978-3-319-44657-8_3

procedure after amendment of the latter the Chicago Convention has introduced the necessity of rulemaking by States according to the Standards contained in the Annexes. However, this requirement is immediately withdrawn by the following words *or which deems it necessary to adopt regulations or practices differing in any particular respect from those established by an international standard, is required to give immediate notification to ICAO of the differences between its own practice and that established by the international standard.* The only obligation remaining is for ICAO to advise the States of differences filed by other member States. This does not mean that ICAO has the mere function of acting as a "mailbox" for its member States which ICAO has regrettably done.

When the author joined ICAO in 1990 ICAO issued a Supplement which contained a collation of all differences filed by States relating to each Annex, with the reasons given by States as to why the compliance of particular Standards were *impracticable*. This gave States the option of taking any action that they deemed fit against a non-complying State, particularly in terms of safety. ICAO has watered down this practice where ICAO no longer publishes Supplements to the Annexes but leaves the task of filing their differences to the States electronically, through ICAO's *Electronic Filing of Differences, EFOD* system. Any State can thus logon to the system and find out the differences filed (if any) by all other States.

The differences to SARPS notified by States were published in Supplements to Annexes. After the Council adopted an Annex it was sent to ICAO member States for their comments and notification of disapproval of Standards with a date identified by the Council of the Annexes effective date which is within 3 months of submission. This was an interim edition of the Annex, referred to as the "Green Edition", which is dispatched to States with a covering explanatory letter. This covering letter also gave the various dates associated with the introduction of the Annex including its effective date. Once the Annex became effective, the States had 3 months to indicate disapproval of adopted amendments to SARPs. Unless a majority of the States indicated their disapproval on or before the time allocated to them to respond with their disapprovals, the Council declared the Annex to have come into force at a particular date.

By adopting the current electronic practice, ICAO has effectively abdicated its obligation of notifying members States of differences as required by the words . . .*in any such case, the Council has to make immediate notification to all other states of the difference which exists between one or more features of an international standard and the corresponding national practice of that State* of Article 38 where now it is the States themselves that inform each other of their differences through a mere ICAO portal. The Council of ICAO has conveniently ignored Article 55 of the Chicago Convention which should be tied to the obligation under Article 38 where the Council has to conduct research into all aspects of air transport and air navigation which are of international importance, communicate the results of its research to the contracting States, and facilitate the exchange of information between contracting States on air transport and air navigation matters, and inter alia to study any matters affecting the organization and operation of international air transport. If this were to be done, The Council could have compelling reason to coerce States to bring their own regulations in line with the Standards of the Annexes to the Convention, with the full involvement of all member States.

At this stage of the discussion it becomes necessary to inquire deeper into the legitimacy of ICAO's core rulemaking powers. Firstly, one has to determine the nature of the Annex provisions themselves and thereafter, the legal legitimacy that could be ascribed to the rulemaking powers of the Council.

SARPs have been the subject of curiosity as well as intrigue, as they are neither here nor there as the preceding discussion showed. To this extent numerous ICAO Assembly Resolutions have addressed the development of SARPs in the Annexes.[1] Resolution A21-21 (Consolidated Statement of Continuing Policies and Associated Practices Related Specifically to Air Navigation), resolves in Appendix A (Formulation of Standards and Recommended Practices and Procedures for Air Navigation Services) that a *Standard* is

> any specification for physical characteristics, configuration, material, performance, personnel or procedure, the uniform application of which is recognized as necessary for the safety of international air navigation and to which Contracting States will conform in accordance with the Convention; in the event of impossibility of compliance, notification to the Council is compulsory under Article 38 of the Convention.

The same Resolution defines a *Recommended Practice* as:

> any specification for physical characteristics, configuration, material, performance, personnel or procedure, the uniform application of which is recognized as desirable in the interest of safety, regularity or efficiency of international air navigation and to which Contracting States will endeavour to conform in accordance with the Convention.

A much later Resolution–Resolution A37-15 (Formulation of Standards and Recommended Practices and Procedures for Air Navigation Services) repeats these definitions verbatim in its Appendix A which resolved that:

> SARPs and PANS shall be amended as necessary to reflect changing requirements and techniques and thus, inter alia, to provide a sound basis for regional planning and the provision of facilities and services; Subject to the foregoing clause, a high degree of stability in SARPs shall be maintained to enable the Contracting States will maintain stability in their national regulations. To this end amendments shall be limited to those significant to safety, regularity and efficiency, and editorial amendments shall be made only if essential; SARPs and PANS shall be drafted in clear, simple and concise language. SARPs shall consist of broad, mature and stable provisions specifying functional and performance requirements that provide for the requisite levels of safety, efficiency and interoperability. Supporting technical specifications, when developed by ICAO, shall be placed in separate documents to the extent possible; In the development of SARPs, procedures and guidance material, ICAO should utilize, to the maximum extent appropriate

[1]Beginning with Resolution A1-13 (Implementation of Standards and Recommended Practices); A1-25 (Future Work of the Technical Divisions; A1-31 (Definition of International Standards and Recommended Practices); A2-42 (Submission of Comments for Proposals on Standards and Recommended Practices); A4-8 (Annexes Prescribing Standards Related to Facilities); A7-9 Notification of Differences From International Standards) and A10-16 (Allocation of Effort Between the Formulation of Standards and Regional Plans and Their Implementation).

and subject to the adequacy of a verification and validation process, the work of other recognized standards making organizations. Material developed by these other standards-making organizations may be deemed appropriate by the Council as meeting ICAO requirements; in this case such material should be referenced in ICAO documentation; To the extent consistent with the requirements of safety and regularity, Standards specifying the provision of facilities and services shall reflect a proper balance between the operational requirements for such facilities and services and the economic implications of providing them;

Contracting States shall be consulted on proposals for the amendment of SARPs and PANS before the Council acts on them, except when the Council may deem urgent action to be necessary. Furthermore, subject to the adequacy of the verification and validation process, technical specifications may be acted upon by the Council without consultation with States. Such material shall however be made available to States upon request; The applicability dates of amendments to SARPs and PANS shall be so established as to allow the Contracting States sufficient time for their implementation;

No Annex or PANS document shall be amended more frequently than once per calendar year.

By way of Associated Practices Associated Practices, The Resolution recognized that the Council should ensure that provisions of SARPs and PANS are completely consistent with each other and that it should endeavour to improve the processing, presentation and usefulness of ICAO documents containing SARPs, PANS and other related provisions, especially for complex systems and their associated applications. To that end the Council was required to promote the development and upkeep of broad system-level, functional and performance requirements. The Council was also requested to continue seeking the most appropriate means of development, translation, processing and dissemination of technical specifications. Contracting States were requested to comment fully and in detail on the proposals for amendment of SARPs and PANS or at least should express their agreement or disagreement on their substance. They should be allowed at least 3 months for this purpose. Furthermore, Contracting States should receive at least 30 days of notification of the intended approval or adoption of detailed material on which they are not consulted. Contracting States were to be allowed a full 3 months for notifying disapproval of adopted SARPs amendments; in establishing a date for notifying disapproval the Council should take into account the time needed for transmission of the adopted amendments and for receipt of notifications from States.

Finally, Appendix A required the Council to ensure that, whenever practicable, the interval between successive common applicability dates of amendments to Annexes and PANS is at least 6 months.

In terms of the Implementation of SARPS Appendix D (Implementation of Standards and Recommended Practices and Procedures for Air Navigation Services) of Resolution A37-15 states:

Whereas Article 37 of the Convention on International Civil Aviation requires each Contracting State to collaborate in securing the highest practicable degree of uniformity in regulations and practices in all matters in which such uniformity will facilitate and improve air navigation;

Whereas in accordance with Article 38 of the Convention any Contracting State which finds it impractical to comply in all respects with any international standard or procedure and deems it necessary to adopt regulations or practices differing therefrom is obliged to give immediate notification to ICAO; and

Whereas it is important that all available means of the Organization be employed in encouraging and assisting

Contracting States in overcoming their difficulties in implementation of SARPs and PANs;

The Assembly resolves that:

1. Contracting States shall be encouraged and assisted in the implementation of SARPs and PANs by available means;
2. the differences between the regulations and the practices of Contracting States and the SARPs and PANS shall be monitored by the Council with the aim of encouraging the elimination of those differences that are important for the safety and regularity of international air navigation or are inconsistent with the objectives of the international Standards; and
3. the Council shall analyse the root cause for non-implementation and take appropriate action.

The Appendix has the following Associated Practices:

1. In encouraging and assisting Contracting States in the application of SARPs and PANs the Council should make use of all existing means including the resources of Headquarters, the ICAO Regional Offices and the United Nations Development Programme;
2. Contracting States should continue, and where necessary should intensify, their efforts to apply at their operating installations practices and procedures that are in accordance with the current SARPs and PANS. In this regard, Contracting States should consider the practicability of modifying the internal processes by which they give effect to the provisions of SARPs and PANs, if such modifications would expedite or simplify the processes or make them more effective;

   (a) The Council should urge Contracting States to notify the Organization of any differences that exist between their national regulations and practices and the provisions of SARPs as well as the date or dates by which they will comply with the SARPs. If a Contracting State finds itself unable to comply with any SARPs, it should inform ICAO of the reason for non-implementation, including any applicable national regulations and practices which are different in character or in principle. The notifications of differences from SARPs received should be promptly issued in supplements to the relevant Annexes. Contracting States should also be requested to publish in their AIPs any significant differences from the SARPs and PANs;
   (b) In the monitoring of the differences from SARPs and PANS, the Council should request reports from Contracting States that have not or have incompletely reported to the Organization the implementation of SARPs; Furthermore, the Council should also request Contracting States that have not

published in their AIPs information on the implementation of SARPs and PANs to publish it.

The ICAO Assembly, at its 4th Session (Montreal 30 May–20 June 1950) adopted Resolution A4-7 (Relation of Procedures for Air Navigation Services to Annexes) Resolved that the Council ensure that Procedures for Air Navigation Services are incorporated in the appropriate Annexes to the Convention as soon as these have become sufficiently stable and that the Council continue to urge Contracting States to notify the Organization of national differences from relevant procedures for air navigation services when such differences affected the safety or regularity of international air navigation. At a later Session during its 7th Assembly (Brighton 16 June–6 July 1953) it was resolved in Resolution A7-9 (Notification of differences from International Standards) that the Council initiate a more effective and simplified programme with regard to the reporting by States of differences, pursuant to Article 38 of the Convention, to the end that the Organization (ICAO) may be better informed of the actual state of implementation among the Contracting States. The Resolution also requested that more emphasis be given to a programme of monitoring outstanding differences. With the objective of encouraging the elimination of those differences which are important for the safety of air navigation or which are inconsistent with the objective of the international standards.

This last statement of Resolution A7-9 indubitably was the precursor to the current ICAO Continuous Monitoring Approach (CMA). It is encouraging that a later Assembly continued this progressive trend of monitoring adhering by States of SARPs and PANs.[2]

3.1 Nature of an Annex

In dealing with this question one immediately hits a snag. As stated earlier, Article 54 l) states that the Council shall adopt, international standards and recommended practices, and, *for convenience* (my emphasis), designate them as Annexes to this Convention. If the Annexes are called as such for convenience, would they form an integral part of the Chicago Convention? Aust is of the view:

> When a treaty has an annex it is normal to provide, though not necessarily in a separate article, that the annex is an integral part of the treaty. Since there are often other documents produced at the time the treaty is adopted, such as agreed minutes, declarations and interpretative exchanges of notes, it is important to know whether they are an integral part of the treaty or merely associated with it.[3]

[2]Resolution A21-21 in Appendix D merely reiterated the significance of Articles 37 and 38 and stated that States should be encouraged to adhere to SARPs and PANs and that their ability to comply with Articles 37 and 38 should be monitored.

[3]Aust (2000), p. 348.

Therefore is accepted legal practice that if a treaty has attachments it will usually say in the text of the treaty that they are integral to the instrument. Such integral portions of a treaty are Annexes, Protocols, Appendices or Schedules. In the context of the 18 Annexes to the Chicago Convention one could say that such long documents could form a series of separate instruments which use terminology different from the Treaty provisions. For instance, if a treaty uses the word "shall" the Annex should usually not use the word. However, both the Chicago Convention and the SARPs of its Annexes use the word "shall" which deviates from this trend. Therefore from a strictly legal perspective, it is arguable that the Annexes to the Chicago Convention are not integral parts of the Convention.

The above notwithstanding, and from a practical perspective, there seems to be no way out other than to consider an Annex in this context as part of the Convention. If one does not do so, there will be no work for ICAO and the international community in following a structured regulatory practice in the safety and security of air navigation and assisting States with deficiencies.

Another difficulty is perceived in Article 38 of the Convention which clearly does not obligate States to adhere to Standards in an Annex. In this context, one wonders what the status of the Annexes are and one could be perplexed as to what ICAO's role in pursuing the Standards of the Annexes with Contracting States is. This ambivalence prevailed until ICAO initiated the proactive move of its safety and security audits whereby ICAO could follow progress of States in complying with SARPs (in particular the Standards) and assist States with overcoming any deficiencies with regard to adhering to the Standards of the Annexes.

The question arises as to whether a Contracting State is formally bound by Standards contained in an Annex to the Chicago Convention, particularly when such a State has no convincing argument that it is impracticable to implement such Standards or when it has not notified the ICAO Council of differences as required. This is a vexed debate, particularly in the face of two blatant facts. The first is that the *travaux preparatoires* to the Convention contains a statement that "the Annexes are given no compulsory force".[4] The second is that, as stated earlier, in Article 54 of the Convention, which lays down the mandatory functions of the Council, it is provided that one of the mandatory functions is to:

> Adopt, in accordance with the provisions of this Convention, international standards and recommended practices; **for convenience** (emphasis added) designate them as Annexes to this Convention; and notify all Contracting States of action taken".[5]

One could argue therefore that the Annexes are not an integral part of the Convention by virtue of the statement in Article 54 and therefore do not form binding law.

---

[4]See Whiteman (1968) p. 404.

[5]Chicago Convention, Chap. 1 in *supra* note 13, Article 54 (l).

There have been numerous views of legal scholars who have cautioned against this approach and advocated that the words of the Convention should not be taken literarily. One commentator is of the view that:

> The debate is largely academic. Whether or not ICAO standards are formally binding in the treaty law sense, they are highly authoritative in practice. This reflects their recognized importance for the safety and efficiency of civil air travel and the thorough process by which they are promulgated.[6]

It is therefore arguable that all Standards contained in the ICAO Annexes are formally binding on Contracting States, except when a State opts out of under the procedure set forth in the Convention in Article 38. ICAO's international Standards are identified by the words "Contracting States shall" and have a mandatory flavour (infused by the word 'shall') while Recommended Practices identified by the words 'Contracting States may' have only an advisory and recommendatory connotation (infused by the word 'may'). It is interesting that at least one ICAO document[7] requires States under Article 38 of the Convention, to notify ICAO of all significant differences from both Standards and Recommended Practices, thus making all SARPS regulatory in nature.

The legal effect and the compulsive nature of the Standards and Recommended Practices of the ICAO Annexes have to be recognized if a meaningful implementation of the Annexes to the Chicago Convention were to be carried out by Contracting States. Milde states:

> The Chicago Convention, as any other legal instrument, provides only a general legal framework which is given true life only in the practical implementation of its provisions. Thus, for example, Article 37 of the Convention relating to the adoption of international standards and recommended procedures would be a very hollow and meaningless provision without active involvement of all Contracting States, Panels, Regional and Divisional Meetings, deliberations in the Air Navigation Commission and final adoption of the standards by the Council. Similarly, provisions of Article 12 relating to the rules of the air applicable over the high seas, Articles 17 to 20 on the nationality of aircraft, Article 22 on facilitation, Article 26 on the investigation of accidents, etc., would be meaningless without appropriate implementation in the respective Annexes. On the same level is the provision of the last sentence of Article 77 relating to the determination by the Council in what manner the provisions of the Convention relating to nationality of aircraft shall apply to aircraft operated by international operating agencies.[8]

---

[6]Kirgis (1995), p. 109 at 126. There is a similar process in operation under the World Meteorological Organization, whereby a certain amount of decision making authority is given to the WMO Congress. Article 9 (a) of the WMO Convention provides that all members shall do their utmost to implement the decisions of the Congress. Article 9(b) allows any member to opt out by notifying the Secretary General, with reasons if it finds it impracticable to give effect to the technical requirement in question. WMO Convention, reprinted in *International Organization and Integration*, (P Kapteyn et al. eds) 2nd Revised Edition, 1981, pt. I.B.1.9 a. Also in *WMO Basic Documents*, No. 1. WMO Doc. No. 15 at 9 1987.

[7]*Aeronautical Information Services Manual*, ICAO Doc 8126 -0 AN/872/3.

[8]Milde (1989), pp. 203–208. See also Schenkman (1955), p. 163.

Milde goes on to say that the manner in which the International Civil Aviation organization has exercised its regulatory functions in matters relating to the safety of international air navigation and the facilitation of international air transport provides a fascinating example of international law making. He further observes that the Organization has consequently not had to contend with any of the post war ideological differences that have impeded international law making on politically sensitive issues.[9]

Policy decisions of ICAO are usually adopted and transmitted through the Council and in this respect the Council is a powerful and visible body in international aviation.[10] Furthermore, a decision taken by the Council is juridically dignified by Article 86 of the Convention, where the Article provides that unless the Council decides otherwise, any decision by the Council on whether an international airline is operating in conformity with the provisions of the Convention shall remain in effect unless reversed in appeal. The Council also has powers of sanction granted by the Convention, if its decision is not adhered to.[11] Schenkman states:

The power of sanctions in this field is an entirely new phenomenon, attributed to an aeronautical body. . .none of the pre-war instruments in the field of aviation had the power of sanctions as a means of enforcement of its decisions.[12]

A most interesting aspect of the ICAO Council remains to be that one of its mandatory functions is to consider any subject referred to it by a Contracting State for its consideration.[13] or any subject which the President of the Council or the Secretary General of the ICAO Secretariat desires to bring before the Council. Although the Council is bound to consider a matter submitted to it by a Contracting State it can refrain from giving a decision as the Council is only obligated to consider a matter before it.

3.2 Can the Council Make Law and Rules?

The words "legislative power" have been legally defined as "power to prescribe rules of civil conduct",[14] while identifying law as a "rule of civil conduct". The word "quasi" is essentially a term that makes a resemblance to another and classifies it. It is suggestive of comparative analogy and is accepted as:

> the conception to which it serves as an index and its connection with the conception with which the comparison is instituted by strong superficial analogy or resemblance.[15]

---

[9] *Id.* p. 210.

[10] Sochor (1991), p. 58.

[11] Chicago Convention, Chap. 1 in *supra*, note 13, Article 87.

[12] Schenkman, *op.cit* at p. 162.

[13] Chicago Convention, Chap. 1 in *supra*, note 13, Article 54 (n).

[14] *Schaake* v. *Dolly* 85 Kan. 590., 118 Pac. 80.

[15] *People* v. *Bradley* 60 Ill. 402, at 405. Also, *Bouviers Law Dictionary and Concise Encyclopedia* 3 ed. Vol 11, Vernon Law Book Co., New York 1914.

The question *stricto sensu* according to the above definition is therefore whether the ICAO Council now has power to prescribe rules of civil conduct (legislative power) or in the least a power that resembles by analogy the ability to prescribe rules of conduct (quasi-legislative power). Since legislative power is usually attributed to a State, it would be prudent to inquire, on a general basis, whether the ICAO Council has law making powers (in a quasi-legislative sense). Therefore, all references hereafter that may refer to legislative powers would be reflective of the Council's law making powers in a quasi-legislative sense.

Article 54(l) of the Chicago Convention prescribes the adoption of international Standards and Recommended Practices (hereafter, SARPS) and their designation in Annexes to the Convention, while notifying all Contracting States of the action taken. The adoption of SARPS was considered a priority by the ICAO Council in its Second Session (2 September-12 December 1947)[16] which attempted to obviate any delays to the adoption of SARPS on air navigation as required by the First Assembly of ICAO.[17] SARPS inevitably take two forms: a negative form e.g. that States shall not impose more than certain maximum requirements; and a positive form e.g. that States shall take certain steps as prescribed by the ICAO Annexes.[18]

Article 37 of the Convention obtains the undertaking of each Contracting State to collaborate in securing the highest practical degree of uniformity in regulations, standards, procedures and organization in relation to international civil aviation in all matters in which such uniformity will facilitate and improve air navigation. Article 38 obligates all Contracting States to the Convention to inform ICAO immediately if they are unable to comply with any such international standard or procedure and notify differences between their own practices and those prescribed by ICAO. In the case of amendments to international Standards, any State which does not make the appropriate amendment to its own regulations or practices shall give notice to the Council of ICAO within 60 days of the adoption of the said amendment to the international Standard or indicate the action which it proposes to take.

The element of compulsion that has been infused by the drafters of the Convention is compatible with the "power to prescribe rules of civil conduct" on a *stricto sensu* legal definition of the words "legislative power" as discussed above. There is no room for doubt that the 18 Annexes to the Convention or parts thereof lay down rules of conduct both directly and analogically. In fact, although there is a conception based on a foundation of practicality that ICAO's international Standards that are identified by the words "Contracting States shall" have a mandatory flavour (infused by the word "shall") while Recommended Practices identified by the words "Contracting States may have only an advisory and" recommendatory connotation

[16]Proceedings of the Council 2nd Session 2 September-12 December 1947, Doc 7248 - C/839 at 44–45.

[17]ICAO Resolutions A - 13 and A - 33 which resolved that SARPS relating to the efficient and safe regulation of international air navigation be adopted.

[18]ICAO Annex 9, Facilitation, Foreword.

(infused by the word "may"), it is interesting that at least one ICAO document requires States under Article 38 of the Convention, to notify ICAO of all significant differences from both Standards and Recommended Practices, thus making all SARPS regulatory in nature.[19]

Another strong factor that reflects the overall ability and power of the Council to prescribe civil rules of conduct (and therefore legislate) on a strict interpretation of the word is that in Article 22 of the Convention each Contracting State agrees to adopt all practical measures through the issuance of special regulations or otherwise, to facilitate and expedite air navigation... It is clear that this provision can be regarded as an incontrovertible rule of conduct that responds to the requirement in Article 54(l) of the Convention. Furthermore, the mandatory nature of Article 90 of the Convention—that an Annex or amendment thereto shall become effective within 3 months after it is submitted by the ICAO Council to Contracting States is yet another pronouncement on the power of the Council to prescribe rules of State conduct in matters of international civil aviation. *A fortiori*, it is arguable that the Council is seen not only to possess the attribute of the term "jurisfaction" (the power to make rules of conduct) but also the term "jurisaction" (the power to enforce its own rules of conduct). The latter attribute can be seen where the Convention obtains the undertaking of Contracting States not to allow airlines to operate through their air space if the Council decides that the airline concerned is not conforming to a final decision rendered by the Council on a matter that concerns the operation of an international airline.[20] This is particularly applicable when such airline is found not to conform to the provisions of Annex 2 to the Convention that derives its validity from Article 12 of the Convention relating to rules of the air.[21] In fact, it is very relevant that Annex 2, the responsibility for the promulgation of which devolves upon the Council by virtue of Article 54(l), sets mandatory rules of the air, making the existence of the legislative powers of the Council an unequivocal and irrefutable fact.

Academic and professional opinion also favours the view that in a practical sense, the ICAO Council does have legislative powers. Milde concludes that ICAO has regulatory and quasi-legislative functions in the technical field and plays a consultative and advisory role in the economic sphere.[22] A similar view had earlier been expressed by Buergenthal who states:

---

[19] *Aeronautical Information Services Manual*, ICAO Doc 8126 -0 AN/872/3. ICAO Resolution A1-31 defines a Standard as any specification for physical characteristics...the uniform application of which is recognised as *necessary*... and one that States *will conform to*. The same resolution describes a Recommended Practice as any specification for physical characteristics... which is recognised as *desirable* ...and one that member States *will endeavour to conform to*...Buergenthal (1969), p. 10 also cites the definitions given in ICAO's Annex 9 of SARPS.

[20] Article 86 of the Convention.

[21] Article 12 stipulates that over the high seas, the rules in force shall be those established under the Convention, and each contracting State undertakes to insure the prosecution of all persons violating the applicable regulations.

[22] Milde., *op.cit.* 122.

> the manner in which the International Civil Aviation organization has exercised its regulatory functions in matters relating to the safety of international air navigation and the facilitation of international air transport provides a fascinating example of international law making... the Organization has consequently not had to contend with any of the post war ideological differences that have impeded international law making on politically sensitive issues.[23]

Paul Stephen Dempsey endorses in a somewhat conservative manner, the view that ICAO has the ability to make regulations when he states:

> In addition to the comprehensive, but largely dormant adjudicative enforcement held by ICAO under Articles 84–88 of the Chicago Convention, the Agency also has a solid foundation for enhanced participation in economic regulatory aspects of international aviation in Article 44, as well as the Convention's Preamble.[24]

A significant attribute of the legislative capabilities of the ICAO Council is its ability to adopt technical standards as Annexes to the Convention without going through a lengthy process of ratification.[25] Eugene Sochor refers to the Council as a powerful and visible body in international aviation.[26] It is interesting however to note that although by definition, the ICAO Council has been considered by some as unable to deal with strictly legal matters, since other important matters come within its purview,[27] this does not derogate the compelling facts that reflect the distinct law making abilities of ICAO. Should this not be true, the functions that the Convention assigns to ICAO in Article 44—that ICAO's aims and objectives are to "develop the principles and techniques of international air navigation and to foster the planning and development of international air transport"—would be rendered destitute of effect.

Under the Interim Agreement[28] the PICAO Council was required to act as an arbitral body on any differences arising among member States relating to matters of international civil aviation which may be submitted to it, wherein the Interim Council of PICAO was empowered to render an advisory report or if the parties involved so wished, give a decision on the matter before it.[29] The Interim Council, which was the precursor to the ICAO Council, set the stage therefore for providing the Council with unusual arbitral powers which are not attributed to similar organs of the specialised agencies of the United Nations system.[30] *A fortiori*, since the ICAO Council is permanent and is almost in constant session, Contracting States

---

[23] Buergenthal (1969), p. 9.

[24] Dempsey (1987), p. 302.

[25] Sochor (1991), p. 58.

[26] *Ibid.*

[27] Tobolewski (1979), pp. 349–359.

[28] See Chap. 1 in *infra* note 37.

[29] Interim Agreement, Article 111, Section 6(i).

[30] Schenkman (1955), p. 160.

could expect any matter of dispute brought by them before the Council to be dealt with, without unreasonable delay.[31]

Most Contracting States have, on their own initiative, enacted dispute-settlement clauses in their bilateral air services agreements wherein provision is usually made to refer inter-State disputes relating to international civil aviation to the ICAO Council, in accordance with Chapter XV111 of the Convention. In this context, it is also relevant to note that the President of the Council is empowered by the Convention to appoint an arbitrator and an umpire in certain circumstances leading to an appeal from a decision of the Council.[32]

A most interesting aspect of the ICAO Council remains to be that one of its mandatory functions is to consider any subject referred to it by a Contracting State for its consideration.[33] or any subject which the President of the Council or the Secretary General of the ICAO Secretariat desires to bring before the Council.[34] Although the Council is bound to consider a matter submitted to it by a Contracting State it can refrain from giving a decision as the Council is only obligated to consider a matter before it.

3.3 Rulemaking in Safety Oversight

Paragraph 2.1.1. of the *Safety Oversight Manual* of ICAO defines safety oversight as:

> a function by means of which States ensure effective implementation of the safety related Standards and Recommended Practices (SARPs) and associated procedures in the Annexes to the Convention on International Civil Aviation and related ICAO Documents.[35]

The ICAO Assembly at its 29th Session (1992), adopted Resolution A29-13 which reaffirmed that each individual State's responsibility for safety oversight is one of the tenets of the Convention on International Civil Aviation (Chicago Convention).

---

[31]See statement of R. Kidron, Israeli Head Delegate, Statement of the Second Plenary Meeting of the Seventh Assembly on June 17, 1953, reported in *ICAO Monthly Bulletin*, August-October 1953, at 8.

[32]Article 85.

[33]Rules of Procedure for the Council. *op.cit.* Section 1 V, Rule 24 (e). Also, Article 54(n) stipulates that one of the mandatory functions of the Council is to consider any matter relating to the Convention which any contracting State refers to it.

[34]Rules of Procedure for the Council, *op.cit.* Section 1 V Rule 24 (f). The two additional multilateral agreements stemming from the Convention and providing for the exchange of traffic rights—the Air Services Transit Agreement and the Air Transport Agreement, also contain provisions that empower the ICAO Council to hear disputes and "make appropriate findings and recommendations..." see Air Services Transit Agreement Article 11 Section 1, and the Air Transport Agreement Article 1 V Section 2.

[35]ICAO Doc 9734, AN/959, 2nd ed. (2006) Part A.

The Assembly, at its 37th session adopted Resolution A37-5 (The Universal Safety Oversight Audit Programme USOAP continuous monitoring approach) which recognized that safety oversight and the safety of international civil aviation in general, is the responsibility of the Contracting States, both collectively and individually.

According to the Chicago Convention, safety oversight and a State's responsibility pertaining thereto can be subsumed into two broad areas: nationality and registration of the aircraft and responsibilities that flow therefrom; and territorial jurisdiction of that State. Accordingly, there are certain mandatory responsibilities of a State in ensuring safety oversight.

Article 17 of the Convention provides that aircraft have the nationality of the State in which they are registered. Article 18 prohibits the registration of aircraft in more than one State, which effectively precludes dual nationality of aircraft and responsibility of more than one State.

The registration of an aircraft in a particular State devolves upon that State certain safety related obligations. For example Article 12 of the Chicago Convention states:

> Each Contracting State undertakes to adopt measures to insure that every aircraft flying over or manoeuvring within its territory and that every aircraft carrying its nationality mark, wherever such aircraft may be, shall comply with the rules and regulations relating to the flight and manoeuvre of aircraft there in force. Each Contracting State undertakes to keep its own regulations in these respects uniform, to the greatest possible extent, with those established from time to time under this Convention. Over the high seas, the rules in force shall be those established under this Convention. Each Contracting State undertakes to insure the prosecution of all persons violating the regulations applicable.

Article 31 of the Convention provides:

> Every aircraft engaged in international navigation shall be provided with a certificate of airworthiness issued or rendered valid by the State in which it is registered.

Along the same lines, Article 32 provides:

> *a)* The pilot of every aircraft and the other members of the operating crew of every aircraft engaged in international navigation shall be provided with certificates of competency and licenses issued or rendered valid by the State in which the aircraft is registered.
>
> *b)* Each Contracting State reserves the right to refuse to recognize, for the purpose of flight above its own territory, certificates of competency and licenses granted to any of its nationals by another Contracting State.

In the context of equipment on board aircraft, Article 30 of the Convention requires that over the territory of States other than their State of registration, aircraft shall carry radio transmitting apparatus only if a license to install and operate such apparatus has been issued by the appropriate authorities of the State in which the aircraft is registered. The use of radio transmitting apparatus in the territory of the Contracting State whose territory is flown over shall be in accordance with the regulations prescribed by that State.

The only exception to these mandatory principles is found in Article 83 *bis*, where, for purposes of expediency, when an aircraft registered in a Contracting

State is operated pursuant to an agreement for the lease, charter or interchange of the aircraft or any similar arrangement by an operator who has his principal place of business or, if he has no such place of business, his permanent residence in another Contracting State, the State of registry may, by agreement with such other State, transfer to it all or part of its functions and duties as State of registry in respect of that aircraft under Articles 12, 30, 31 and 32 (a). In such an instance the State of registry is relieved of responsibility in respect of the functions and duties transferred.

In pursuance of the above obligations, one could validly conclude that Article 37 of the Chicago Convention imposes an obligation on each Contracting State to undertake to collaborate in securing the highest practicable degree of uniformity in regulations, standards, procedures, and organization in relation to aircraft, personnel, airways and auxiliary services in all matters in which such uniformity will facilitate and improve air navigation. These Standards and Recommended Practices are contained in the 18 Annexes to the Chicago Convention, all of which except Annexes 9 (Facilitation) and 17 (Security) are applicable to safety oversight either directly or indirectly.

3.4 Regional Safety Oversight

Regional governance under State responsibility is an undeniable necessity in ensuring safety in air transport. However, since international air transport crosses boundaries and all regions of the world, a certain stringent global regulatory system is required, and this objective cannot be reached unless the safety oversight system is de-centralized into safety agencies in each region. This is because although air transport is still considered the safest mode of travel, constant and diligent vigilance in ensuring the safety of aviation is required. The International Civil Aviation Organization (ICAO), which is the global forum for aviation, provides this guidance and direction and encourages States to form regional civil aviation bodies in regions where they do not exist. Since almost all regional civil aviation bodies have their own Constitutions, these Constitutions should recognize the need for increased cooperation with ICAO and ICAO should actively seek such an inclusion. Cooperation could include assignment of tasks related to oversight, accident investigation, sharing of information and the conduct of training in collaboration with ICAO.

Some of the measures that are suggested in this article include, the initiation by ICAO where appropriate, of periodic meetings with regional civil aviation bodies and the setting up of panels that include members from ICAO and each regional body on a selective basis. This panel could recommend and monitor issues of cooperation, including cooperation between the various regional organizations.

There is also the compelling need to define the role that regional organizations and regional civil aviation bodies would play in working closely with ICAO; and the adoption of a policy with regard to cooperation with regional organizations and regional civil aviation bodies. ICAO should also ascertain the role to be played by the regional offices in coordinating ICAO cooperation with such bodies. Consideration should be given to providing appropriate resources in regional offices where necessary.

This article also discusses in some depth the various regional safety oversight organizations agencies (RSOOs) and examines the legal and regulatory basis of ICAO's role with regard to the establishment and functions of RSOOs with reference to selected regional oversight organizations around the world.

The role played by Regional Safety Oversight Organizations (RSOOs)[36] has sustained serious discussions in ICAO. and in particular in the Council[37] of that Organization over the past year. At its 187th Session on 10 June 2009, the Council accepted several principles with regard to the role of ICAO in regional governance[38] which were placed before it by a multidisciplinary group comprising some Representatives on the Council and members of the ICAO Secretariat, which had been tasked with producing a report on ICAO and Regional Governance, by the Council.

At its meeting, the Council agreed ICAO should enhance its cooperation with regional organizations and regional civil aviation bodies and vice-versa, both in the technical and economic fields and should ensure that the interests of States which do not belong to regional civil aviation bodies should not be jeopardized or compromised in the above context. The Council also recognized that while ICAO encourages the activities of States and regional civil aviation bodies in facilitating the implementation of Standards and Recommended Practices of the Annexes to the Convention on International Civil Aviation (Chicago Convention) (SARPs), States ultimately remained responsible for their obligations under the Convention on International Civil Aviation, notwithstanding whatever arrangements States may conclude with their regional civil aviation bodies. It was also agreed that ICAO should encourage States to form regional civil aviation bodies in regions where they do not exist, and that ICAO should define the role that regional organizations would play in working closely with ICAO.

---

[36]Sometimes referred to as Regional Safety Oversight Agencies (RASAs).

[37]The ICAO Council is a permanent body responsible to the Assembly. It is composed of 36 Member States elected by the Assembly. In electing the members of the Council, the Assembly gives adequate representation to States of chief importance to air transport; States not otherwise included which make the largest contribution to the provision of facilities for international air navigation; and States not otherwise included whose designation will ensure that all the major geographic areas of the world are represented on the Council. The mandatory and permissive functions of the Council are stipulated in Articles 54 and 55 of the Convention on International Civil Aviation respectively. The Council has its genesis in the Interim Council of the Provisional International Civil Aviation Organization (PICAO). PICAO occupied such legal capacity as may have been necessary for the performance of its functions and was recognized as having full juridical personality wherever compatible with the Constitution and the laws of the State concerned. See Interim Agreement on International Civil Aviation, opened for signature at Chicago, December 7 1944, Article 3. Also in Hudson, *International Legislation*, Vol 1X, New York: 1942–1945, at 159. For a detailed discussion on the functions of the Council See Abeyratne (1992), pp. 387–394.

[38]C-WP/13339, 12/05/09.

Article 55a) of the Chicago Convention states that the Council may, where appropriate and as experience may show to be desirable, create subordinate air transport commissions on a regional or other basis and define groups of States with or through which it may deal to facilitate the carrying out of aims of the Convention. Article 65 of the Convention allows the Council to enter into agreements with other international bodies for the maintenance of common services with and for common arrangements concerning personnel and, with the approval of the Assembly, allows the Council to enter into such other arrangements as may facilitate the work of the Organization.

This provision prompted the ICAO Assembly, at its First Assembly held on 6–27 May 1947 to adopt Resolution A1-10, which recognized that there were a number of public organizations whose activities affect or are affected by ICAO and that the work of ICAO and the advancement of international civil aviation will be enhanced by close cooperation with such organizations. The Resolution authorized the Council to make appropriate arrangements with public international organizations whose activities affect international civil aviation and suggested that such arrangements be established through informal working arrangements rather than formal arrangements, wherever practicable.

At its 10th Session conducted in Caracas from 19 June to 16 July in 1956, the ICAO Assembly adopted Resolution A10-5, which established a policy framework for ICAO and the European Civil aviation Conference (ECAC) which had its focus on regional cooperation. An agreement effective 12 July 1969 was signed by ICAO and ECAC which allowed the appointment of ICAO staff to the Secretariat of ECAC, and the provision of qualified and expert staff to the latter. A similar agreement effective 1 January 1978 was signed between ICAO and the African Civil Aviation Commission (AFCAC) which provided *inter alia* that ICAO will provide, to the extent possible, secretariat services to AFCAC. There is also an agreement, which became effective on 1 January 1979 between ICAO and the Latin Civil Aviation Commission (LACAC) which called for close cooperation between the two Organizations and the provision of secretariat services to LACAC by ICAO.

There are numerous other instances of such regional cooperation which followed such as the signing of a memorandum of understanding by ICAO and LACAC on 1 October 1999 followed by an MoU between ICAO and ECAC on 11 November 1999. These were to be followed by a management service agreement between ICAO and AFCAC which came into effect on 1 January 2007.

These regional bodies are by themselves not RSOOs, although they could, and indeed should play an integral role in assisting States in their oversight functions and the RSOOs in their work. In this regard, it is critical to recognize that regional governance and regional safety oversight are prerogatives which devolve consequent responsibility on the State which cannot be delegated. The RSOO acts as an agent[39] of the State (which is the Principal) with delegated functions from the

[39]An agency is a consensual relationship created by contract or law where the Principal grants authority to agents to act on behalf of or under the control of the Principal to deal with a third party.

Principal. ICAO, to the extent of its empowerment by its member States, can assist in the oversight process, offer expertise, advice, technical support and even manage an RSOO if necessary.

Therefore, ICAO's position with regard to RSOOs is that it would give its full cooperation to regional governance as determined by States through carefully formulated policy which would in no way abdicate or delegate ICAO's responsibilities under the Chicago Convention. In the agency equation the State remains the Principal and the RSOO remains the Agent and ICAO remains the organization empowered by the States to carry out audits and report results thereof.

3.5 The Regional Safety Oversight Manual

ICAO's perspectives on regional safety oversight are reflected in its *Regional Safety Oversight Manual*[40] which provides guidance for States that wish to form a regional safety oversight system. It formulates a regional strategy which attenuates and brings together the efforts, experiences and resources of Contracting States. From ICAO's perspective the reasons for adopting a strategy to establish RSOOs are to: eliminate a duplication of effort by standardizing regulatory and enforcement provisions over a large area of aviation activities; achieve economies of scale leading to efficiency and effectiveness; pool human and financial resources; institute effective regional programmes through the joint action of States; address external factors and constraints more effectively; develop and implement a safety management system[41] that would allow for the implementation of similar standards and procedures to measure the safety performance of civil aviation organizations in the region; supplement shortfalls in the scope of domestic and bilateral interventions; prove organizational ability by testing activities before making important commitments under national programmes; meet industry expectations; demonstrate improved regional solidarity; improve the objectivity and independence of inspectors; and develop a capability for drafting and amending regulations and procedures.[42]

ICAO believes that RSOOs should have goals which reflect national priorities, and recommends that States consider providing adequate and efficient resources and ensure coordination between high level government officials who are responsible for aviation safety. The most incontrovertible principle ICAO believes in is, as mentioned earlier, that the responsibility for safety oversight within the State remains with the State and cannot be delegated.[43] The critical activities of a State

[40]ICAO Doc 9734 AN/959 Part B (The Establishment and Management of a Regional Safety Oversight System).

[41]For a detailed discussion on safety management systems see Abeyratne (2007), pp. 7–13.

[42]*Id.* Para 2.2.4 at p. 2–3.

[43]*Id.* Para 2.2.5 at p. 2–4.

are identified in the *Manual* as: the licensing of operational personnel; the certification of aircraft, air operators, aerodromes, and maintenance organizations; the control and supervision of licensed personnel, certified products and approved organizations; the provision of air navigation services[44]; and aircraft accident and incident investigation.[45]

ICAO's role, according to the *Manual*, is to provide assistance to States that are willing to enter into a cooperative agreement for the establishment and management of an RSOO on the basis of an agreement between ICAO and the interested parties. ICAO may also manage an RSOO until such time as the State concerned develops an ability to perform the task. The Organization may also provide technical and logistical support as well as necessary information and documents that may be needed by an RSOO and also, upon a request of a State monitor the effectiveness of an RSOO. Where necessary and as requested, ICAO could, according to the Manual, provide advice or propose action required in the proper running of an RSOO.[46]

In this regard the Symposium was also advised that ICAO has conducted a series of safety audits throughout the world and information of these audits were available.

3.6 Conclusion

In this chapter we have discussed various ICAO instruments—from Annexes and their SARPs to Assembly Resolutions and guidance material in the form of manuals. These are useless if not properly implemented. On this score, ICAO does not pursue studies on how these are implemented with the exception of the safety and security audits performed and that too ICAO's evaluation goes only as far as determining whether the Standards in the Annexes are adhered to. Rulemaking is quite different, where the ICAO provisions or their content and even their basic sense, get into the rule books of the member States of ICAO. Articles 54 and 55 of the Chicago Convention as discussed, give ICAO a head start which should not be ignored.

The first step towards a more forceful and compelling role for ICAO's pronouncements is to recognize all the above categories of guidance that come from the ICAO Council and Assembly as international norms. These norms would have to be made acceptable to a State's internal discourse and policy making process. ICAO's international norms must match the cultural construct of a State and offer practical advantages and value to the structure of the domestic institutions of that

---

[44]Including meteorological information, aeronautical telecommunications, search and rescue services, charts and the distribution of information.

[45]*Id*. Para. 2.4.5 at p. 2–6.

[46]*Id*. Para 3.5 at p. 3–5.

State. A good example lies in the Headquarters Agreement between the Government of Canada and ICAO. This agreement bestows many advantages to the international civil servants of the Organization. For instance, Article 2 of the Agreement stipulates that ICAO possesses juridical personality and has the legal capacities of a body corporate, including the capacity to contract; to acquire and dispose of immovable and movable property; and to institute legal proceedings. This principle now is an acceptable rule in Canada without it even being entered into the statute books of the country. Other provisions that are inarticulate rules in Canada are that ICAO, its property and its assets, wherever located and by whomsoever held, enjoy the same immunity from suit and every form of judicial process as is enjoyed by foreign states. The Government of Canada accords to the headquarters premises the same protection as is given to diplomatic missions in Canada and the property and assets of the Organization, wherever located and by whomsoever held, are immune from search, requisition, confiscation, expropriation and any other form of interference, whether by executive, administrative, judicial, or legislative action, except with the consent of and under the conditions agreed to by the Secretary General of the Organization. ICAO is exempt from all direct taxes other than charges for public utility services as well as from customs duties, taxes and prohibitions and restrictions on imports and exports in respect of articles imported or exported by the Organization in furtherance of its functions.

Cortell and Davis note:

> When such a cultural match exists, domestic actors are likely to treat the international norm as a given, instinctively recognizing the obligations associated with the norm. Domestic salience under such conditions is automatic. Conversely, when the international norm conflicts with understandings, beliefs, or obligations established in the domestic sphere, domestic actors may then find appeals to the international norm to be ineffective in garnering support for a particular policy. Gary Goertz and Paul F. Diehl note that "although Britain and France may face the same international norms... the unique national experience of a country will make its propensity to follow that norm different.[47]

Against this reality, ICAO has to approach effective rulemaking in two stages. The first step is the conduct of a serious empirical study under Article 55 of the Chicago Conventions that would bring about a thorough analysis of what norms of ICAO are followed by whom and for what reasons, together with the reasons that impel States not to follow certain ICAO norms. The second step is for ICAO to match the more adaptable Standards of the Annexes with general political philosophy and culture of its member States and formulate general norms that could be incorporated into an arrangement with the States that require their adherence in principle to such norms along with their assurance that they would consider all Standards of the Annexes to the Chicago Convention that accord with the general philosophy of such norms would be considered rules in their jurisdictions.

The Preamble to the Chicago Convention speaks of principles and arrangements that States adhere to, giving legitimacy *in limine* to such an arrangement between

---

[47]Cortell and Davis (Spring 2001), pp. 66–87 at 74.

the States and ICAO. The Convention as well as its Annexes are replete with instances of "arrangements" under the auspices of ICAO. One such example lies in the instance of communicable diseases that could be spread through air transport. ICAO has already put into action a systemic approach to a possible outbreak of communicable disease. At the 35th Session of the ICAO Assembly, held in September/October 2004, ICAO Contracting States adopted Resolution A35-12, which declares that the protection of the health of passengers and crews on international flights is an integral element of safe air travel and that conditions should be in place to ensure its preservation in a timely and cost effective manner. Through this Resolution, the Council has been requested to review existing Standards and Recommended Practices (SARPs) of relevant Annexes to the Chicago Convention and adopt new SARPs as necessary, while maintaining institutional arrangements to coordinate efforts by Contracting States and other members of the international civil aviation community.

Another example of salience lies in the area of the Passenger Name Record (PNR) where ICAO guidelines easily mesh with a State's cultural and political construct in general terms. Through the PNR Data Guidelines ICAO has introduced uniform measures for PNR data transfer and the subsequent handling of that data by the States concerned. The guidelines are both durable and easy to follow, making them cost effective for the parties concerned. They would ensure accuracy of information, while at the same time protecting the data subject against encroachment of his privacy. The Guidelines call for completeness of data and the need for timely submissions and effective collection of data. They also ensure that data management will be efficient and efficacious.

From a practical perspective, the guidelines also provide useful directions assisting States in designing data requirements and procedures, in order to minimize technical difficulties that might prove too onerous and may impair the implementation of the uniform measures suggested. The Guidelines also contain detailed instructions with a view to assisting both air carriers and States on PNR data transfer from an operator's system to a State and the management of the data including arrangements for storage and protection States are enabled, by the guidelines, to design systems and establish arrangements that are compatible with the guidelines while not impairing their ability to implement their laws and enforce them. The guidelines do not interfere with the preservation of national security and public safety of a State.

Arguably, one of the most important features of the unified PNR data guidelines is that, by their very nature, they would effectively obviate the complexities that aircraft operators could face with regard to legal, technical and financial issues if they were to be required to respond to multiple, unilaterally imposed or bilaterally agreed PNR data transfer requirements that differ substantially from one another.

It must be noted that States also have the responsibility of enacting explicit legal provisions concerning data transfer. Such legislation should clearly elaborate on the reasons for requiring PNR data, or provide explanatory material accompanying such laws or regulations, as appropriate. Since an aircraft operator is obliged to comply with the laws of both the State from which it transports passengers (State of departure) and the State to which these passengers are transported (State of destination. When a destination State legislates with regard to its PNR data transfer requirements, it should do so cognizant of the fact that existing laws of other States may affect operators' ability to comply with these requirements. Therefore, where there could be an inconsistency between two legal regimes of the departure State and the destination State, or where a conflict arises between any two States, or where an operator advises of a conflict, The ICAO guidelines suggest that the States involved should consult each other to determine what might be done to enable affected operators to continue to operate within the bounds of the laws in both States.

Home Country Measures (HCM) that imbue international norms should not stop at arrangements incorporating such norms into domestic rules. There must be follow up measures and ICAO already has experiences analogically in its conduct of safety and security audits. ICAO's mission statement, which admits of cooperation between States in ensuring safety, security, environmental protection, capacity building and the development of air transport can be invoked in this context, where the developed-developing country equation where the assistance of developed countries could be utilized as a catalyst to the implementation of rules across the board would be another beneficial approach towards domestic rulemaking in air transport.

References

Abeyratne RIR (1992) Law making and decision making powers of the ICAO council - a critical analysis. Zeitschrift Fur Luft-und Weltraumrecht 41(4):387–394

Abeyratne RIR (2007) State responsibility for safety management systems. J Aviat Manag 2(2):7–13

Aust A (2000) Modern treaty law and practice. Cambridge University Press, New York, p 348

Buergenthal T (1969) Law making in the international civil aviation organization. Syracuse University Press, Syracuse, p 9

Cortell AP, Davis Jr JW (Spring, 2001) Understanding the domestic impact of international norms: a research Agenda. Int Stud Rev 2(1):66–87

Dempsey PS (1987) Law and foreign policy in international aviation. Transnational Publishers, New York, p 302

Kirgis Jr FL (1995) Specialized law making processes. In: Schachter O, Joiner C (eds) United Nations legal order, vol 1. The American Society of International Law, Washington, pp 109–126, Chap. 2

Milde M (1989) The Chicago convention - after forty years. Ann Air Space Law IX:203–208

Schenkman J (1955) International civil aviation organization. Librairie E. Dross, Geneve, p 160

Sochor E (1991) The politics of international aviation. McMillan, London, p 58

Tobolewski A (1979) ICAO's legal syndrome. Ann Air Space Law 1:349–359

Whiteman M (1968) Digest of international law. Kluwer, Amsterdam 3(2):404

Chapter 4
Principles of Rulemaking

In a democracy, when a rule is made within the jurisdiction of a country, it could either be made as a direct or indirect import from a treaty or international norm, or a sui generis rule stemming from an exigency faced by that country. The former could be exemplified by any significant event, such as the earthquake in Ecuador of April 2016 or the attacks in the United States of 11 September 2011. In the latter instance the Attorney General of the United States made several rules in responses to the attacks directed at the conduct of citizens and suspects. In the air transport context, a good example is the principle enunciated by the Montreal Convention of 1999,[1] Article 19 of which states that the carrier is liable for damage occasioned by delay in the carriage by air of passengers, baggage or cargo. The provision goes on to say that nevertheless, the carrier is not liable for damage occasioned by delay if it proves that it and its servants and agents took all measures that could reasonably be required to avoid the damage or that it was impossible for it or them to take such measures. The normative sense of this treaty provision has been made into Regulation 261 of 2004 by The European Parliament and the European Council and judicially interpreted by The European Court of Justice. In essence Regulation 261/2004[2] elaborates on Article 19 of the Montreal Convention, which is what rulemaking is all about, in that States could take a recognized international norm and adopt rules and regulations to comport with special exigencies and social mores of their internal requirements and principles of justice.

Arguably the best definition of a rule came from Justice Oliver Wendell Holmes who said:

[1]Convention For The Unification Of Certain Rules For International Carriage By Air Done At Montreal On 28 May 1999.

[2]Regulation establishes, under the conditions specified herein, minimum rights for passengers when: they are denied boarding against their will; their flight is cancelled; or their flight is delayed. For a substantial discussion on Regulation 261/2004 see Verheyen (2015), pp. 659–677.

R. Abeyratne, *Rulemaking in Air Transport*, DOI 10.1007/978-3-319-44657-8_4

> a rule is the skin of a living policy . . . it hardens an inchoate normative judgment into the frozen form of words.... Its issuance marks the transformation of policy from the private wish to public expectation. . . the framing of a rule is the climactic act of the policy making process.[3]

A commentator adds helpfully:

> Rules like legislation, attempt to structure the future. By creating new conditions, eliminating existing ones, or preventing others from coming into being, rule implement legislation that seeks to improve the quality life. The term 'future effect' is thus a crucial element in the definition of rules because it allows a clear contrast to situations in which agencies issue decisions, acting in their judicial capacity. .... An order applies existing rules to past or existing circumstances. Although an order may have a future effect . . . its primary purpose is not the creation its primary purpose is not the creation of policy or law to create new conditions.[4]

Rulemaking is a complex and developed process, which takes that form due to the precision of a rule that is required and the purpose the rule is expected to serve. The process can lead to the repeal of an existing rule; issuance of a new rule; or an amendment to an existing rule. There are three categories of rules. The first category is called legislative or substantive rules which usually implement a multilateral treaty or statute. These rules have the force of law. There is only one such set of rules stemming from the Annexes to the Chicago Convention and those are contained in Annex 2—aptly called *Rules of the Air*. There is no derogation from the Standards of this Annex (and Annex 2 contains only Standards,[5] and is derived from Article 12 of the Chicago Convention[6]) based on the doctrine of

---

[3]Quoted by Prof. Diver (1989), p. 199.

[4]Kerwin (1994), p. 6.

[5]In October 1945, the Rules of the Air and Air Traffic Control (RAC) Division at its first session made recommendations for Standards, Practices and Procedures for the Rules of the Air. These were reviewed by the then Air Navigation Committee and approved by the Council on 25 February 1946. They were published as Recommendations for Standards, Practices and Procedures—Rules of the Air in the first part of Doc 2010, published in February 1946. The RAC Division, at its second session in December 1946–January 1947, reviewed Doc 2010 and proposed Standards and Recommended Practices for the Rules of the Air. These were adopted by the Council as Standards and Recommended Practices relating to Rules of the Air on 15 April 1948, pursuant to Article 37 of the Convention on International Civil Aviation (Chicago, 1944) and designated as Annex 2 to the Convention with the title International Standards and Recommended Practices—Rules of the Air. They became effective on 15 September 1948. On 27 November 1951, the Council adopted a complete new text of the Annex, which no longer contained Recommended Practices. The Standards of the amended Annex 2 (Amendment 1) became effective on 1 April 1952 and applicable on 1 September 1952.

[6]Article 12 pertaining to rules of the air provides: Each contracting State undertakes to adopt measures to insure that every aircraft flying over or maneuvering within its territory and that every aircraft carrying its nationality marks, wherever such aircraft may be, shall comply with the rules and regulations relating to the flight and maneuver of aircraft there in force. Each contracting State undertakes to keep its own regulations in these respects uniform, to the greatest possible extent, with those established from time to time under this Convention. Over the high seas, the rules in force shall be those established under this Convention. Each contracting State undertakes to insure the prosecution of all persons violating the regulations applicable.

incorporation flowing through customary international law, where customary rules could be considered part of the national law. However, such custom should not be inconsistent with already existing legislation or judicial decisions of last instance or final authority.[7] There is a long *cursus curiae* in support of this principle.[8]

The doctrine of incorporation is essentially a rule of construction and, as already discussed, is a product of the British judiciary of the eighteenth Century. Perhaps the most compelling thrust of the incorporation of custom into national law through the judiciary is contained in the dictum of Lord Alverstone in *West Rand Central Gold Mining Company* v. *R*[9] where his Lordship observed:

> Whatever has received the common consent of civilized nations must have received the assent of our country, and that to which we assented along with other nations in general may properly be called international law, and as such will be acknowledged and applied by our municipal tribunals to decide questions to which doctrines of international law may be relevant.[10]

The second type of rule is called non-legislative rules or guidance, which in the air transport context is merely persuasive. Good examples of such guidance are the Recommended Practices of the Annexes and the various Manuals issued by ICAO on both the economic and the technical aspects of air transport. In the United States such rules take various forms such as interpretive rules where the rules inform the public of the interpretation is of the agency which adopts such rules of the legislative instrument that the rule/s are derived from For example, the agency could define the world "air transport" which appears in a statute. There are also policy statements which elaborate on procedure that a rule sets out, a good example for which would be rules laying down aircraft accident investigation. These could be tied in with management and procedural rules. For example, Australia, which investigated the disappearance in March 2014 of Malaysian Airlines Flight MH 370 followed Chapter 6, paragraph 6 of ICAO Annex 13 to provide information on the progress of the investigation on the flight, recognizing the Annex provision as a rule.

There are also rules which may give policy statements that explain how discretionary powers are used by an authorized agency. However, an agency is effectively precluded from issuing a legislative rule unless it is granted or delegated the

---

[7]Blackstone, *Commentaries*, iv, ch 5; Oppenheim, i. 39–40; See also the dictum of Lord Finley in the *Lotus* (1927) PCIJ Ser. A, no. 10. p. 54.

[8]*Triquet* v. *Bath*, (1764), 3 Burr. 1478; per Mansfield LJ; *Buvot* v. *Barbuit* 91737) Cases t. Talb. 281. *Dolder* v. *Lord Huntingfield* (1805), 11 Ves. 283; *Vivesh* v. *Becker* (1814), 3 M&S. 284; *Wolff* v. *Oxholm* (1817), 6 M. &S 92, 100–106; *Novello* v. *Toogood* (183), 1, I.B. & C, 554; *De Wutz* v. *Hendricks*(1984), 2 Bing. 314, 315; *Emperor of Austria* v. *Day*, (1861), 30 LJ, Ch. 690, 70; *Trendtex Trading Corporation* v. *Central Bank of Nigeria* [1977] 1 QB 529 CA, Cf.; *R.* v. *Secretary of State*, *ex parte* Thakrar [1974] 1 QB 694, CA; *International Tin Council Appeals* [1989] 3 WLR 969, HL;

[9][1905] 2 KB. 391.

[10]*Id*. 396.

authority to do so by statute or a statutory instrument. The statutory delegation can range from broad discretionary authority to a very specific mandate.

4.1 The United States Example

A good example of effective rulemaking is seen in the *Administrative Procedure Act*[11] of the United States where, through a highly democratic process which involves the participation of the public, a rule is brought into effect. The Act is explicit in the requirements for notice on the rulemaking process which include: the time, place, and nature of public rulemaking proceedings; reference to the legal authority under which the rule is proposed; and either the terms or substance of the proposed rule or a description of the subjects and issues involved. Once adequate notice is provided, the agency is required to give interested persons a meaningful opportunity to comment on the proposed rule through the submission of written "data, views, or arguments.":

> The comment period may result in a vast rulemaking record as persons are permitted to submit nearly any piece of information for consideration by the agency. While there is no minimum period of time for which the agency is required to accept comments, in reviewing an agency rulemaking, courts have focused on whether the agency provided an "adequate" opportunity to comment—of which the length of the comment period represents only one factor for consideration.[12]

The FAA's authority to issue rules on aviation safety is found in 49 U.S.-C. Subtitle I, section 106(f), describes the authority of the FAA Administrator. Subtitle VII, Aviation Programs, describes in more detail the scope of the agency's authority. Section 40101(d)(1) provides that the Administrator shall consider in the public interest, among other matters, assigning, maintaining, and enhancing safety and security as the highest priorities in air commerce. Section 40105(b)(1)(A) requires the Administrator to exercise his authority consistently with the obligations of the U.S. Government under international agreements.

States or groups of States exchange common principles of rulemaking with a view to common rating their policies and procedures. An example is the rulemaking agreement between the Federal Aviation Administration (FAA) of the United States and The European Aviation Safety Administration (EASA). The broad principles of this agreement are based on mutual communication where the Parties say that the objectives of the rulemaking cooperation arrangement are to: exchange rulemaking intentions and priorities of the Participants to align as much as possible their respective rulemaking programmes; identify rulemaking initiatives of common interest that through regulatory collaboration would allow the FAA and EASA to:

[11]5 U.S.C. § 551(a). 2 5 U.S.C. §§ 551(a), 701-06.

[12]Lubbers (2006). v. U.S., 846 F.2d 765, 772 (D.C. Cir. 1988)). However, some statutes require minimum comment periods. See, e.g., 42 U.S.C. § 6295(p)(2).

and avoid unnecessary divergence and duplication of work, maximize available resources, and facilitate further harmonization.[13]

Under the Agreement the Parties agree to maintain an up to date inventory of rulemaking tasks that have been identified as being of common interest, including identification of the focal points and information on the types of common actions agreed to and their current status. Where appropriate, the FAA and EASA intend to make available to the public the list of rulemaking tasks of common interest and status of the work. Furthermore, representatives of the FAA and EASA responsible for rulemaking give each other the flexibility of attending the meetings of the joint coordination bodies established under the Agreement, such as the Certification Oversight Board, Joint Maintenance Coordination Board, and Bilateral Oversight Board to ensure, inter alia, that the discussions on rulemaking cooperation in the above bodies are consistent with the overall priorities identified under these Guidelines. The Participants also intend that attendance at meetings at the Bilateral Oversight Board be in accordance with the provisions of the Board's Internal Governing Procedures.

An interesting fact is that within the United States, exemptions from internal rules in air transport are permitted even if they are at variance with or different from SARPs of the ICAO Annexes. The granting of an exemption is generally viewed as an alternative method of complying with a regulatory requirement. Exemptions are transmitted under Title 14 of the Code of Federal Regulations (14 CFR) part 11. A grant of exemption and each specific condition and limitation is a regulatory requirement. A petition for exemption may be submitted to the Federal Aviation Administration (FAA) by any interested person. In accordance with part 11, § 11.83, persons who desire to use an exemption outside the United States must specifically request this condition when petitioning for the exemption. Such a petition must include the reason(s) why a person desires to use the exemption outside of the United States. If no reason is provided in the petition, the FAA will limit the exemption for use within the United States. Before the FAA extends an exemption for use outside the United States, it must verify that the exemption would be in compliance with the ICAO SARPs as contained in the Annexes to the Chicago Convention. If it would not be in compliance, but the FAA still believes it would be in the public interest to allow the petitioner to do so, the FAA will file a difference with ICAO. However, a foreign country still may not allow a person to operate in that country without meeting the ICAO Standard. This illustrates the dichotomy between ICAO material and domestic rulemaking, which has been purely predicated by the obfuscation of clarity and the ambivalence brought to bear by Article 38 of the Chicago Convention (which has already been discussed). The FAA states:

> Some exemptions have been granted to an organization of certificate holders (such as Airlines for America (A4A)), instead of to an individual certificate holder. A certificate holder requesting use of an exemption that has been granted to an organization is not

---

[13] *Rulemaking Cooperation Guidelines for the Federal Aviation Administration and the European Aviation Safety Agency*, 1.2.

> required to submit a separate petition. The appropriate principal inspector (PI) may review the request to verify if the certificate holder meets the criteria stated in the exemption granted to the organization. If the certificate holder meets the criteria and has the necessary policies and procedures to comply with the conditions and limitations stated in the exemption, the PI may approve use of the exemption by amending operations specification (OpSpec)/management specification (MSpec)/training specification (TSpec)/letter of authorization (LOA) A005, Exemptions and Deviations.[14]

A glaring example of an FAA response to Annex provisions pertains to the FAA Response to Annex 19 (Safety Management). ICAO's Annex 6, Part 1 titled, International Commercial Air Transport—Aeroplanes, required that by January 1, 2009 "States shall require, as part of their safety programme, that an operator implement a safety management system (SMS) acceptable to the State of the Operator." The FAA observes that Specific SMS Requirements. ICAO's, Annex 6, Amendment 33, requires "...from November 18, 2010...that an operator implement [and maintain] a safety management system...[in accordance with the ICAO SMS] Framework contained in appendix 7." This requirement adds SMS specifics to the January 2009 requirement in the form of four components and 12 elements. FAA SMS guidance material was revised to incorporate these changes.

The FAA filed a "difference" with ICAO detailing that it is not currently in full compliance with the ICAO requirement, but said it was considering SMS rulemaking. The FAA's difference was neither a deviation nor an exemption, but a notification to ICAO member states of the inability to meet the January 1, 2009 deadline. The FAA explained in its notice of difference or deviation that the FAA rulemaking process requires thorough analysis and stakeholder input and therefore requires more time to complete regulatory action.

The FAA observed in its notice that consequent upon considering a difference filed by an ICAO member State, other member states decide whether to honor a difference on the part of an international operator who enters and operates within their airspace. In this context, The FAA had been advised that both Transport Canada (the Canadian equivalent of the FAA) and EASA or any of their member States, did not intend to restrict operations within their airspace due to noncompliance with ICAO SMS requirements.

Despite ICAO's relevant Annex provisions, The FAA did not immediately make internal rules accordingly. Even in the absence of such rules, many aviation service providers joined the FAA's SMS Pilot Project, or electing to voluntarily implement an SMS within their organization. With a growing number of aviation service providers in various levels of the pilot project, there were inevitable questions regarding the approval or acceptance of SMS documentation and questions about operations within ICAO member states' airspace.

Title 5, United States Code (U.S.C.) § 553(b)(3)(B) authorizes agencies to dispense with notice and comment procedures for rules when the agency for

[14]FAA Doc 8900.1 CHG 380, Volume 3 General Technical Administration Chapter 2 Exemptions, Deviations, Waivers, And Authorizations, Section 1 Exemptions, Deviations, Waivers, and Authorizations.

"good cause" finds that those procedures are "impracticable, unnecessary, or contrary to the public interest." In this instance, the FAA finds that notice and public comment to the immediately adopted final rule, as well as any delay in the effective date of this rule, are contrary to the public interest due to the immediate need to address the potential hazard to civil aviation that now exists in a portion of the Simferopol (UKFV) FIR, as described in the Background section of this notice.

Three months prior to the shooting down of Malaysian Airlines Flight MH 17 over Ukrainian airspace in July 2014 the FAA was alerted to the Russian Federation establishing a Flight Information Region (FIR) over a part of Ukraine. This was one such instance where the FAA showed good cause in obviating bureaucratic obscurity and getting on with enacting a rule. The background to the measure taken by the Russian Federation created, in the view of the FAA, confusion to air operators of two authorities (Ukrainian and Russian) controlling the same FIR. On March 28, 2014, the Russian Federation issued a Notice-to-Airmen (NOTAM) purporting to establish unilaterally a new FIR, effective April 3, 2014, in a significant portion of the Simferopol (UKFV) FIR. The affected airspace included sovereign Ukrainian airspace over the Crimean Peninsula and the associated Ukrainian territorial sea, as well as international airspace managed by Ukraine over the Black Sea and the Sea of Azov under a regional air navigation agreement approved by ICAO. The FAA claimed that the action taken by the Russian Federation contradicted international law, including provisions of the Chicago Convention and the Standards established in Annex 11 to the Chicago Convention. Ukraine rejected the Russian Federation's purported establishment of a new FIR within the existing Simferopol (UKFV) FIR and continued to provide air traffic control services in both Ukrainian territorial airspace and international airspace assigned to Ukraine.

In response to the Russian Federation's actions, Ukraine established a prohibited area over the Crimean Peninsula for flight operations below flight level 290 by means of a NOTAM and closed various air traffic services (ATS) route segments. The Russian Federation further responded by the issuance of a NOTAM that rejected and directly conflicts with Ukrainian NOTAMs concerning the establishment of the prohibited area and the route segment closures. On April 2, 2014, ICAO's Regional Director for Europe and the North Atlantic Regions issued a state letter to countries and their civil aviation authorities highlighting the possible existence of serious risks to the safety of international civil flights. It was ICAO's position that, due to the unsafe situation where more than one ATS provider may be controlling flights within the same airspace from April 3, 2014, 0600 Universal Time Coordinated (UTC) onwards, consideration should be given to implementing measures to avoid the airspace and to circumnavigate the Simferopol (UKFV) FIR with alternative routings.[15]

[15]Prohibitions Against Certain Flights in the Simferopol (UKFV) Flight Information Region, https://www.regulations.gov/#!documentDetail;D=FAA-2014-0225-0001.

On May 21 2010 The FAA issued a similar rule—Special Federal Aviation Regulation No. 110—Prohibition Against Certain Flights Within the Territory and Airspace of Afghanistan which applied to: all U.S. air carriers and U.S. commercial operators; all persons exercising the privileges of an airman certificate issued by the FAA, except such persons operating U.S.-registered aircraft for a foreign air carrier; and all operators of U.S.-registered aircraft, except where the operator of such aircraft is a foreign air carrier. The prohibition extended to any person so described who were barred by the Regulation of conducting a flight within the territory and airspace of Afghanistan below flight level (FL 160). The rule permitted U.S. civil aircraft operations by persons below flight level (FL) 160 within the territory and airspace of Afghanistan, only when approved by the FAA as provided in the Rule.[16]

4.2 The Rulemaking Process

In any jurisdiction, the rulemaking process starts with the supremacy of the law that is enacted by parliament. To any rule adopted must be ascribed the legitimacy of the law, which would also prescribe the manner and form in which the rule must be drafted and adopted and the time limit set to promulgate the rule. Essential to this initial process is the identification by the legislature of the mission to be accomplished by the rule as well as the extent of the powers and discretion of the instrumentality of State assigned with the task of making the rule.

The second stage of rulemaking consists of identifying content and the process that would be initiated if deadlines for rulemaking are not met by the empowered agency. If necessary, advisory committees are appointed to assist in the process. It is at this stage that appropriate officials are identified, particularly for purposes of enforcement of the rule, and advance notice of rulemaking is initiated. This is followed by stages three and four where determination that final authorization for rulemaking has been obtained, after which priorities are set. The legal requirements for the making of the rule are evaluated at this point, followed by the information gathering process. After this comes the fifth stage where the rule is given its first draft which inevitably follows a thorough analysis of the elements of the rule. The stages to follow involve internal reviews of the rule; policy analysis; external review of the draft rule, public participation where written submissions are entertained after which the rule is finally adopted. As one can see, rulemaking is both a lengthy and thorough process which comports with the fundamental principles of democracy and participation of all key stakeholders. There is also a post-rulemaking process where technical corrections, if necessary could be made as well as petitions for reconsideration of a rule can be considered.

Noteworthy is the example of Rulemaking Cooperation Guidelines for the FAA and Transport Canada Civil Aviation (TCCA), which is a bilateral agreement

[16]FR Doc. 2010–12670 Filed 5–25–10; 8:45 am.

between the two countries. This is a common element in developed States which are eager to set a level playing field in rulemaking. Later, under the rulemaking process of Europe, we will discuss similar agreements signed by the EU with other countries. FAA, TCCA and the Joint Aviation Authorities (JAA) of the EU have established such agreements. Getting back to Agreement between The FAA and TCCA, The Participants consider as the primary driver, their understanding that harmonization can best be achieved through effective communication during the definition and early stages of implementation of their respective rulemaking programmes. They also believe they should make the best use of scarce available resources to produce rules, and that cooperation in this field can be furthered without affecting their independence when deciding on the final rules they best see fit to fulfil their statutory obligations. The Agreement was entered into on a purely voluntary basis preserving the independence of the Parties and are not intended to create binding obligations under international law. Additionally, both parties agreed that no provision of the Agreement should be construed to impair the authority of the FAA or TCCA to develop and promulgate aviation regulations within the limits of their enabling legislation and regulations.

The objectives of the rulemaking cooperation arrangement are to: exchange rulemaking intentions and priorities of the Participants to align as much as possible their respective rulemaking programmes; identify rulemaking initiatives of common interest that through regulatory collaboration would allow the FAA and TCCA to: avoid unnecessary divergence and duplication of work, maximize available resources, and further harmonization. Another aspect of cooperation pertains to defining the corresponding working methods to be followed by the Participants when executing tasks which have been identified as of common interest.

With regard to each rulemaking project The FAA and TCCA agree to develop a work plan. Each work plan should describe: the working method; technical points of contact; project implementation schedule and meeting dates; description of the technical documents that either the FAA or TCCA intends to make available for review and discussion. These may include jointly developed issue papers, analyses, research results and other technical documents of a non-confidential nature, except that the FAA and TCCA, if their national procedures or rules so require, may decide not to make available copies of documents; participation in work groups, and any other cooperative activities mutually determined by TCCA and the FAA to be beneficial.

4.3 The ICAO Process

When the aforementioned process is compared with the rulemaking process of ICAO there are two dimensions to consider. The first is the treaty making process where at the apex sits the Council of ICAO—36 member States—who send their representatives to Montreal to be resident at ICAO (in other words, ICAO has a resident Council) which decides whether to recommend to the Legal Committee of the Council either to deliberate on developing a draft treaty on a particular subject or develop a protocol either to replace provisions of an existing treaty or to supplement an already existing treaty. I some instances, this process leads to lapses which both the Legal Committee and the Council (the representatives of which are by no means legal experts) fail to pick up on, as has been discussed in the first chapter of this book. The Secretariat—in particular the Legal Affairs and External Relations Bureau—which acts as the Secretary to the Legal Committee, which is expected to have some expertise on the subject under discussion, sometimes fails to advise the Committee accordingly or is ignorant of an evolving issue and its legal rectitude, which compounds an error. This anomaly leads to the refusal of States to ratify a multilateral treaty, resulting in some treaties being relegated to the shelf. Two such glaring instances are found in the Beijing Convention and the Protocol to the Tokyo Convention.[17]

The second dimension of ICAO rulemaking is the development of the Annexes to the Chicago Convention. As already discussed, the Annexes by no means contain compulsory rules for States to adopt, except for the provisions of Annex 2 on Rules of the Air. However, the Standards of the Annexes may have some persuasive authority. The process usually starts with the Council of ICAO requiring its subordinate body—the Air Navigation Commission—to develop an Annex. The initiative of the Council could have its genesis either in the ICAO Assembly or in a high level conference of ICAO comprising the member States officials at high level. This has happened in the development of 17 of the 19 Annexes (Except Annexes 9 and 17 on Facilitation and Security respectively). An example is the most recent Annex—Annex 19 on safety management. Here, The ICAO High-level Safety Conference of 2010,[18] in its Recommendation 2/5 suggested that ICAO develop, in close collaboration with States, international and national organizations, a new Annex dedicated to safety management responsibilities and processes which would address the safety management responsibilities of States framed under the State Safety Programme (SSP). The Conference stated that the new Safety Management Annex should facilitate the provision of State and air carrier safety information to the travelling public, in addition to specifying the high level safety responsibilities of States. The perceived benefits of such an Annex were: that it would address safety risks proactively; manage and support strategic regulatory and infrastructure developments; re-enforce the role played by the State in managing safety at the State level, in coordination with service providers; and stress the concept of overall safety performance in all domains.

Consequently, The Air Navigation Commission (ANC) proposed, in a working paper submitted to the Council, the new safety management Annex be developed in two phases—the first phase to be focused on the reorganization of the existing Standards and Recommended Practices (SARPs) and supporting guidance material,

[17]See Abeyratne (2011), pp. 243–255. Also by the same author, Abeyratne (2014), pp. 47–58.

[18]Directors General of Civil Aviation Conference on a Global Strategy for Aviation Safety (Montréal, 20 to 22 March 2006) (DGCA/06).

and the second phase to be focused on further development of the Safety Management Annex and related provisions in other Annexes. The Council accepted this proposal. The Commission commenced its work, basically on the foundation of provisions of other existing Annexes and in accordance with the SARPs contained in Annex 1—Personnel Licensing, Annex 6—Operation of Aircraft, Annex 8—Airworthiness of Aircraft, Annex 11—Air Traffic Services, Annex 13—Aircraft Accident and Incident Investigation and Annex 14—Aerodromes, Volume I—Aerodrome Design and Operations. The new Annex 19 incorporated provisions for State Safety Programmes (SSP).

The Annex, when completed, was submitted for approval by the Council. It was adopted by the Council on 25 February 2013 and became effective on 15 July 2013. Annex 19 became applicable on 14 November 2013. Article 90 of the Chicago Convention on adoption and amendment of Annexes drives the applicability and effectiveness of an Annex. : Adoption and amendment of Annexes. It says:

> The adoption by the Council of the Annexes described in Article 54, subparagraph (l), shall require the vote of two-thirds of the Council at a meeting called for that purpose and shall then be submitted by the Council to each contracting State. Any such Annex or any amendment of an Annex shall become effective within three months after its submission to the contracting States or at the end of such longer period of time as the Council may prescribe, unless in the meantime a majority of the contracting States register their disapproval with the Council.

Once an amendment becomes "effective", changes can only be made by the usual Annex amendment process, i.e. effective date +3 months: deadline for States to submit differences: effective date +4 months. an amendment becomes applicable to all States (i.e. States expected to have incorporated provisions of amendment into their national legislation).

ICAO standards and other provisions are developed in the following forms: Standards and Recommended Practices—collectively referred to as SARPs; Procedures for Air Navigation Services—called PANS; Regional Supplementary Procedures—referred to as SUPPs; and Guidance Material in several formats.

A Standard is defined as any specification for physical characteristics, configuration, material, performance, personnel or procedure, the uniform application of which is recognized as necessary for the safety or regularity of international air navigation and to which Contracting States will conform in accordance with the Convention; in the event of impossibility of compliance, notification to the Council is compulsory under Article 38 of the Convention.

A Recommended Practice is any specification for physical characteristics, configuration, material, performance, personnel or procedure, the uniform application of which is recognized as desirable in the interest of safety, regularity or efficiency of international air navigation, and to which Contracting States will endeavour to conform in accordance with the Convention. States are invited to inform the Council of non-compliance.

Although Standards specifically demand that States adhere to certain minimum standards, on a general basis, SARPs are formulated and couched in broad terms and target essential requirements. For complex systems such as communications equipment, SARPs material is constructed in two sections: core SARPs—material of a fundamental regulatory nature contained within the main body of the Annexes, and detailed technical specifications placed either in Appendices to Annexes or in manuals.

The differences to SARPS notified by States were originally published in Supplements to Annexes as part and parcel of the Annex document in hard form. However, with the advent of the electronic format, there is a special ICAO portal that store differences which are entered by the States themselves.

Technical operating practices and material which are too detailed for Standards or Recommended Practices are published in Procedures for Air Navigation Services (or PANS) which elaborate upon basic SARPs principles and offer more focused direction. PANS are essentially global in application, subscribing to the two key words of air transport operations and air navigation—standardization and harmonization. Under Annex 15, The Council invites Contracting States to publish any differences in their Aeronautical Information Publications when knowledge of the differences is important to the safety of air navigation.

Another facet of guidance which gain do not come under the strict rubric of "rulemaking" are Technical Instructions attached to or related to an Annex. For example, the provisions for Annex 18, Dangerous Goods, are supplemented by Technical Instructions for the Safe Transport of Dangerous Goods by Air. While these detailed instructions do not have the status of SARPs or PANS, they do have a special status by which the Contracting States are requested to achieve compliance.

In terms of Regional application of ICAO policy guidelines, there are the Regional Supplementary Procedures (or SUPPs) which have application in the respective ICAO regions. Although the material in Regional Supplementary Procedures is similar to that in the Procedures for Air Navigation Services, SUPPs do not have the worldwide applicability of PANS.

Guidance Material is produced to supplement the SARPs and PANS and to facilitate their implementation. Guidance material is issued as Attachments to Annexes or in separate documents such manuals, circulars and lists of designators/addresses. Usually it is approved at the same time as the related SARPS are adopted.

There are also various ICAO Manuals that provide information calculated to supplement and/or amplify the Standards and Recommended Practices and Procedures for Air Navigation Services. They are specifically designed to facilitate implementation and are amended periodically to ensure their contents reflect current practices and procedures.

Lower down the scale of guidance and communication, ICAO Circulars contain specialized information of interest to Contracting States. Unlike manuals, circulars are not normally updated.

Where the development of SARPS of Annexes are concerned, initially, and for technical SARPs, proposals are first analyzed by the ANC. Depending on the nature of the proposal, the Commission may assign its review to a specialized working group. Meetings are, of course, the main vehicle for progress in the air navigation field, although much of the preparatory work is accomplished by correspondence. It is through a variety of meetings that most of the work is finalized and the necessary consensus reached.

In the development, a number of consultative mechanisms are used:

Air Navigation meetings are divisional-type meetings devoted to broad issues in the air navigation fields. They can be either divisional meetings dealing with issues in one or more related fields or air navigation conferences normally having a "theme" covering issues in more than one field. All Contracting States are invited to participate in these meetings with equal voice. Interested international organizations are invited to participate as observers.

ANC panels are technical groups of qualified experts formed by the ANC to advance, within specified time frames, the solution of specialized problems which cannot be solved adequately or expeditiously by the established facilities of the ANC and the Secretariat. These experts act in their expert capacity and not as representatives of the nominators.

Air Navigation study groups are small groups of experts made available by States and international organizations to assist the ICAO Secretariat, in a consultative capacity, in advancing progress on technical tasks.

Council technical committees are established to deal with problems involving technical, economic, social and legal aspects, for the resolution or advancement of which expertise is required that is not available through the normal Council means, are also instrumental in developing ICAO SARPs.

In summary, technical issues dealing with a specific subject and requiring detailed examination are normally referred by the ANC to a panel of experts. Less complex issues may be assigned to the Secretariat for further examination, perhaps with the assistance of an air navigation study group.

These various groups report back to the Air Navigation Commission in the form of a technical proposal either for revisions to SARPs or for new SARPs, for preliminary review. This review is normally limited to consideration of controversial issues which, in the opinion of the Secretariat or the Commission, require examination before the recommendations are circulated to States for comment.

The original recommendations for core SARPs along with any alternative proposals developed by the Air Navigation Commission are submitted to Contracting States and selected international organizations for comment. Detailed technical specifications for complex systems are made available to States upon request and are submitted to a validation process. States are normally given 3 months to comment on the proposals.

Standards developed by other recognized international organizations can also be referenced, provided they have been subject to adequate verification and validation.

The comments of States and international organizations are analyzed by the Secretariat and a working paper detailing the comments and the Secretariat proposals for action is prepared.

The Commission undertakes the final review of the recommendations and establishes the final texts of the proposed amendments to SARPs, PANS and associated attachments. The amendments to Annexes recommended by the

Commission are presented to the Council for adoption under cover of a "Report to Council by the President of the Air Navigation Commission".

The Council reviews the proposals of the Air Navigation Commission and adopts the amendment to the Annex if two-thirds of the members are in favor.

Within 2 weeks of the adoption of an Annex amendment by the Council, an interim edition of the amendment, referred to as the "Green Edition", is dispatched to States with a covering explanatory letter. This covering letter also gives the various dates associated with the introduction of the amendment.

Policy prescribes that Contracting States be allowed three months to indicate disapproval of adopted amendments to SARPs. A further period of one month is provided for preparation and transit time, making the Effective Date approximately 4 months after adoption by Council. There should be a period of 4 months between an amendment's Effective Date and its Applicability Date. However, this can be longer or shorter as the situation requires. The Notification Date is normally one month prior to the Applicability Date.

Provided a majority of States have not registered disapproval, the amendment will become effective on the Effective Date.

On the Notification Date, which is 1 month prior to the Applicability Date, the States must notify the Secretariat of any differences that will exist between their national regulations and the provision of the Standard as amended. The reported differences are then published in supplements to Annexes.

Immediately after the Effective Date, a letter is sent announcing that the amendment has become effective and the Secretariat takes action to issue the "Blue Edition" which is the form of the amendment suitable for incorporation in the Annex or PANS.

On the Applicability Date, States must implement the amendments unless, of course, they have notified differences. To limit the frequency of Annex and PANS amendments, the Council has established one common applicability date for each year. This date is chosen from the schedule for the regulation of amendments to Aeronautical Information Regulation and Control (AIRAC) for the month of November.

The result of this adoption procedure is that the new or amended Standards and Recommended Practices become part of the relevant Annex.

It takes on average 2 years from the Preliminary Review by the ANC to the applicability date. Although this process may seem lengthy at first glance, it provides for repeated consultation and extensive participation of States and international organizations in producing a consensus based on logic and experience.

Cooperation and consensus have thus provided international aviation with the vital infrastructure for safe and efficient air transport. The third "C", compliance, brings this comprehensive regulatory system to life.

Attachments to Annexes, although they are developed in the same manner as Standards and Recommended Practices, are approved by Council rather than adopted.

Regional Supplementary Procedures, because of their regional application, do not have the same line of development as the previously mentioned amendments; they also must be approved by Council.

The proposed amendments to PANS are approved by the Air Navigation Commission, under power delegated to it by the Council, subject to the approval by the President of the Council after their circulation to the Representatives of the Council for comment.

Manuals and circulars are published under authority of the Secretary General in accordance with principles and policies approved by Council.

Under the Convention on International Civil Aviation, the implementation of SARPs lies with Contracting States. To help them in the area of safety, ICAO established in 1999 a Universal Safety Oversight Audit Programme. The Programme consists of regular, mandatory, systematic and harmonized safety audits carried out by ICAO in all Contracting States.

The objective is to promote global aviation safety by determining the status of implementation of relevant ICAO SARPs, associated procedures and safety-related practices. The audits are conducted within the context of critical elements of a State's safety oversight system. These include the appropriate legislative and regulatory framework; a sound organizational structure; technical guidance; qualified personnel; licensing and certification procedures; continued surveillance and the resolution of identified safety concerns.

Since its inception, the Programme has proved effective in identifying safety concerns in the safety-related fields under its scope, while providing recommendations for their resolution. The Programme is being gradually expanded to include aerodromes, air traffic services, aircraft accident and incident investigation and other safety-related fields.

While providing additional assistance in the form of regional safety oversight seminars and workshops, the programme also provides ICAO with valuable feedback to improve existing SARPs and create new ones.

The experience gained with the safety oversight programme was successfully adapted to aviation security. In 2002, the Universal Security Audit Programme was launched to similarly help States identify deficiencies in the implementation of security-related SARPs. The format may in the future be applied to other areas of civil aviation.

ICAO claims that cooperation, consensus, compliance and an unfailing commitment to the on-going implementation of SARPs have made it possible to create a global aviation system that has evolved into the safest mode of mass transportation ever conceived. The flight crew of today's commercial aircraft, as their predecessors and those that will follow, can count on a standardized aviation infrastructure wherever they fly in the world.

Getting back to the example used earlier of an Annex, The SARPs in Annex 19 are intended to assist States in managing aviation safety risks. Given the increasing complexity of the global air transportation system and its interrelated aviation activities required to assure the safe operation of aircraft, this Annex supports the continued evolution of a proactive strategy to improve safety performance. The foundation of this proactive safety strategy is based on the implementation of a State safety programme (SSP) that systematically addresses safety risks. SARPs are given a particular definition in Annex 19, where a Standard is any specification for physical characteristics, configuration, matériel, performance, personnel or procedure, the uniform application of which is recognized as necessary for the safety or regularity of international air navigation and to which Contracting States will conform in accordance with the Convention; in the event of impossibility of compliance, notification to the Council is compulsory under Article 38. A Recommended Practice is any specification for physical characteristics, configuration, materiel, performance, personnel or procedure, the uniform application of which is recognized as desirable in the interest of safety, regularity or efficiency of international air navigation, and to which Contracting States will endeavor to conform in accordance with the Convention.

4.4 The European Example

The European Union,[19] through the European Parliament and European Commission has an elaborate system of rulemaking, which will be discussed later in this segment. However, an interesting development occurred while this book was being written. On 20 April 2016, the European Commission transmitted formal antitrust charges to *Google* claiming that the company "abused its dominant position by imposing restrictions on Android device manufacturers and mobile network operators" and "implemented a strategy on mobile devices to preserve and strengthen its dominance in general internet search."[20] There was widespread concern that Lufthansa which imposed a surcharge of 16 Euro on each air ticket not bought through its website, could be liable to be charged with abuse of dominant position. Article 102 of the Treaty on the Functioning of the European Union (TFEU)

[19]The European Union was created as a political and economic community with supranational and inter-governmental features. It is composed of 27 member states primarily located in Europe. The member States which created the EU contemporaneously delegated to the Union the exercise of certain national competencies. In 1963 the European Court of Justice handed down a decision which inter alia confirmed that the EC Treaty which established the Union went beyond the boundaries of an international agreement that confers mutual obligations between States by constituting a new order of international law. Member States have, by this act transferred certain powers to the European Community, thereby creating a community that can legally represent member States in the international scene, having its own institutions and legal capacity. In effect, the member States have limited their sovereign rights in certain fields by creating a body that limits the exercise of their national competencies in particular areas and binds themselves and their nationals. The European Union works through the European Commission which was created by the Treaty of Rome and exercises the competencies of the EU.

[20]What EC Anti-Trust Charges Against Google Might Have in Common With Airlines? http://www.eturbonews.com/70550/what-ec-antitrust-charges-against-google-might-have-common-airli.

prohibits abusive conduct by companies that have a dominant position[21] on a particular market.[22] Of relevance to this concern is European Council Regulation (EC) No 1/2003 of 16 December 2002 on the implementation of the rules on competition laid down in Articles 81 and 82 of the Treaty, Article 1 of which states that agreements, decisions and concerted practices caught by Article 81(1)[23] of the Treaty which do not satisfy the conditions of Article 81(3) of the Treaty shall be prohibited, no prior decision to that effect being required. Agreements, decisions and concerted practices caught by Article 81(1) of the Treaty which satisfy the conditions of Article 81(3)[24] of the Treaty shall not be prohibited, no prior decision to that effect being required. The abuse of a dominant position referred to in Article 82 of the Treaty is prohibited, no prior decision to that effect being required.

---

[21]To be in a dominant position is not in itself illegal. A dominant company is entitled to compete on the merits as any other company. However, a dominant company has a special responsibility to ensure that its conduct does not distort competition. Examples of behaviour that may amount to an abuse include: requiring that buyers purchase all units of a particular product only from the dominant company (exclusive purchasing); setting prices at a loss-making level (predation); refusing to supply input indispensable for competition in an ancillary market; charging excessive prices.

[22]Article 102 stipulates:" Any abuse by one or more undertakings of a dominant position within the internal market or in a substantial part of it shall be prohibited as incompatible with the internal market in so far as it may affect trade between Member States. Such abuse may, in particular, consist in: (a) directly or indirectly imposing unfair purchase or selling prices or other unfair trading conditions; (b) limiting production, markets or technical development to the prejudice of consumers; (c) applying dissimilar conditions to equivalent transactions with other trading parties, thereby placing them at a competitive disadvantage; (d) making the conclusion of contracts subject to acceptance by the other parties of supplementary obligations which, by their nature or according to commercial usage, have no connection with the subject of such contracts. Such abuse may, in particular, consist in: (a) directly or indirectly imposing unfair purchase or selling prices or other unfair trading conditions; (b) limiting production, markets or technical development to the prejudice of consumers; (c) applying dissimilar conditions to equivalent transactions with other trading parties, thereby placing them at a competitive disadvantage; (d) making the conclusion of contracts subject to acceptance by the other parties of supplementary obligations which, by their nature or according to commercial usage, have no connection with the subject of such contracts.

[23]Article 81 (1) prohibits as incompatible with common market principles, all agreements between undertakings, decisions by associations of undertakings, and concerted practices which may affect trade between Member States and which have as their object or effect the prevention, restriction, or distortion of competition within the common market. The provision speaks of an agreement or concerted practice between two or more undertakings, or a decision by an association of undertakings; which has as its object or effect the prevention, restriction or distortion of competition; an appreciable effect on competition; and an appreciable effect on trade between Member States.

[24]Even if an agreement is caught by Article 81(1) it may benefit from an exemption under Article 81(3). Companies must assess for themselves whether an agreement meets the criteria for exemption. The Article 81(3) criteria are that the agreement contributes to improving production or distribution, promotes technical or economic progress, allows consumers a fair share of the resulting benefit, does not impose restrictions which are not indispensable to achieving those objectives, and does not eliminate competition. If these criteria are all met, the agreement may be exempt from the application of Article 81(1).

The European Aviation Safety Agency (EASA) can be considered a good study on the European air transport rulemaking process. EASA in 2014, underwent a critical organizational change. There were two major policy changes that year: the dissolution of the Rulemaking Directorate and the transfer of rules development activities to the Certification Directorate and the newly created Flight Standards Directorate; and the assignment of all programming activities to the newly created Strategy and Safety Management Directorate. These two changes were expected to bring about the integration of the rulemaking activities with other activities (certification, standardization and organization approvals) in the same field and the creation of poles of technical competences per department in each directorate; and the adoption of a top-down, fully consistent and coherent approach to the programming of the Agency key activities.

The EASA Executive Director Decision 2015/236/ED of 11 December 2015 is the key policy decision which decided to establish a rulemaking programme for EASA for the years 2016–2020.[25] The rulemaking programme was designed to contain the rules which were expected to be issued in the year 2016 and formulate an indicative plan ahead for the years 2017–2020. The rulemaking programme would be subject to annual review taking into consideration the identified priorities and the resources available. The programme concentrated on two main areas—safety and the environment and had two key objectives for implementation and application: the first was the establishment of a level playing field.[26] The rulemaking projects falling under this category are driven principally by the need to ensure that all players in a certain segment of the aviation market can benefit from the same set of rules, thereby promoting fair competition and free movement of persons and services. The broad principle of equality of opportunity to compete, which is the cornerstone of the Chicago Convention as enunciated in its Preamble is resonated by this EASA philosophy. The second limb was efficiency and proportionality[27] which called for the need to support technological and business advancements as well as to ensure that rules are cost-effective in achieving their objective. Naturally, these projects will also contribute to maintaining or even increasing the current level of safety.

The EASA rulemaking process is defined systematically in its programme to have three main components: driver; strategic objective; and issue and activity objective. For example, a driver for a safety management rule is identified as

[25]The previous issue of the Rulemaking Programme was that of 2014–2017 in its revised version dated December 2013.

[26]The key stakeholders that would benefit from a level playing field are airlines, manufacturers and operators other than airlines maintenance organisations (MOs)/service providers/continuing airworthiness management organisations (CAMOs) training organisations (TOs) aerodrome operators air traffic management (ATM)/air navigation services (ANS) systems and constituents GA Individuals (pilots, mechanical engineers, air traffic controllers (ATCOs)) Remotely piloted aircraft systems (RPAS).

[27]This criterion applied to aerodrome operators, airlines, general aviation, manufacturers, operators other than airlines RPAS and other related categories such as pilots and mechanical engineers.

efficiency and strategic objective as implementation of the performance-based environment. The issue and activity objectives are to work with authorities and organizations to implement safety management. revision; adoption of the revision with the objective of making the rules less prescriptive, relying more on industry standards; and provision of support to Member States (MS) in implementing the new Air OPS Regulation in accordance with the agreed strategy.

Taking another example on the economic field, in developing the European Community's external aviation policy, the first step was to establish an agenda and guidelines. This agenda used established regulation on bilateral air services negotiations of the European Union countries, namely Regulation (EC) No 847/2004 of the European Parliament and of the Council of 29 April 2004, on the negotiation and implementation of air service agreements between Member States and third countries. This regulation recognized that The European Court of Justice had confirmed the exclusive competence of the EU to negotiate, sign and conclude such agreements when they deal with matters within its competence. The Court has also confirmed the right of EU air carriers to benefit from the right of establishment within the EU, including their right to non-discriminatory market access to routes between all Member States and third countries (nationality clause).

Accordingly the Regulation asserted that The EU must revise the elements in existing bilateral agreements that infringe EU law. However, given the large number of bilateral agreements, Member States are authorised to negotiate with third countries to conclude a new agreement or modify an existing one, provided that no EU negotiations have been entered into. Although in this case they must act in accordance with the obligations laid down in this Regulation, to ensure that the agreement is compatible with EU law.

The new Regulation establishes a procedure for notifying and authorizing the bilateral negotiations conducted by Member States with a view to ensuring the introduction of standard clauses to make existing agreements compliant with EU law. The Regulation also imposes certain obligations on Member States to ensure that non-discriminatory procedures are established for the consultation of stakeholders and for the distribution of traffic rights during negotiations. A Member State may enter into negotiations with a third country concerning a new air service agreement or the modification of an existing air service agreement, its Annexes or any other related bilateral or multilateral arrangement, the subject matter of which falls partly within the competence of the EU, provided that any relevant standard clauses, developed jointly between Member States and the Commission, are included in such negotiations and the notification procedure is complied with.

Where a Member State intends to enter into such negotiations it shall notify the Commission of its intentions in writing. If, within 15 working days of receipt of the notification, the Commission concludes that the negotiations are likely to undermine the objectives of EU negotiations underway with the third country and/or lead to an agreement which is incompatible with EU law, it shall inform the Member State accordingly. A Member State is not permitted to enter into any new arrangement with a third country, which reduces the number of EU air carriers which may be designated to provide services between its territory and that country.

On the basis of this philosophy the Agenda for the Community's external aviation policy was set, based on a 2012 Communication from the Commission to the European Parliament, The Council, The European Economic and Social Committee and the Committee of the Regions, called The EU's External Aviation Policy—Addressing Future Challenges. The overall policy of this communication was that aviation is and will remain essential for connecting Europe with the rest of the world. The communication said that over the last two decades, by removing historic barriers, the EU had transformed and integrated fragmented national aviation markets into the single largest and most open regional aviation market in the world. The communication averred to the earlier policy of 2005[28] and stated that while the Communication concludes that the policy established in 2005 goes in the right direction, there was a compelling need to recognize that, 7 years later, the world of aviation was a very different place and that European aviation urgently needed a stronger framework where fair and open competition can thrive, and this can be ensured by a much more coordinated European approach to external aviation relations. Placing the consumer in the paramount position the 2012 communication called for competitiveness in forging a shared political readiness to push ahead with EU-level negotiations where the added value and economic benefits have been demonstrated.

In order to achieve this objective, The EU considered the necessity for the use of the full range of tools available, including Council authorizations of EU-level negotiations with major partners as well as European neighborhood countries, and, where necessary, to defend ourselves more effectively against unfair practices. The EU needed to show leadership in driving change to international ownership and control regimes that will ensure that EU-based global carriers stay prominent in the global network for years to come. In doing so, the EU thought it imperative to recognize that the EU was not only looking to strengthen the competitiveness of the entire value chain of European aviation, and all elements within that, but doing so in the interest of the end-consumer.

As a result of such policy determination, EASA has entered into bilateral arrangements on rulemaking with some countries. One such agreement is between EASA and TCCA (Canada) where TCCA and the European Aviation Safety Agency (EASA) agree that they should actively promote mutual rulemaking co-operation to maintain and further improve the achieved level of harmonization of their rules. They also agree that harmonization can best be achieved through constant communication during the definition and implementation of their respective rulemaking programmes.

A key objective of such an agreement is the sharing of resources and the supplementation of scarce resources of both parties, so that rules can be produced co-operation can be furthered without affecting their independence when deciding on the final rules they best see fit to fulfil their statutory obligations.

---

[28]Communication from the Commission, Developing the Agenda for the Community's External Aviation Policy, SEC (2005, 336), Brussels, 11.03.2005, COM 2005, 79 Final.

The EASA/ TCCA agreement establishes the process through which such objectives can be met. As TCCA and EASA agree to promote rulemaking co-operation, the agreement remains purely voluntary and is a basis for the procedure to be developed for implementing the provisions on regulatory co-operation in the Agreement on Civil Aviation Safety between Canada and the European Community. The objectives of this rulemaking co-operation arrangement are to: exchange rulemaking intentions and priorities thereof to align as much as possible the rulemaking programmes of TCCA and EASA; identify rules of common interest that TCCA and EASA can develop jointly to (1) avoid unnecessary divergence and duplication of work, (2) maximize available resources, and (3) further harmonization; and establish processes for developing those rules of common interest.

One of the features of the agreement is that nothing in the agreement affects the autonomy of either Party to exercise their independence when deciding on the necessary rules for the protection of the travelling public. Neither TCCA nor EASA is bound by the decisions of the other. Communication on a regular basis between the two Parties is so that they can coordinate their respective rulemaking programmes. Each rulemaking office is required to designate a coordinator, through which the regular communications of this arrangement will be facilitated. At least once a year, at a mutually-agreed opportune time, TCCA and EASA pledge to: review the functioning of this rulemaking co-operation arrangement; discuss their future rulemaking programmes, including priorities thereof and related documentation such as preliminary regulatory impact assessments. To that end, TCCA and EASA have agreed to exchange their respective rulemaking programmes at least six weeks before the meeting at which the programmes will be discussed. Upon receipt, TCCA and EASA will review the rulemaking programmes in a detailed manner to identify those rulemakings eligible for possible cooperation and potential focal points. They will also identify rulemakings of common interest; examine possible co-operative working methods for joint action when appropriate (based on the below chapter on implementation) and discuss possible changes in the rulemaking programmes and working methods imposed by changing priorities along with other possible contentious issues.

Arguably the most important principle in the Agreement is that both EASA and TCCA agree, when either of them initiates drafting a proposed rule to inform the other: when deciding the proposed composition of the rulemaking team; when deciding changes to the scope of the rulemaking or the rulemaking team; before presenting the proposed draft to the authorities; when reviewing the comments received and drafting responses; when deciding on changes to proposed regulatory text based on comments received; and before publication of the final rule.[29]

One of the achievements of the EU's rulemaking activities has been its ability to get other States to buy into its safety rules. One such example is the Extended Cooperative Arrangement on Aviation Safety between EASA and The General

[29]TCCA Standards Branch, Ottawa and EASA Rulemaking, Cologne January 15, 2008. See https://www.tc.gc.ca/eng/civilaviation/standards/int-easarulemaking-3670.htm.

Civil Aviation Authority (GCAA) of The United Arab Emirates.[30] In the arrangement, the Preamble refers to GCAA's decision to implement European Union rules on aviation safety and the mutual intention of both Parties to enhance professional qualifications of staff involved in the regulation and oversight of aviation activities. As a result, activities of both Organizations have the common objective under the cooperation agreement to deepen mutual cooperation on aviation safety regulation, safety promotion and oversight, professional staff development and coordination of technical cooperation projects. The scope of the cooperation extends to rulemaking cooperation; aviation safety promotion and sharing of safety information; and aviation training and professional staff development.

Another interesting example of European rulemaking lies in the field of aircraft emissions, where the EU adopted a strict policy that ultimately involved the entire aviation community and ICAO. The European Commission[31] published a proposal in December 2006[32] for a directive on the inclusion of aviation into the European Union's trading scheme for stationary sources. This proposal was placed before Committee on Aviation Environment Protection (CAEP/7)—a subsidiary body of the ICAO Council—by the Commission. At the meeting, the European Commission noted that CAEP had, at its sixth meeting in 2004, agreed that an aviation-specific emissions trading system based on a new legal instrument under ICAO auspices seemed sufficiently unattractive that it should not be pursued further. This notwithstanding, the 35th session of the ICAO Assembly, through Resolution 35-5

[30]https://www.easa.europa.eu/document-library/working-arrangements/united-arab-emirates.

[31]The European Commission (formally the Commission of the European Communities) is the executive body of the European Union. Alongside the European Parliament and the Council of the European Union, it is one of the three main institutions governing the Union. Its primary roles are to propose and implement legislation, and to act as 'guardian of the treaties' which provide the legal basis for the EU. The role of the European Commission has many parallels with the executive body of a national government, but also differences. The Commission consists of 27 Commissioners, one from each member state of the EU supported by an administrative body of about 23,000 European civil servants divided into departments called Directorate-General. The term "the Commission" is generally used to refer both to the administrative body in its entirety, and to the team of Commissioners who lead it. Unlike the Council of the European Union, the Commission is intended to be a body independent of member states. Commissioners are therefore not permitted to take instructions from the government of the country that appointed them, but are supposed to represent the interests of the citizens of the EU as a whole.

[32]In September 2005, the European Commission adopted a Communication on reducing the climate change impact of aviation. The Communication recognised that, although aviation's share of overall greenhouse gas emissions is still modest (about 3 %), the rapid growth in emissions in the sector undermines progress to reduce emissions made in other sectors and that the combined effect of existing measures would not be sufficient to offset the growth in aviation emissions. The Communication concluded that including aviation in the EU Emission Trading Scheme (EU ETS) would be the most cost-efficient and environmentally effective way forward and indicated that the Commission would put forward a proposal for legislation by the end of 2006. See Commission of the European Communities, 2006. Proposal for a Directive of the European Parliament and of the Council amending Directive 2003/87/EC so as to include aviation activities in the scheme of greenhouse gas emission allowance trading within the Community, COM(2006) 818 final, Brussels.

of the ICAO Assembly subsequently endorsed the implementation of international open emissions trading through voluntary emissions trading or the incorporation of international aviation into State's existing emissions trading Schemes. The European Commission had opted for the latter option and incorporated certain principles in its Proposal.

Broadly, the European proposal admitted of operators being allocated allowances each giving them a right to emit one tonne of carbon dioxide per year. The total number of allowances allocated sets a limit on the overall emissions from the activities covered by the Scheme. By 30 April each year operators must surrender allowances to cover their actual emissions. Operators can trade allowances so that emissions reductions can be made where they are most cost-effective. In addition to allowances allocated under the Scheme, operators can also use credits from emission-reduction projects under the Kyoto Protocol (Joint Implementation and Clean Development Mechanism) to cover their emissions.

Under the Commission's proposal, Directive 2003/87/EC[33] was to be amended to include the aviation sector in the European Union's Emissions Trading Scheme (EU ETS). This was an example of rulemaking by the European Commission on its own initiative. Initially, in 2011, only flights between EU airports would be included in the Scheme. From 2012 this would be extended to all flights arriving at or departing from an EU airport. Where a third country puts in place measures to reduce the climate change impact of aviation, the Scheme would not apply to flights arriving from that country.

The objective of the proposal was to provide a model for aviation emissions trading that can be a point of reference in the EU's contacts with key international partners and to promote the development of similar systems worldwide. The Commission also supports the objective of a global agreement aimed at effectively tackling aviation emissions at global level.

The key aspects of the proposal are that aircraft operators would be the entities responsible for complying with the obligations imposed by the Scheme. The Scheme would exclude flights by State aircraft, flights under visual flight rules, circular flights ('circuits'), flights for testing navigation equipment or for training purposes, rescue flights and flights by aircraft with a maximum take-off weight of less than 5700 kg. Under the proposal, each aircraft operator, including operators from third countries, would be administered by one Member State only in order to avoid duplication and an excessive administrative burden on aircraft operators. The Scheme would only cover CO_2 emissions. The Commission will carry out a

[33]The European Union Emission Trading Scheme (EU ETS) is the largest multi-national, greenhouse gas emissions trading scheme in the world and is a main pillar of EU climate policy. Under the Scheme, each participating country has a National Allocation Plan (NAP) specifying caps on greenhouse gas emissions for individual power plants and other large point sources. Each facility gets a maximum amount of emission "allowances" for a particular period (e.g. 2005–2007). To comply, facilities can either reduce their emissions or purchase allowances from facilities with an excess of allowances. Progressively tightening caps are foreseen for each new period, forcing overall reductions in emissions.

thorough impact assessment and will put forward a further proposal to address nitrogen oxide (NOx) emissions by the end of 2008.

Another feature of the proposal was that, in contrast to the existing Scheme, the method of allocating allowances would be harmonised at the level of the EU and not at Member State level. The Scheme calls for the total number of allowances to be allocated to the aviation sector to be determined by reference to average emissions from aviation in the years 2004–2006. The majority of allowances were to be allocated free of charge on the basis of a benchmark to aircraft operators which submit an application (the earliest application relating to 2008 data). There is also provision for a small proportion of allowances to be auctioned.[34] The percentage of allowances to be auctioned would be equal to the average percentage proposed to be auctioned by EU Member States auctioning allowances in the 2008–2012 period (expected to be around 3 %). Thereafter the percentage auctioned would be decided in the light of the results of the general review of the EU ETS due for completion in late 2007.

The Scheme required aircraft operators, like other participants in the Community Scheme, to monitor their emissions of carbon dioxide and report them to the competent authority of their administering Member State by 31 March each year. The reports were to be independently verified to make sure that they are accurate. The basic principles for monitoring, reporting and verifying emissions set out in the proposal were elaborated by guidelines. If necessary, aircraft operators were entitled to buy allowances from other sectors in the Scheme to cover increases in their emissions Aircraft operators would also be able to use project credits—so-called Emission Reduction Units (ERUs) and Certified Emission Reductions (CERs)—from the Joint Implementation or Clean Development Mechanisms (JI/CDM) provided for in the Kyoto Protocol up to a harmonised limit equivalent to the average of the limits applied by EU Member States for other sectors in the EU ETS. The Scheme was to also apply to domestic aviation which would be treated in the same way as international aviation.

One of the issues that this rulemaking proposal raised was, if it were to become EU law, the jurisprudential significance of the requirements the proposal imposes on the parties concerned. The tenets of international law as well as the recommendations of the ICAO Assembly and the Council call for mutual agreement between States. The *Vienna Convention for the Protection of the Ozone Layer* of 1985[35] requires that States Parties take appropriate measures in accordance with the provisions of the Convention and of those protocols in force to which they are party to protect human health and the environment against adverse effects resulting or likely to result from human activities which modify or are likely to modify the ozone layer

[34]The details of how auctioning would work such as appropriate design and timing will be set out in a further Regulation to be adopted by the Commission. Auctioning proceeds would be used to mitigate and adapt to the impacts of climate change and to cover administrative costs.

[35]The Convention was Opened for Signature Vienna, 22 March 1985 and entered into Force on 22 September 1988.

by co-operating by means of systematic observations, research and information exchange in order to better understand and assess the effects of human activities on the ozone layer and the effects on human health and the environment from modification of the ozone layer. It also calls for States to adopt appropriate legislative or administrative measures and co-operate in harmonizing appropriate policies to control, limit, reduce or prevent human activities under their jurisdiction or control should it be found that these activities have or are likely to have adverse effects resulting from modification or likely modification of the ozone layer. One of the mainstays of the Convention is the requirement that States co-operate in the formulation of agreed measures, procedures and standards for the implementation of this Convention, with a view to the adoption of protocols and annexes and co-operate with competent international bodies to implement effectively this Convention and protocols to which they are party. Therefore the legal issue is whether a unilateral measure by the European Union (which other States might not necessarily agree to) would be determined destitute of legal effect and therefore unenforceable at international law.

One of the factors that stymied the European Commission's attempt at initiating rulemaking in the emissions trading process pertaining to aircraft emissions was the supremacy of treaty law. Principle 12 of the 1992 Rio Declaration on Environment and Development states:

> States should cooperate to promote a supportive and open international economic system that would lead to economic growth and sustainable development in all countries, to better address the problems of environmental degradation. Trade policy measures for environmental purposes should not constitute a means of arbitrary or unjustifiable discrimination or a disguised restriction on international trade. Unilateral actions to deal with environmental challenges outside the jurisdiction of the importing country should be avoided. Environmental measures addressing transboundary or global environmental problems should, as far as possible, be based on an international consensus.[36]

The last sentence of this Principle is of particular relevance. Member States of ICAO, at the Organization's 36th Session of the Assembly (Montreal, 18--28 September 2007) adopted Resolution A36-22[37], which, in Appendix A declares that ICAO is the lead United Nations Agency in matters involving international aviation,[38] and urges ICAO member States, in Appendix L not to implement an emissions trading system on other member States' aircraft operators except on the basis of mutual agreement between those States.[39] It is encouraging that the formal

[36]The Rio Declaration on Environment and Development, often shortened to *Rio Declaration*, was a short document produced at the 1992 United Nations "Conference on Environment and Development" (UNCED), informally known as the earth Summit. The Rio Declaration consisted 27 principles intended to guide future sustainable development around the world.

[37]Consolidated statement of continuing ICAO policies and practices related to environmental protection, *Assembly Resolutions in Force* (As of 28 September 2007), ICAO Doc 9902, 1–54 to 1–74.

[38]*Id*, Appendix A, at 1–55.

[39]*Id*. Appendix L, at 1–73.

EU position with regard to ICAO is that ICAO is the natural forum to develop a global solution.[40] Mr. Daniel Calleja, Air Transport Director at the European Commission, in an interview with the *ICAO Journal* has stated that the EU is committed to processes that have been launched by ICAO's GIACC. Mr. Calleja also stated at the same interview that the EU is ready to change its position if a more global solution can be agreed upon.[41] This could be the ultimate approach for a globally acceptable trading mechanism.

Member States of ICAO, at the Organization's 36th Session of the Assembly (Montreal, 18–28 September 2007) adopted Resolution A36-22[42], which, in Appendix A declares that ICAO is the lead United Nations Agency in matters involving international aviation,[43] and urges ICAO member States, in Appendix L not to implement an emissions trading system on other member States' aircraft operators except on the basis of mutual agreement between those States.[44] However, The Portuguese Delegation, representing the European Union (EU) and the other States of the European Civil Aviation Conference (ECAC), that is 42 States in total, expressed a reservation on the text contained in Appendix L. In their view, the resolving clauses in the Appendix lacked legal foundation in the Convention on International Civil Aviation (Chicago Convention) and therefore could not be used to diminish their rights. Accordingly, these States reserved the right to apply market based measures of the type referred to in Appendix L on a non-discriminatory basis to all operators of all States providing services to, from or within their territories.[45]

One of the reasons given by the EU and ECAC States for the reservation was that they supported a comprehensive approach to reducing aviation emissions, encompassing progress on technology and standards, operational measures, and market-based measures. These States were of the view that it was necessary to pursue such a comprehensive approach actively since, as confirmed by the 4th Assessment Report from the Intergovernmental Panel on Climate Change (IPCC),[46] none of the abovementioned measures would have a sufficient impact on aviation

[40]Calleja (2008), pp. 14–15.

[41]*Ibid.*

[42]Consolidated statement of continuing ICAO policies and practices related to environmental protection, *Assembly Resolutions in Force* (As of 28 September 2007), ICAO Doc 9902, 1–54 to 1–74.

[43]*Id*, Appendix A, at 1–55.

[44]*Id*. Appendix L, at 1–73.

[45]Assembly Thirty Sixth Session, Executive Committee Report, A36-WP/355. p/53, 17-10.

[46]The IPCC is a scientific intergovernmental body set up by the World Meteorological Organization (WMO) and by the United Nations Environment Programme (UNEP). Its constituency is made of the governments. The IPCC is open to all member countries of the World Meteorological Organization (WMO) and The United Nations Environmental Programme (UNEP). Governments of member States participate in plenary Sessions of the IPCC where main decisions about the IPCC work programme are taken and reports are accepted, adopted and approved. They also participate in the review of IPCC Reports. Hundreds of scientists all over the world contribute to the work of the IPCC as authors, contributors and reviewers. As a United Nations body, the IPCC work aims at the promotion of the United Nations human development goals.

emissions in isolation. Therefore, it was stated on behalf of the EU and ECAC States that the European Community was considering a legislative proposal[47] to incorporate emissions from international aviation into its existing emissions trading scheme. This measure, it was claimed, demonstrated the European Community's commitment to taking meaningful action to reduce aviation emissions, whilst allowing air transport to continue to develop and sustainably grow, taking into account the particular situation of developing countries.

Accordingly, The European Parliament, on 8 July 2008, voted to expand the European Union's Emissions Trading Scheme (EU ETS)[48] to cover aviation engine emissions by requiring that all airlines leaving from or landing at airports in the EU will have to buy pollution credits commencing in 2012.[49] According to this requirement, 85 % of the emissions certificates will be allocated for free and 15 % will be auctioned. The reduction target will be calculated on the basis of airlines' annual emissions between 2004 and 2006. In the first period (2012) the cut in airlines emissions would be 3 % and in the period to follow commencing 2013 the emissions would be cut by 5 %. Research flights and small airlines producing low emissions would be excluded.

A key factor in the debate was the position of ICAO in the EC rulemaking process. ICAO is a specialized agency of the United Nations and therefore the law applicable to the United Nations in general applies to ICAO, and to its resolutions.[50] As per established law on the subject, the distinct and unequivocal answer to the question as to whether the 42 States which constituted membership of the EU and ECAC at the time had a legal right to tabulate their reservation and have it carried through under international law, is clearly in the affirmative. The record of the United Nations over its six decades of history is that member States have on occasion, but in a consistent manner, refused to automatically comply with the corporate will of the Organization.[51] *Brownlie* has expressed the view that decisions by international conferences and organizations can in principle only bind those States accepting them.[52] Shaw, referring to the binding force of United Nations General; Assembly Resolutions states:

---

[47]See generally, Abeyratne (2007), pp. 358–375.

[48]For a detailed discussion on the nature of the EU ETS, See Abeyratne (2008), pp. 5–9.

[49]*Washington Aviation Summary*, July 2008, at 10.

[50]Article 57 of the United Nations Charter provides that the various specialized agencies, established by intergovernmental agreement and having wide international responsibilities, as defined in their basic instruments, in economic, social, cultural, educational, health, and related fields, shall be brought into relationship with the United Nations in accordance with the provisions of Article 63, which provides that the Economic and Social Council may enter into agreements with any of the agencies referred to in Article 57, defining the terms on which the agency concerned shall be brought into relationship with the United Nations. Such agreements shall be subject to approval by the General Assembly. It may co-ordinate the activities of the specialized agencies through consultation with and recommendations to such agencies and through recommendations to the General Assembly and to the Members of the United Nations.

[51]Zoller (1987), p. 32.

[52]Brownlie (1990), p. 691.

> . . .one must be alive to the dangers in ascribing legal value to everything that emanates from the Assembly. Resolutions are often the results of political compromises and arrangements and, comprehended in that sense, never intended to constitute binding norms. Great care must be taken in moving from a plethora of practice to the identification of legal norms.[53]

With regard to the practice of other international organizations, a little more caution might be required, as a resolution might create a custom. Non binding instruments form a special category that is sometimes referred to as "soft law" which is definitely not law in the sense of enforceability.[54]

ICAO's conferred powers enable the Organization to adopt binding regulations by majority decision (which is usually unnecessary as most of ICAO policy is adopted through consensus). However, States could opt out of these policies or make reservations thereto, usually before such policy enters into force. This is because States have delegated power to ICAO to make decisions on the basis that they accept such decisions on the international plane. In such cases States could contract out and enter into binding agreements outside the purview of ICAO even on subjects on which ICAO has adopted policy. The only exception to this rule lies in the adoption of Standards in Annex 2 to the Chicago Convention on Rules of the Air, in particular navigation over the high seas and other overflight areas where freedom of flight prevails which all Contracting States are bound to follow in order to maintain global safety.

One of the reasons given by the States for tabling their reservation is that contrary to usual practice, the resolution was not adopted by consensus and that no meaningful effort has been made to reflect in Appendix L the views of a substantial number of members of ICAO. Yet another reason was that there is no provision in the Chicago Convention which may be construed as imposing upon the Contracting Parties the obligation to obtain the consent of other Contracting Parties before applying market-based measures referred to in Appendix L to operators of other States in respect of air services to, from or within their territory. It was claimed that, on the contrary, the Chicago Convention recognizes expressly the right of each Contracting Party to apply on a non-discriminatory basis its own air laws and regulations to the aircraft of all States.

The claim by the EU and ECAC States that there was a lack of consensus in adopting Resolution A36-22 is an interesting one. Consensus[55] is considered an egalitarian way of reaching international agreement:

---

[53]Shaw (2003), p. 110.

[54]*Id.* 111. See also Tammes (1958), p. 265.

[55]Consensus is reached when any one of the following occurs:

1. all are in agreement (unanimity);
2. most are in agreement and those who disagree are content that the discussion has been both full and fair and that the proposal expresses the general "mind of the meeting"; the minority therefore gives consent;
3. the meeting acknowledges that there are various opinions, and it is agreed that these be recorded in the body of the proposal (not just in the minutes);
4. it is agreed that the matter be postponed;
5. it is agreed that no decision can be reached. See, Frequently Asked Questions (2003), p. 42.

> The consensus system assures that decision-making at a multilateral negotiation of a convention will not be dominated by the numerical superiority of any group of nations. Rather, procedural significance will be given to the variations in the power of nations. Since it is difficult to obtain acceptance of voting systems that overtly recognize the differences in nations' importance, the consensus approach permits the maintenance of an egalitarian procedure which in practice may assure that multilateral negotiations reflect the real geopolitical power of the participating nations.[56]

Throughout its legislative history, ICAO has had a sustained history of reaching agreement through consensus. Therefore, if the States were not able to reach consensus on Appendix L they have only themselves to blame. In this context, it is worthy of note that the ICAO Assembly, at its First Session held in Montreal from 6 to 27 May 1947 resolved that:

> Universal membership in the International Civil Aviation Organization is desirable to achieve its maximum usefulness in promoting safety in the air and the efficient and orderly development of air transport.[57]

The universal solidarity of ICAO Contracting States that was recognized from the outset at the Chicago Conference which brings to bear the need for States to be united in recognizing the effect of ICAO policy and decisions. Therefore, it is incontrovertible that universal participation in ICAO by the contracting States is indispensable if ICAO were to effectively implement the provisions of the Chicago Convention. Sixty years of symbiotic existence have shown that States need ICAO no less than ICAO needs their membership.

Another issue is that, notwithstanding that the 42 States of the EU and ECAC are not obligated to follow the provisions of Annex L to Resolution A36-22 in view of their reservation, they are deemed to have accepted the rest of the Resolution, which *inter alia* recognizes that ICAO plays a leadership role in international civil aviation matters related to the environment. This, and the fact that ICAO is an Organization established by the Chicago Convention of 1944 and is composed of an Assembly, a Council and such other bodies as may be necessary[58] are relevant to the issue at hand and accords ICAO the profile of a global forum. The Assembly and the Council are composed of Contracting States. The Assembly, composed of 190 Contracting States, is the supreme legislative body. Therefore it would not be incorrect to assume that any resolution adopted or decision taken by ICAO can be imputed to ICAO's Contracting States which have delegated powers on the Organization. However, States retain the powers to act unilaterally and they are not bound to comply with obligations flowing from the Organization's exercise of conferred powers. States which have delegated powers on ICAO have the legal

---

[56]Charney (1978), p. 43.

[57]Resolution A1-9, ICAO Doc 7375-C/852, 1947 pp. 242–243. The same philosophy of universality was extended to the United Nations in general at the first session of the United Nations—that the United Nations looked forward to the time when universal membership in the system of the international organization established by the Charter of the United Nations would be possible and actual. Captain Schenkman (1955), p. 87.

[58]Chicago Convention, *supra*, Article 43.

right under public international law to take measures against a particular exercise by ICAO of conferred powers which is considered to be *detournement de pouvoir, ultra vires* or an internationally wrongful act with which the objecting States do not wish to be associated. A State could also distance itself from the State practice of other Contracting States if such activity is calculated to form customary international law that could in turn bind the objecting State if it does not persist in its objections.[59]

A significant issue in the determination of ICAO's effectiveness as an international organization is the overriding principle of universality and global participation of all its 190 Contracting States in the implementation of ICAO policy. This principle, which has its genesis in the Chicago Conference of 1944, has flowed on gaining express recognition of legal scholars. This is what makes ICAO unique as a specialized agency of the United Nations and establishes without any doubt that ICAO is not just a tool of cooperation among States.

Another serious criticism of the EC attempt at extending the ETS to aviation by an internal rule is that rulemaking is an endogenous process and should only be effective and applicable to the domestic scene. The complaint against EU ETS is that the European Union is exercising extra territorial jurisdiction by extending the scheme in 2012 to all flights arriving at or departing from an EU airport and exempting from the scheme flights arriving in the territory of the Union membership from a third country which puts in place measures to reduce the climate change impact of aviation. This brings to bear the need to inquire into the status of the European Union as well as the issue of extra territoriality in the context of the applicable principles of public international law. The only exception to the prohibition of extra territorial application of a law or rule is the "effects theory" of extra territorial jurisdiction which goes beyond the principles of sovereignty. This theory relates to a situation where a State assumes jurisdiction beyond its territorial limits on the ground that the behaviour of a party is adversely affecting the interests of that State by producing "effects" within its territory. It does not matter whether all the conduct and practices take place in another State or whether part of the conduct is within the State adopting the legislation. In the latter instance, the conduct of the party would come under the "objective territorial principle" where part of the offence takes place within the jurisdiction. In the case of aircraft engine emissions, the applicable principles would come under both headings as trans-boundary pollution of the environment by an aircraft which flies into Europe may involve the emissions of gases in one State that could cross boundaries and affect Europe.

Although it is true that the Chicago Convention recognizes the right of each Contracting Party to apply on a non-discriminatory basis its own air laws and regulations to the aircraft of all States it is quite tenuous to suggest that the Convention *ipso facto* gives States the right to apply their laws outside their territories.

A commentator makes the point:

---

[59]See Sarooshi (2005), p. 110.

> EAs (European Agencies) exercise de jure or de facto rulemaking powers. Admittedly, such powers are of limited relevance, which reflects both the political reluctance of EU institutions to grant EAs genuine rulemaking powers and a certain shyness of EAs themselves to fight to acquire rulemaking powers on the ground. Nevertheless, these powers are used by EAs as one of the various instruments through which the implementation of EU legislation is carried out and the objective of the smooth functioning of the relevant policy sectors is pursued.[60]

He goes on to say that there are two main types of rulemaking in Europe: where Agencies of the Commission are called upon to be technical actors in adopting rules to be implemented or to issue soft law instruments when they are called upon to issue such. Moreover, two main types of EAs' rulemaking can be identified. EAs may be called to participate, as technical actors, in procedures leading to the adoption of binding implementing rules, either assisting the Commission or directly adopting technical rules. They may also be called upon to issue soft law such as guidance and communications. A fitting conclusion to the legal legitimacy and profile of European rulemaking comes from another commentator[61] who says:

> Consequently, one must not fall back on over-idealisation and misunderstandings. Scholarly efforts in European Union Law should not strive to achieve unreachable idealistic goals or deny undisputable developments, but should aim at further developing the theory and doctrine(s) of rulemaking in the European legal area in a way that enable EU rulemaking to fulfil the requirements of democracy and the rule of law, but that also makes it rational and efficient. There may be many appropriate ways to analyse EU rulemaking without falling into one of the traps of oversimplification. Legal scholarship, I submit, should do so by using the basic categories it developed over time, and in a way that – more or less – transcends the borders between jurisdictions.[62]

Rulemaking in the European Union has generally gone on the basis that the subject of an agreement falls partly within Community competence and partly within the competence of its Member States. As a corollary to this premise the EU considers it imperative to ensure close cooperation between the Member States and the Community institutions, such as during the negotiations for the conclusion of the agreement and the fulfillment of the obligations. The obligation to cooperate flows from the requirement of unity in the international representation of the Community. Community institutions and Member States should take all measures necessary to ensure the best possible cooperation in that regard. It is also a recognized principle that The cooperation procedure between Member States and the Commission established by this Regulation should not interfere with the division of powers between the Community and the Member States, in accordance with Community law, as interpreted by the European Court of Justice.

In this context, of particular interest to air transport is Regulation (EC) no. 847/2004 of the European Council and Parliament of 29 April 2004 on the negotiation and implementation of air service agreements between Member States and

[60]Chiti (2013), pp. 93–110.

[61]Matthias Ruffert.

[62]The 'public law approach' in international law developed by von Bogdandy et al. (2010), p. 3.

third countries. According to Rule 847, all existing bilateral agreements between Member States and third countries that contain provisions contrary to Community law should be amended or replaced by new agreements that are wholly compatible with Community law. The rule also stipulates that member States may wish to change existing agreements and provide for the management of their implementation pending the entry into force of the agreement concluded by the Community and that Member States conducting negotiations takes account of Community law, broader Community interests and ongoing Community negotiations. They could involve air carriers in the bilateral air services negotiations, but if they involve one carrier, they must involve all air carriers with an establishment in the territory of the Member State concerned are treated equally.

The establishment in the territory of a Member State means the actual pursuit of the business of air transport on the basis of established agreements; legal form of such an establishment, whether a branch or a subsidiary with legal personality, in this respect should not be the determining factor. In the case of a business on the territory of several Member States, as laid down in the Treaty, would be to prevent any circumvention of national law, it should ensure that each of the establishments fulfills the obligations which it, in accordance with Community law, can be imposed by national legislation It regulates its activities. In order to ensure that the rights of Community carriers are not unduly restricted, the bilateral agreements on the provision of air transport should not be included of any new agreement on reducing the number of Community air carriers which may be designated to operate air services on a given market.

Member States are expected to establish non-discriminatory and transparent procedures for distributing traffic rights between Community air carriers. Member States in the application of those procedures should adequately take into account the need to preserve continuity of air services. The measures necessary for the implementation of this Regulation should be adopted in accordance with Council Decision 1999/486/EC of 28 June 1999 laying down the procedures for the exercise of implementing powers conferred on the Commission. Any Member State may invoke the confidentiality provisions of the bilateral agreements, which were negotiated and request the Commission to not transmit the information to the other Member States.

The European Community may adopt measures, in accordance with the principle of subsidiarity as set out in Article 5 of the Rome Treaty. In accordance with the principle of proportionality, as set out in that Article, this Regulation does not go beyond what is necessary to achieve these objectives, since the objectives of this Regulation, namely the coordination of negotiations with third countries following the conclusion of air services agreements, the need to ensure a harmonized approach to the implementation and application of these agreements and confirmation of their compliance with Community legislation, Member States can not be sufficiently achieved by them therefore, due to the scope of applicability of the Regulation throughout the Community, be better achieved at Community level. Where a Member State concludes an agreement or amendments to an agreement or annex to the latter from which limit the use of traffic rights or the number of

Community air carriers which fulfill the conditions for the use of traffic rights, that Member State is required to ensure the distribution of traffic rights among eligible Community air carriers on the basis of non-discriminatory and transparent process.

Another noteworthy example of rulemaking in Europe is Regulation 868/2004 of the European Parliament and the Council concerning protection against subsidisation and unfair pricing practices causing injury to Community air carriers in the provision of air services from countries not members of the European Community. This rule was adopted amid concerns about unfair pricing practices by certain non-EU carriers on the transatlantic market. Its objective is to protect EU air carriers against subsidisation and unfair pricing practices causing them injury in the supply of air services from non-EU countries.

Rule 868/2004 exemplifies an important of practicality in European rulemaking as it has not been applied for the reason that EU legislative framework in practice does not guarantee protection of EU air carriers against subsidisation and unfair pricing practices from third country airlines. The EU industry argues that the Regulation is not practicable as it has been modelled on tools used in anti-dumping for goods and is not properly adapted to the specificities of the air transport sector. Difficulties have arisen because of the approach of the regulation which is based on trade defence notions and practices (e.g. "like air service2") which are difficult if not impossible to apply in air transport unless better adapted to the special features of the sector which is regulated by bilateral air services agreements between sovereign states.

The EU legislative framework in practice does not guarantee protection of EU air carriers against subsidisation and unfair pricing practices from third country airlines. Regulation 868/2004 has never been used. The EU industry argues that the Regulation is not practicable as it has been modelled on tools used in anti-dumping for goods and is not properly adapted to the specificities of the air transport sector. The considerable difficulties for EU stakeholders to use the Regulation are mostly due to its approach based on trade defence notions and practices (e.g. "like air service") which are difficult if not impossible to apply in air transport unless better adapted to the special features of the sector which is regulated by bilateral air services agreements between sovereign states.

Regulation 1008/2008 is another example of rulemaking pertaining to operating licences of aircraft. Given the growing importance of air carriers with operational bases in several Member States and the need to ensure the efficient supervision of these air carriers, the same Member State should be responsible for the oversight of the air operator certificate and of the operating licence. Article 4 of the rule stipulates the conditions that are applicable to the grant of an operating licence, which are that an undertaking, to be qualify as a recipient of a licence should have: its principal place of business is located in that Member State; hold a valid AOC (air operator's certificate) issued by a national authority of the same Member State whose competent licensing authority is responsible for granting, refusing, revoking or suspending the operating licence of the Community air carrier; have one or more aircraft at its disposal through ownership or a dry lease agreement; have, as its main occupation the operation of air services in isolation or combined with any other commercial operation of aircraft or the repair and maintenance of aircraft; have its company structure allowing the competent licensing authority to implement relevant provisions of the rule.

Member States and/or nationals of Member States should own more than 50 % of the undertaking and effectively control it, whether directly or indirectly through one or more intermediate undertakings, except as provided for in an agreement with a third country to which the Community is a party and the undertaking must meet applicable financial conditions. Public policy linked with European rulemaking is seen in Regulation (EU) No 598/2014 of the European Parliament and of the Council of 16 April 2014 on the establishment of rules and procedures with regard to the introduction of noise-related operating restrictions at Union airports within a Balanced Approach. This approach was adopted along the lines suggested by ICAO at its 6th Worldwide Air Transport Conference held in 2012 which called for an airport-by-airport approach where the following procedural steps allow for identification of the most suitable solution for the noise issue at the airport in question: (a) assessment of the current and future noise impact at the airport concerned, compared to the noise objective to be achieved; (b) evaluation of the likely costs and benefits of the various measures available; (c) selection of measures with the goal to achieve maximum environmental benefits most cost-effectively; (d) provision for dissemination of the evaluation results; (e) provision for consultation with stakeholders at different stages from assessment to implementation; and (f) provision for dispute resolution.

Another example, as already mentioned, of European rulemaking in accordance with overall public policy both at local and global level is found in Regulation 421/2014 where the European Commission relented on it original stance that aircraft engine emissions must be brought within the purview of its emissions trading scheme (EU/ETS).

The European Commission published a proposal in December 2006 for a directive on the inclusion of aviation into the European Union's trading scheme for stationary sources. This proposal was placed before the 7th Meeting of the Committee on Aviation Environmental Protection (CAEP/7) held in January-February 2007 by the Commission. At the meeting, the European Commission noted that CAEP had, at its sixth meeting in 2004, agreed that an aviation-specific emissions trading system based on a new legal instrument under ICAO auspices seemed sufficiently unattractive that it should not be pursued further. This notwithstanding, the 35th session of the ICAO Assembly, through Resolution 35-5 of the ICAO Assembly subsequently endorsed the implementation of international open emissions trading through voluntary emissions trading or the incorporation of international aviation into State's existing emissions trading Schemes. The European Commission had opted for the latter option and incorporated certain principles in its Proposal.

Broadly, the European proposal admits of operators being allocated allowances each giving them a right to emit one tonne of carbon dioxide per year. The total number of allowances allocated sets a limit on the overall emissions from the activities covered by the Scheme. By 30 April each year operators must surrender allowances to cover their actual emissions. Operators can trade allowances so that emissions reductions can be made where they are most cost-effective. In addition to allowances allocated under the Scheme, operators can also use credits from emission-reduction projects under the Kyoto Protocol (Joint Implementation and Clean Development Mechanism) to cover their emissions.

Under the Commission's proposal, Directive 2003/87/EC was to be amended to include the aviation sector in the European Union's Emissions Trading Scheme (EU ETS). Initially, in 2011, only flights between EU airports would be included in the Scheme. From 2012 this would be extended to all flights arriving at or departing from an EU airport. Where a third country puts in place measures to reduce the climate change impact of aviation, the Scheme would not apply to flights arriving from that country.

The objective of the proposal was to provide a model for aviation emissions trading that can be a point of reference in the EU's contacts with key international partners and to promote the development of similar systems worldwide. The Commission also supports the objective of a global agreement aimed at effectively tackling aviation emissions at global level.

The key aspects of the proposal were that aircraft operators would be the entities responsible for complying with the obligations imposed by the Scheme. The Scheme would exclude flights by State aircraft, flights under visual flight rules, circular flights ('circuits'), flights for testing navigation equipment or for training purposes, rescue flights and flights by aircraft with a maximum take-off weight of less than 5700 kg. Under the proposal, each aircraft operator, including operators from third countries, would be administered by one Member State only in order to avoid duplication and an excessive administrative burden on aircraft operators. The Scheme would only cover CO2 emissions. The Commission will carry out a thorough impact assessment and will put forward a further proposal to address nitrogen oxide (NOx) emissions by the end of 2008.

Another feature of the proposal was that, in contrast to the existing Scheme, the method of allocating allowances would be harmonised at the level of the EU and not at Member State level. The Scheme calls for the total number of allowances to be allocated to the aviation sector to be determined by reference to average emissions from aviation in the years 2004–2006. The majority of allowances would be allocated free of charge on the basis of a benchmark to aircraft operators which submit an application (the earliest application relating to 2008 data). There was also provision for a small proportion of allowances to be auctioned. The percentage of allowances to be auctioned would be equal to the average percentage proposed to be auctioned by EU Member States auctioning allowances in the 2008–2012 period (expected to be around 3 %). Thereafter the percentage auctioned would be decided in the light of the results of the general review of the EU ETS due for completion in late 2007.

The Scheme required aircraft operators, like other participants in the Community Scheme, to monitor their emissions of carbon dioxide and report them to the competent authority of their administering Member State by 31 March each year. The reports would be independently verified to make sure that they are accurate.

The basic principles for monitoring, reporting and verifying emissions set out in the proposal would be elaborated by guidelines. If necessary, aircraft operators would be able to buy allowances from other sectors in the Scheme to cover increases in their emissions Aircraft operators would also be able to use project credits—so-called Emission Reduction Units (ERUs) and Certified Emission Reductions (CERs)—from the Joint Implementation or Clean Development Mechanisms (JI/CDM) provided for in the Kyoto Protocol up to a harmonised limit equivalent to the average of the limits applied by EU Member States for other sectors in the EU ETS. The Scheme would also apply to domestic aviation which would be treated in the same way as international aviation.

There were strong protests from the international aviation community at ICAO, alleging that bringing aircraft engine emissions within the EU/ETS would be an extra territorial measure that was incompatible with global agreement already reached in the 1992 Rio Conference (Earth Summit), Principle 12 of which stated that unilateral actions to deal with environmental challenges outside the jurisdiction of the importing country should be avoided and that environmental measures addressing transboundary or global environmental problems should, as far as possible, be based on international consensus. Member States of ICAO, at the Organization's 36th Session of the Assembly (Montreal, 18–28 September 2007) adopted Resolution A36-22, which, in Appendix A declares that ICAO is the lead United Nations Agency in matters involving international aviation, and urges ICAO member States, in Appendix L not to implement an emissions trading system on other member States' aircraft operators except on the basis of mutual agreement between those States . It is encouraging that the formal EU position with regard to ICAO is that ICAO is the natural forum to develop a global solution . Mr. Daniel Calleja, Air Transport Director at the European Commission, in an interview with the ICAO Journal has stated that the EU is committed to processes that have been launched by ICAO's GIACC. Mr. Calleja also stated at the same interview that the EU is ready to change its position if a more global solution can be agreed upon.

On the subject of computer reservations systems, Regulation 80/2009 offers an interesting dimension. This regulation, which was designed to ensure optimal protection of the consumer, recognized inter alia that technological and market developments allow for a substantial simplification of the legislative framework by giving more flexibility to system vendors and air carriers to negotiate booking fees and fare content and that this should allow them to adapt in a flexible way to the needs and requests of travel agents and consumers and to distribute more efficiently their transport products. Accordingly, the regulation effectively precluded a system vendor from attaching unfair and/or unjustified conditions to any contract with a participating carrier or require the acceptance of supplementary conditions which, by their nature or according to commercial usage, have no connection with participation in its CRS. There was also a condition of participation in that a participating carrier could not at the same time be a participant in another system or that a participating carrier may not freely use alternative reservation systems such as its own Internet booking system and call centres.

A system vendor was required to load and process data provided by participating carriers with equal care and timeliness, subject only to the constraints of the loading method selected by individual participating carriers, while being required to publicly disclose, unless this is otherwise made public, the existence and extent of a direct or indirect capital holding of an air carrier or rail-transport operator in a system vendor, or of a system vendor in an air carrier or rail-transport operator. A system vendor had to provide a principal display or displays for each individual transaction through its CRS and was required to include therein the data provided by participating carriers in a neutral and comprehensive manner and without discrimination or bias. Criteria to be used for ranking were not to be based on any factor directly or indirectly relating to carrier identity and shall be applied on a non-discriminatory basis to all participating carriers. The principal display (s) should not, under any circumstances, mislead the user, shall be easily accessible and shall respect the rules set out in the regulation.

Rulemaking is both a powerful tool as well as a superimposed layer of social conduct which often call the legislature to tone it down or control it. It also shows the populace where power resides and how to participate effectively in the rulemaking process. Arguably the most useful tool of the rulemaking process is the ability of rules to keep a government going and keep democracy flourishing. It is for this reason that rulemaking in air transport becomes important, given the exponential growth of demand for air transport. Rulemaking in competition and liberalization in air transport both in the west and the east becomes critically important given the fact that:

> Challenges to air transport liberalization persist in many parts of the world where rigid bilateral air transport agreements and regulations take centre stage and hinder the prospect of economic development. The wider economic benefit is realized through increased connectivity between cities and the flow of people, which has enabled the proliferation of markets for goods, services, capital and technology. According to the International Air Transport Association (IATA), the number of unique city-pair connections by air will double in 2016 from what it was twenty years' prior, reaching more than 17,000.[63]

It is for this reason that the primary use of this book, it is hoped, is to generate a serious interest in the aviation community of the need to study rulemaking in air transport from a research orientation. As already mentioned, The Chicago Convention gives the Council of ICAO ample flexibility to study this issue, particularly as an adjunct to States responses to the Standards contained in the Annexes by sending out a questionnaire to all its member States to submit to the ICAO Secretariat a compendium of their regulations pertaining to air navigation and air transport. Such a compendium could be analysed and critical areas identified and defined which in turn could be the subject of consideration both by the Council and the ICAO Assembly which could influence States to incorporate ICAO policy, whether it comes from the Annexes or other policy material.

[63] 2015 *ACI Airport Economics Report*, at 25.

References

Abeyratne R (2007) Emissions trading- recommendations of CAEP/7 and the European perspective. Air Space Law XXXII(4–5):358–375
Abeyratne R (2008) The authority of the European Union to unilaterally impose an emissions trading scheme. Air Space Law 21(4):5–9
Abeyratne R (2011) The beijing convention of 2010: an important milestone in the annals of aviation security. Air Space Law 36(3):243–255
Abeyratne R (2014) A protocol to amend the Tokyo convention of 1963: some unanswered questions. Air Space Law 39(1):47–58
Brownlie I (1990) Principles of public international law, 4th ed. Clarendon Press, Oxford, p 691
Calleja D (2008) Striving toward meaningful solutions, an interview. ICAO J 04:14–15
Charney JI (1978) United States interest in a convention on the law on the sea: the case for continued efforts. Vand J Transnatl Law 11:39–43
Chiti E (2013) European agencies' rulemaking: powers, procedures and assessment. Eur Law J 19 (1):93–110
Diver C (1989) Dean of Pennsylvania law school. In: Hawking K, Thompson J (eds) Making regulatory policy. Oxford University Press, Oxford, p 199
Frequently asked questions: the special commission on orthodox participation in the world council of churches. Ecum Rev (2003) 55(1):42
Kerwin CM (1994) Rule making - how government agencies write law and make policy. CQ Press, Washington, p 6
Lubbers JS (2006) A guide to federal agency rulemaking, vol. 296, 4 edn. Florida Power & Light
Matthias Ruffert J. The Many Faces of Rulemaking in the EU, http://ssrn.com/abstract=2592092
Sarooshi D (2005) International organizations and their exercise of sovereign powers. Oxford University Press, p 110
Schenkman J (1955) International civil aviation organization. Librairie E. Droz, Geneve, p 87
Shaw MN (2003) International law, 5th edn. Cambridge University Press, p 110
Tammes AJP (1958) Decisions of international organs as a source of international law. Recueil 94:265
Verheyen W (2015) 10 Years of 261/2004: any excuses left? Eur Transp Law 6:659–677
von Bogdandy A, Dann P, Goldmann M (2010) Developing the publicness of public international law: towards a legal framework for global governance activities. In: von Bogdandy A, Wolfrum R, von Bernstorff J, Dann P, Goldmann M (eds), The exercise of public authority by International Institutions. Oxford University Press, Oxford, p 3
Zoller E (1987) The corporate will of the United Nations and the rights of the minority contributors. Am J Int Law 81(3):32

Chapter 5
Judicial Review of Rulemaking and Administrative Action

5.1 The Aviation Perspective

Rules often represent delegated authority stemming from a higher source such as a treaty provision that has been incorporated into domestic legislation and empowers a high executive such as a minister to make rules accordingly. A rule can bestow a right to prescribe a requirement, such as the prerogative of the Federal Aviation Administration (FAA) in the case of *Tseng* v. *El Al Israel Airlines Ltd*[1] where the United States Court of Appeal, Second Circuit, held that every air carrier in the United States was required by FAA regulations to have in place security procedures to prevent terrorist attacks and to deny transport to anyone who does not consent to be searched upon request. In the case of *Sturgeon* v. *Frost, Alaska Regional Director of the National Park Service, et al.*[2] concerning the application of a regulation relating to hovercraft operated in a national park in the United States the courts interpreted the regulation which said "If the State, a Native Corporation, or other owner desires to convey any such lands, the Secretary may acquire such lands in accordance with applicable law (including this Act), and any such lands shall become part of the unit, and be administered accordingly" to apply to all federal lands and waters administered by the Park.

Going back to Europe, the well cited *Sturgeon* case,[3] where the Fourth Chamber of the European Court of Justice determined in 2009 the scope of application of Regulation (EC) No 261/2004—Article 2(l) and Articles 5, 6 and 7 on the concept of flight 'delay' and 'cancellation', the court was charged with ascertaining and

[1]Nos. 331, 857, Dockets 96-7447, 96-7619, decided: June 13, 1997. See http://caselaw.findlaw.com/us-2nd-circuit/1054892.html.

[2]No. 14–1209. Argued January 20, 2016—Decided March 22, 2016.

[3]*Christopher Sturgeon, Gabriel Sturgeon and Alana Sturgeon* v *Condor Flugdienst GmbH* (C-402/07) and *Stefan Böck and Cornelia Lepuschitz* v *Air France SA* (C-432/07). See ECLI:EU:C:2009:716.

R. Abeyratne, *Rulemaking in Air Transport*, DOI 10.1007/978-3-319-44657-8_5

determining whether a flight delay must be regarded as a flight cancellation for the purposes of Articles 2(l) and 5 of Regulation No 261/2004 where the delay is long; whether Articles 5, 6 and 7 of Regulation No 261/2004 must be interpreted as meaning that passengers whose flights are delayed may, for the purpose of the application of the right to compensation laid down in Article 7 of that regulation, be treated as passengers whose flights are cancelled, and whether a technical problem in an aircraft is covered by the concept of 'extraordinary circumstances' within the meaning of Article 5(3) of Regulation No 261/2004. The court held that according to a general principle of interpretation, a Community act must be interpreted, as far as possible, in such a way as not to affect its validity. Likewise, where a provision of Community law is open to several interpretations. Furthermore, it was the decision of the Court that preference must be given to that interpretation which ensures that the provision retains its effectiveness.

In that regard, the Court held that all Community acts must be interpreted in accordance with primary law as a whole, including the principle of equal treatment, which requires that comparable situations must not be treated differently and that different situations must not be treated in the same way unless such treatment is objectively justified.

The Court concluded that in view of the objective of Regulation No 261/2004, which was to strengthen protection for air passengers by redressing damage suffered by them during air travel, situations covered by the regulation must be compared, in particular by reference to the type and extent of the various types of inconvenience and damage suffered by the passengers concerned and that in the instance at hand, the situation of passengers whose flights are delayed should be compared with that of passengers whose flights are cancelled.

To take this issue further, in the 2013 case of *McDonagh* v. *Ryanair Limited*[4] where the plaintiff was a passenger on a Ryanair flight and was delayed in carriage for several days due to the closure of European airspace as a result of the Icelandic volcano *Eyjafjallajökul* of 2010, the plaintiff averred that Ryanair had, blatantly ignored Article 5 of Regulation 261/2004 and not looked after her during her forced layover. Article 5 of Regulation No 261/2004, headed 'Cancellation', states that in case of cancellation of a flight, the passengers concerned will be offered assistance by the operating air carrier and be offered assistance by the operating air carrier, as well as, in event of re-routing when the reasonably expected time of departure of the new flight is at least the day after the departure as it was planned for the cancelled flight, the assistance according to other relevant provisions of the Regulation. Furthermore Regulation 261/2004 stipulates that a stranded passenger will have the right to compensation by the operating air carrier unless she is informed of the cancellation at least 2 weeks before the scheduled time of departure; or she is informed of the cancellation between 2 weeks and 7 days before the scheduled time

[4]REQUEST for a preliminary ruling under Article 267 TFEU from the Dublin Metropolitan District Court (Ireland), made by decision of 10 November 2010, received at the Court on 10 January 2011, in the proceedings.

of departure and is offered re-routing, allowing them to depart no more than 2 h before the scheduled time of departure and to reach her final destination less than 4 h after the scheduled time of arrival; or she is informed of the cancellation less than 7 days before the scheduled time of departure and is offered re-routing, allowing her to depart no more than 1 h before the scheduled time of departure and to reach her final destination less than 2 h after the scheduled time of arrival.

Ryanair claimed the exception in the Regulation that exempts the carrier of the above responsibilities under extraordinary circumstances, claiming that the Icelandic volcano did not constitute extraordinary circumstances (which still obligated the carrier to provide necessary care) but constituted "super" extraordinary circumstances which totally exempted the carrier from any responsibility in that regard. The court held that in accordance with everyday language, the words 'extraordinary circumstances' literally refer to circumstances which are 'out of the ordinary'. It was the view of the court that in the context of air transport, they refer to an event which is not inherent in the normal exercise of the activity of the carrier concerned and is beyond the actual control of that carrier on account of its nature or origin. In other words, that they related to all circumstances which are beyond the control of the air carrier, whatever the nature of those circumstances or their gravity.

The Court found justification in the fact that Regulation No 261/2004 contained nothing that would allow the conclusion to be drawn that it recognises a separate category of 'particularly extraordinary' events, beyond 'extraordinary circumstances' referred to in Article 5(3) of that regulation, which would lead to the air carrier being exempted from all its obligations, including those under Article 9 of the regulation.

Next, the court opined that as for the context of and the aims pursued by Article 5 of Regulation No 261/2004, which prescribes the obligations of an air carrier in the event of cancellation of a flight, it must be noted, first, that when exceptional circumstances arise, Article 5(3) exempts the air carrier only from its obligation to pay compensation under Article 7 of that regulation. The approach of the European legislature in adopting the regulation placed, in the eyes of the Court the obligation on the air carrier to provide care under the regulation as a necessary element whatever the event which has given rise to the cancellation of the flight. Second, it was clear to the Court that the regulation aimed at ensuring a high level of protection for passengers and takes account of the requirements of consumer protection in general, inasmuch as cancellation of flights causes serious inconvenience to passengers.

The court went on to say that if circumstances such as those at issue in the main proceedings went beyond the scope of 'extraordinary circumstances' within the meaning of Regulation No 261/2004 due in particular to their origin and scale, such an interpretation would go against not only the meaning of that notion in everyday language but also the objectives of that regulation. Such an interpretation would in fact mean that air carriers would be required to provide care pursuant to Article 9 of Regulation No 261/2004 to air passengers who find themselves, due to cancellation of a flight, in a situation causing limited inconvenience, whereas passengers, such as the plaintiff in the main proceedings, who find themselves in a particularly vulnerable state in that they are forced to remain at an airport for several days would be denied that care.

In the light of the foregoing, the Court was convinced that the answer is that Article 5 of Regulation No 261/2004 must be interpreted as meaning that circumstances such as the closure of part of European airspace as a result of the eruption of the *Eyjafjallajökull* volcano constitute 'extraordinary circumstances' within the meaning of that regulation which do not release air carriers from their obligation laid down in Articles 5(1)(b) and 9 of the regulation to provide care.

This gives rise to the now entrenched European position that the notion of extraordinary circumstances must be interpreted strictly when Regulation 261/2004, as clarified by the 2008 decision in *Friederike Wallentin-Hermann* v. *Alitalia*[5] where the ECJ held that political instability or meteorological conditions incompatible with the operation of the flight are relevant only if they create an unexpected risk, but are not directly an exemption. As an example, a technical problem in an aircraft should be considered "extraordinary" only if it is the result of an event that is not normal to the activity of the aircraft.

In Air France v. Folkers[6]—a case with circumstances to those of *Sturgeon,* the court held that since [the relevant] inconvenience materializes, with regard to delayed flights, on arrival at the final destination, a delay must be assessed, for the purposes of the compensation provided for in Article 7 of Regulation No 261/2004, in relation to the "scheduled arrival time at that destination".

In April 2004 The International Air Transport Association (IATA) filed an application for judicial review at the UK High Court to challenge Regulation 261/2004 on the ground that the Regulation seriously endangered the interests of the consumer and that airlines, although acknowledging that they should compensate passengers for denied boarding, they cannot be expected to pay compensation for areas beyond their control. IATA claimed *inter alia* that delays or cancellations due to inclement weather, air traffic control strikes or government security requirements are not within airline control, yet the new ruling penalizes the airline for all situations equally. *A fortiori,* IATA claimed:

> The EU is a signatory to the Montreal Convention which limits a carrier's liability for delays and cancellations in extraordinary circumstances like inclement weather. How can airlines run a business when the regulator gives us two conflicting guidelines? The wisdom of the internationally agreed Montreal convention should form the basis of the EU's thinking as the accepted global standard.[7]

The formal European view[8] distinguishes between Regulation 261/2004 and the Montreal Convention with regard to the argument that in the face of an international treaty which many States' members of the European Union have ratified, the

[5]ECJ in case C-549/07.

[6]Case C-11/11, see http://eutopialaw.com/2013/03/18/sturgeon-revisited-yet-again-case-c-1111-air-france-v-folkerts/.

[7]http://www.iata.org/pressroom/pr/Pages/2004-04-21-01.aspx.

[8]See http://blogs.law.nyu.edu/transnational/2011/10/the-capacity-of-the-court-of-justice-of-the-european-union-to-promote-homogeneous-application-of-uniform-laws-the-case-for-air-carrier-liability-for-flight-delays-and-cancellations/.

Regulation is destitute of effect in terms of its compensatory quantifications. Although the EU accepts that there are two uniform laws in the EU regarding air carrier liability whose interpretation falls to the ECJ—*i.e.* Regulation (EC) No 261/2004 and the Montreal Convention, which forms part of EU Law, by Council Decision 2001/539/EC of 5 April 2001 the two instruments should not give rise to a dichotomy that ascribes ambivalence and confusion to the issue. The European opinion is that the Montreal Convention is exclusively concerned with delays, whereas Regulation 261/2004 does not create any compensation rights in cases of flight delays, but is applicable only to cases of denial of boarding as referred to in Article 4, and cancellation of flights as addressed in Article 5 which in turn creates a compensable right of a lump sum payment for an amount determined under Article 7. On the other hand, it is contended that the Montreal Convention sets in Article 19 its applicability in cases of flight delays, with a liability cap of SDR 4150 as stated in Article 22.

In support of this argument the European submission cites the decision in the *Sturgeon* case as its *cursus curiae*. It goes on to say that there is a delay in the case where none of the elements of the trip but the times of departure and arrival are altered. If the number of the flights changes or new boarding passes are issued, we therefore face a cancellation.

5.2 Treaty v. Regulation

The above discussion brings to bear the curious judicial anomaly that exists in the European Union between treaty and rule. At the apex of the issue is the fact that while the European Union is a membership of States and as such cannot be part of a multilateral international treaty as can individual States, yet the Union promulgates rules of adherence to its member States. The rulings of the European Court of Justice in the context of Regulation 261/2004 illustrates the point that while the Court interpreted both the provisions of the Montreal Convention as well as the Regulation, it did not take into consideration the exclusionary nature of that international treaty when it is considered with domestic legislation. The principle that, although EU member states have exclusive competence to negotiate and ratify international treaties, and the Union is precluded from such practice, the member States cannot enter into any treaty that dispends a lack of harmonization within the EU and that in such an instance the Union can adopt a law that binds all States and obviates such disharmony, which then will take precedence over such individual acts of treaty making, was established in 1971.[9]

[9]*Commission of the European Communities* v. *Council of the European Communities*, Case 22-70, [1971] ECR 263. There could be what are called "mixed agreements" where both the EU and member States are in consonance over treaties, and in such instances The European Court of Justice has jurisdiction to interpret such treaties to make sure that provisions therein ensure harmony throughout the Union in terms of their implementation.

In the context of the situation discussed above, one could certainly ask the question as to what the legal position of a member State of the Union would be when it is faced with Article 27 of The Vienna Convention on the Law of Treaties which stipulates that a Party to the treaty may not invoke a domestic rule or law to offer justification for non-compliance with a treaty. This principle, coupled with the exclusivity principle of the Montreal Convention of 1999 which establishes that, where the relevant convention applies, the remedies available to the passenger are those exclusively under that convention, arguably makes confusion worse confounded.[10]

It is appropriate to cite the decision handed down by The United Kingdom Supreme Court in *Stott* v *Thomas Cook Tour Operators Limited*[11] in which the court held that plaintiff Mr. Stott was unable to recover damages against the carrier for humiliation and discomfort pursuant to the UK Disability Regulations 2007, because those damages were precluded by the Montreal Convention, which would apply to his carriage by air.

The compatibility of Regulation 261/2004 with the Montreal Convention becomes relevant in the discussion of the position of treaty v. regulation. The conjoining of the EU and its member States in accepting the legal legitimacy and applicability of the treaty makes it a mixed agreement.[12] Apart from Regulation 261/2004 there is Regulation 2027/97 which applies to compensation for death or injury to passengers. This regulation, in its preamble refers to the Warsaw regime (The Montreal Convention was in its incipient stage of development in October 1997 when the Regulation was promulgated) and sets down the purpose of the Regulation to be to lay down the obligations of Community air carriers in relation to liability in the event of accidents to passengers for damage sustained in the event of death or wounding of a passenger or any other bodily injury suffered by a passenger, if the accident which caused the damage so sustained took place on board an aircraft or in the course of any of the operations of embarking or disembarking. Both these regulations establish a clear link between them and treaty law.

Article 29 of the Montreal Convention is unequivocal in that it stipulates that in the carriage of passengers, baggage and cargo, any action for damages, however founded, whether under the Convention or in contract or in tort or otherwise, can only be brought subject to the conditions and such limits of liability as are set out in the Convention without prejudice to the question as to who are the persons who have the right to bring suit and what are their respective rights. In any such action, punitive, exemplary or any other non-compensatory damages are not recoverable.

---

[10]See *Cousins* v *Nimvale Pty Ltd* [2013] WADC 175, where the District Court of western Australia held that, in the case of the parents of two deceased passengers, they had a right to seek dependency loss under Australian legislation, which gives effect to the relevant Treaty. However their claims for damages for nervous shock fell outside the scope of the legislation (and treaty), and in such a context, the parents had the right to separately claim against the carrier for their nervous shock under common law negligence or any other relevant statute.

[11][2014] UKSC 15.

[12]*Supra*, note 9.

In the 1997 case of *Sidhu* v. *British Airways*[13] the decision of Lord Hope comes out very clear that the exclusivity principle enunciated in Article 1(1) of the Warsaw Convention, that it applied to all international carriage, clearly underscored the fact that the word "all" effectively precluded any possibility of supremacy of domestic law over the treaty in the context of application of principles of liability in air transport. In the current context, similarly, Article 1 of the Montreal Convention stipulates that the Convention applies to "all" international carriage of persons, baggage or cargo performed by aircraft for reward. It applies equally to gratuitous carriage by aircraft performed by an air transport undertaking.

Across the pond, the Tseng case in the United States established the same judicial principal that a plaintiff cannot invoke local laws in a situation covered by the Warsaw Convention.[14] Next door, in Canada, the Supreme Court in 2014 held in *Thibodeou* v. *Air Canada*[15] the Montreal Convention prevails over any local laws or rules within the area of its competence and application in the context of specific provisions the treaty contains.

A contrary approach can be seen in the European decision in *More* v. *KLM*[16] which concerned a flight cancellation where it was held that the principle contained in Regulation 261/2004 took precedence over both the Warsaw Convention (Article 29) and Montreal Convention (Article 35) in the context of their delay-compensation principles that governed time limits for bringing an action for delay. which were irrelevant in the face of the Regulation. The More case followed an earlier European decision—*Bogiatzi*[17]—which held that, since the European Union was not a party to either Convention (although certain European Union member States were), those treaties could not be considered as applicable legal instruments, particularly in the face of a European regulation on the subject. In a more recent (2014) case the distinction was made clearer. In *Dawson* v. *Thomson Airways Ltd.*,[18] where the plaintiff sought compensation for a delay incurring 6 h, which clearly was addressed by Rule 261/2004, the court ruled that the 2-year limitation period prescribed under Article 35 of the Montreal Convention was subservient at best to the Regulation's provision on the subject.

This dichotomy between North American approaches—between the American and Canadian perspectives on the one hand, and the European approach on the other—seemingly brings to bear the clash between legal instruments embraced through State sovereignty in Europe and regulations adopted by the political union (EU) which have taken precedence over the former. A logical and sensible compromise seems to have been reached by the court in *Axel Walz* v. *Clickair SA*[19]

[13][1997] 2 Lloyd's Rep 76.

[14]*El Al Israel Airlines Ltd.*, v. *Tseng*, (1999) 525 U.S. 155.

[15]2014 SCC 67.

[16]Case C-139/11 [2012].

[17]Case C- 301/08 [2009].

[18][2014] EWCA Civ 845.

[19]Case C-63/09 [2010].

which held that any interpretation ascribed to an applicable principle under the applicable European regulation on the one hand and international treaty on the other should be uniform and autonomous, irrespective of differences of terminology contained in local laws of a State (as represented by EU regulations) and international treaty provisions. The *Walz* case involved the determination of damage for the loss of baggage, which had to be determined under both regimes, where the word "damage" does not appear in Article 22(2) of the Montreal Convention which applies to baggage. Although this compromise seems rational, there is still no explanation as why to why the court had to seek a preference, as the Montreal Convention is the legal instrument that should have been applied in this instance. In a contemporaneous case[20] concerning damage to baggage, the court was compelled to examine in detail the relevant provisions of the Montreal Convention on the basis that the Montreal Convention was an integral part of European law.

It would seem that, at the core of the issue of treaty v. regulation lies the concept of State sovereignty. While on the one hand Article 27 of the Vienna Convention on the Law of Treaties explicitly says that domestic laws cannot be cited to overrule provisions of a treaty that has been ratified by a State, on the other hand lies the sacrosanct principle of State sovereignty and the legal legitimacy of a sovereign member of the European Union which ratifies an international treaty that is later considered irrelevant or subservient to a regulation of the Union. A briefing paper on *The Nation, State Sovereignty and the European Union*—Nine Democratic Principles was prepared for distribution at the Annual General Meeting of The European Alliance of EU-Critical Movements(TEAM) in Prague, Czech Republic, 9–10 March 2016 avers that the Europeans are "internationalists on the basis of our solidarity as members of the human race. As internationalists we seek the emancipation of mankind. The human race is divided into nations. Therefore we stand for the self-determination of nations. The right of nations to self-determination was first proclaimed in 1789 in the Declaration of the Rights of Man of the French Revolution. It is now a basic principle of international law, enshrined in the United Nations Charter. As democrats and internationalists we assert the right of those nations that wish it to have their independence, sovereignty and a Nation State of their own, so that they may relate to one another internationally on the basis of equal rights with other nations. The democratic principle of internationalism does not mean that we are called upon to urge people of other nations to assert their right to self-determination; but that we respect their wishes and show solidarity with them if they decide to do that. It is as true of the life of nations as of individuals that separation, mutual recognition of boundaries, and mutual respect—i.e. political equality, neither dominance nor submission—are the pre-requisite of free and friendly cooperation, of internationalism in other words. . ." However, the statement goes on to say: Nations exist as communities before nationalisms and Nation States. To analyse nations and the national question in terms of "nationalisms" is philosophical idealism, looking at the mental reflection rather than the thing it reflects.

[20]*Aurora Souza Rodriguez* v. *Air France SA*, Case C-83/10 [2011].

Nations evolve historically as stable, long-lasting communities of people, sharing a common language and territory, and the common culture and history that arise from that. On this basis develop the solidarities, mutual interests and mutual identification that distinguish a people from its neighbours. Some nations are ancient, some young, some in process of being formed. Like all human groups—for example the family, clan, tribe—they are fuzzy at the edges. No neat definition will encompass all cases. The empirical test is to ask people themselves. If they have passed beyond the stage of kinship society where the political unit is the clan or tribe, people will invariably know what nation they belong to. That is the political and democratic test too. If enough people in a nation wish to establish their own independent State, they should have it. For democracy can exist normally only at the level of the national community and the Nation State. The reason is that it is within the national community alone that there exists sufficient solidarity, mutual identification and mutuality of interest among people as to induce minorities freely to consent to majority rule and obey a common government based upon that. Such solidarity is the basis of shared citizenship".

The most revealing statement comes in the 6th principle which says that "insistence on the sovereignty of one's own State is a natural right as well as a social duty. It is in no way an expression of misguided national egotism. Sovereignty has nothing to do with autarchy or economic self-sufficiency. The national sovereignty of a democratic State is analogous to the freedom and autonomy of the individual. It means that one's domestic laws and foreign relations are exclusively decided by one's own parliament and government, which are elected by and responsible to one's own people. State sovereignty is a result of advancing political culture and is an achievement of modern democracy. It is not an end in itself but is an instrument of juridical independence...".

Although this declaration may not be a binding legal document in the European Union, it clearly sets out the principle of sovereignty of a State, according to which actions taken and international laws ratified by a member State should arguably take precedence over regional regulations.

5.3 ICAO as a Generic Example

In the air transport context, a glaring example would be the setting of aeronautical charges. In this context, one has to go to the root or fundamental basis of policy which consensually emanates from ICAO. A court in determining whether a rule or practice is reasonable as imposed by a charging authority would delve into policy emanating from ICAO. A Conference of ICAO on the Economics of Airports and Air Navigation Services (CEANS), which was held in Montreal on 15–20 September 2008, agreed to submit to the Council of ICAO crucial recommendations for international civil aviation, which will take cooperation between the air transport, airport, and air navigation service industries to a higher level and increase the efficiency and cost effectiveness in the provision and operation of airports and air navigation services around the world. These recommendations are calculated to serve the aviation industry expeditiously in coping with the current challenges that air transport faces.

On the basis that the cost basis of an airport for charging purposes has usually been established by taking into account the costs of operation and maintenance, cost of capital and depreciation of assets (based on historical value in most cases), and a 'reasonable' return on assets, CEANS approached the issue by attempting to build a consensus on possible ways to assess what would constitute a 'reasonable' rate of return and explore the possibility of consolidating several airport cost bases into one cost base for charging purposes.

On differential charges, CEANS recommended that, within their economic oversight responsibilities, States should, where necessary, assess the positive and negative effects associated with specific c forms of differential charges applied by airports on a case-by case basis according to national circumstances. Furthermore, States were called upon to ensure that differential charges are offered on a non-discriminatory basis; that they are transparent in terms of their creation, purpose, and the criteria on which they are offered; that, without prejudice to modulated charging schemes, costs associated with differential charges are not allocated, either directly or indirectly, to those other users not benefit ting from them; and that, if the purpose is to attract and/or retain new air services, they are offered only on a temporary basis. ICAO was called upon to amend Doc. 9082 to reflect the principles of transparency and time limitation for start-up aids in the application of differential charges.

It was the view of CEANS that the recommendations will make ICAO's policies on charges, which regulate the relationship between airports and air navigation services providers (ANSPs) on the one hand, and airlines and other airport and airspace users on the other, more authoritative in practice. The enhanced cooperation suggested by these recommendations would strengthen policies on States' economic oversight responsibility, requirements on implementation of performance management systems by all airports and ANSPs, and the establishment of a clearly defined, regular consultation process by all airports and ANSPs. At the same time, they recommend that States enshrine the main principles of non-discrimination, cost relatedness, transparency, and consultation with users in their national legislation, regulations, or policies as well as all air services agreements between States.

One of the fundamental premises addressed by CEANS is that the protection of users against the potential abuse of dominant position by airports and ANSPs is the primary responsibility of the State and could be discharged by the exercise of economic oversight. It was suggested during the discussions that such oversight could be effectively carried out by diligent monitoring by a State of the commercial and operational practices of these service providers.

There was discussion during CEANS where some delegations suggested that, in order to 'give teeth' to ICAO policy, there should be a recommendation in Doc. 9082 to the effect that amendment to Doc. 9082 should be incorporated by States in their national legislation. It is submitted that such a measure would be tantamount to treading uncharted and dangerous ground. While it is one thing to assert that the only way that ICAO policies could be implemented is for States to opt for incorporating such principles in their legislation, it is something quite different to recommend that States go ahead and do so.

As a necessary compromise and in order to reach a balance, the Conference broadly recognizes the need for economic oversight in the increasingly commercialized and privatized environment for airports and air navigation services. It considered a number of suggestions that were made by the delegates for improving the proposed new text for Doc. 9082. The following conclusions were reached by the Conference:

1. States should bear in mind that economic oversight is the responsibility of States with the objectives, inter alia, to prevent the risk that a service provider could abuse its dominant position, to ensure non-discrimination and transparency in the application of charges, to encourage consultation with users, to ensure the development of appropriate performance management systems, and to ascertain that capacity meets current and future demand, in balance with the efforts of the autonomous/private entities to obtain the optimal effects of commercialization or privatization;
2. States should select the appropriate form of economic oversight according to their specific circumstances, while keeping regulatory interventions at a minimum and as required. When deciding an appropriate form of economic oversight, the degree of competition, the costs and benefits related to alternative oversight forms, as well as the legal, institutional, and governance frameworks should be taken into consideration;
3. States should consider adoption of a regional approach to economic oversight where individual States lack the capacity to adequately perform economic oversight functions;
4. ICAO should amend Doc. 9082 to clarify the purpose and scope of economic oversight for airports and air navigation services with reference to its different forms and the selection of the most appropriate form of oversight.

5.4 Judicial Review of Commissions and Agencies

The European view acknowledges that prior to the *Sturgeon* case, the Montreal Convention was the right instrument to obtain compensation in case of flight delays, and the Regulation was the right instrument to obtain compensation in case of flight cancellations or denials of boarding. Now, both norms are in conflict.

Judicial review of rulemaking is grounded on the administrative action taken in pursuance of implementing a rule. Roscoe Pound, Dean of Harvard Law said in 1920 that genius of administrative action through commissions endangers the doctrine of the supremacy of law. Commissions established for purposes of administering rules poses one of the dangers of impairing the effectiveness of administrative law. In his recently published book "Is Administrative Law Unlawful?[21]"

[21]Hamburger (2013), p. 77.

Philip Hamburger, a professor of law at Columbia University posits that the centralization of power which deviates from a popular mandate or judicial scrutiny leads to a certain insularity brought upon by bureaucratic ineptitude. It is hard to disagree with this premise as the centralization of power would in turn lead to creative inertia and the causal illusion that, in a so called democracy, the system runs smoothly and justly. Often, this centralization of power leads to an erosion of the fundamental implementation of the process of administrative law which is enactment (by the legislature); execution (by the executive) and adjudication (by the courts).

The creation of commissions more often than not vests power in inept and inefficient entities comprised of political appointees with partisan views and vested personal interests. The process suffocates democracy and the rule of law, making sycophants of the executive and the judiciary. It is interesting to inquire how this blatant subterfuge and disingenuous practice can erode the foundations of administrative law.

P.P. Craig, in his book "Administrative Law"[22] states: "The legislature and courts will both be of importance in determining the shape of administrative law. It should never be forgotten that it is the legislature which enacts the policies which are directly constitutive of the administrative state. It will be the legislature which chooses whether these policies should be imbued with, for example, a market oriented neo liberal philosophy or one which is more social democratic in its orientation. In this sense, the shape and nature of administrative law will be profoundly affected by the philosophy which underlies government policy. The courts also have a major influence on the nature of the subject. They will decide what particular constraints to impose on administrative action, and more generally on the overall purpose of judicial review. Administrative law, when viewed this way, is always a combination of what is going on in the political world, combined with the reactions of the judiciary.

What commissions do, as Dean Pound said in 1920, is eliminate the supremacy of the law. In fact, eliminate the law in its totality, giving power to the executive (or executive president as the case may be) to do as she pleases, whether to sack a president and CEO of a company owned by the government, or dispense with a high government official, without giving that person recourse to the law.

At common law which is applicable in England, there lies a remedy in judicial intervention if a government department promulgates advice in a public document that contained directions or advice erroneous in law. In such an instance, as was pronounced by Lord Bridge, in the 1986 *Gillick case*,[23] although in general such non-statutory advice cannot be questioned by judicial review, the exception to this

---

[22]Craig (2003), p. 32.

[23]*Gillick* v *West Norfolk and Wisbech Area Health Authority and another*, [1986] 1 AC 112, [1985] 3 All ER 402.

general rule lay in instances where such advice was inconsistent with the law, where the courts could intervene. The judiciary could also interpret the meaning of codes, circulars and other similar documents, and review the interpretation of such documents by any government entity. There is also the issue of legitimate expectation of the victim of an administrative decision, towards such a decision being consistent with applicable law, and the courts can go into whether such expectation was obviated or eroded.

The courts could also inquire as to whether a decision had relevancy, purpose, reasonableness and was not taken as a result of or corollary to an abuse of discretion. Historically, common law courts have reviewed and exerted control over discretion exercised by public bodies, tribunals and agencies with a view to preventing misuse or abuse of discretion.

The Standing Committee for the Scrutiny of Regulations of Canada has stated:

> When Parliament confers a power to make regulations, the regulation-maker usually exercises this power by drafting the text of the regulation to be enacted. The regulation-maker may also decide that the contents of an existing document are what should be used in the regulation it intends to enact. One way to make the contents of such a document part of the text of the regulation would be to reproduce it word for word in the regulation. Alternatively, the regulation-maker can simply refer to the title of the document in the regulation. The contents of the document will then be said to be "incorporated by reference". The legal effect of incorporation by reference is to write the words of the incorporated document into the regulation just as if it had actually been reproduced word for word. The incorporation by reference of an existing document is no more than a drafting technique, and a regulation-maker need not be granted any specific power in order to resort to this technique. This is referred to as "closed" or "static" incorporation by reference.[24]

Local regulations should not be fettered by extra territorial application of regulations in another country or jurisdiction. In 1964 The New Brunswick Court of Appeal unanimously held that an order of the Board of Commissioners of Public Utilities directing that water rates should be lowered to be equivalent to the rates charged in Maine should the latter be lower than the rates fixed by the Board was ultra vires.[25] The rationale of this determination was that the order purported to delegate to an administrative tribunal in a foreign country the duty of determining rates in New Brunswick which duty, by the Public Utilities Act, is conferred on the Board. Earlier, in 1982 in Quebec, The Superior Court ruled that a municipal by-law referentially incorporating the National Building Code as amended from time to time constituted an unlawful delegation of authority.[26]

The Statutory Instruments Act of 1946 of The United Kingdom provides:

[24]http://www.parl.gc.ca/HousePublications/Publication.aspx?DocId=3204106&Ses=2.

[25]*R.* v. *Board of Commissioners of Public Utilities* (1964), 51 M.P.R. 4.

[26]*Investissements St-Germain et al* v. *Cité de Rimouski* (1982), 22 M.P.L.R. 121. See also: *R.* v. *Ciarniello* (1979), 12 B.C.L.R. 394 (Prov. Ct.); *Mathurin* v. *Lee Coffrages Dominic Ltée.*, [1982] T.T. 261, reversed [1983] C.S. 143 (Que. S.C.).

> Where by this Act or any Act passed after the commencement of this Act power to make, confirm or approve orders, rules, regulations or other subordinate legislation is conferred on His Majesty in Council or on any Minister of the Crown then, if the power is expressed:

(a) in the case of a power conferred on His Majesty, to be exercisable by Order in Council;
(b) in the case of a power conferred on a Minister of the Crown, to be exercisable by statutory instrument, any document by which that power is exercised shall be known as a "statutory instrument" and the provisions of this Act shall apply thereto accordingly.[27]

The Act envisions two different instances: All Orders in Council made pursuant to a Statutory authority or power must be exercised by statutory instruments. Other rules and regulations must be exercised by statutory instruments only when explicitly prescribed for such process.

It must be understood that an administrative agency or commission of inquiry that is empowered to act in accordance with a rule or statutory instrument is neither a tribunal nor a court. It is not a judicial body. Administrative agencies perform the functions of rulemaking, adjudication, and investigation.

Rulemaking is the process by which an administrative agency creates rules that have the force of law through the rulemaking process. These rulemaking agencies' have authority to make rules only to the extent delegated by the legislature and as such do not have unfettered authority. Laws are enacted by the legislature along the lines of policy adopted by government and allows an administrative agency to adopt rules to implement the law enacted. The force of law is ascribed to an agency only when it accords with government policy. When judicial powers are vested on an agency it is called adjudication. A legislative body could delegate judicial powers to the agency.

There are numerous instances where in the United States, federal agencies are statutorily permitted to make policy by either adjudication or rulemaking. Lines are somewhat blurred as to how this happens and based on what principles that agencies must use one procedure rather than the other, as courts have traditionally refused to specify situations in which an agency must use rulemaking or adjudication.

In 1981 the Ninth Circuit Court of Appeals established guidelines for when rulemaking alone must be used.[28] The case concerned an appeal from a prior Federal Trade Commission finding that an automobile dealer, Francis Ford, Inc., had violated section 5 of the Federal Trade Commission (FTC) Act 4 by failing to refund to defaulting consumers' surpluses gained upon resale of repossessed cars. Although important substantive questions were at issue on appeal, 6 the court refused to reach the merits of the case and dismissed it on procedural grounds, ruling that the agency had abused its discretion by relying on adjudication. Such an

[27]Statutory Instruments Act 1946, 1946 CHAPTER 36 9 and 10 Geo 6, 26 March 1946. See http://www.legislation.gov.uk/ukpga/Geo6/9-10/36.

[28]See *Ford Motor Co.* v. *FTC*, 673 F.2d 1008 (9th Cir. 1981), cert. denied, 103 S. Ct. 358 (1982).

abuse occurs, the Ford court held, when an agency uses adjudication to change existing law and to establish rules of widespread application.

Courts generally give substantial deference to the interpretation an agency gives to a statute that the agency is charged with enforcing.[29] Even though the judiciary is not bound by an agency determination, the Appellate Division in the *R&R case* stated that it would not upset a decision unless it was arbitrary, unreasonable or in violation of legislative policies.[30] Furthermore, courts have established that, in exceptional cases, an agency may choose to formulate and enforce a general requirement through a decision in a particular case. An agency may do this when using the rulemaking procedure would frustrate the effective accomplishment of the agency's functions. Adjudicative rulemaking may be appropriate, for example, when the agency is construing a new rule or when a dispute deals with a problem that requires ad hoc resolution because the issue cannot be captured within the bounds of a general rule.[31]

The determination or implementation of a rule by an administrative agency must be considered an administrative rule when all or most of the relevant features of administrative rules are present and preponderate in favor of the rule-making process.[32] Such a conclusion would be warranted if it appears that the agency determination, in many or most of the following circumstances, (1) is intended to have wide coverage encompassing a large segment of the regulated or general public, rather than an individual or a narrow select group; (2) is intended to be applied generally and uniformly to all similarly situated persons; (3) is designed to operate only in future cases, that is, prospectively; (4) prescribes a legal standard or directive that is not otherwise expressly provided by or clearly and obviously inferable from the enabling statutory authorization; (5) reflects an administrative policy that (a) was not previously expressed in any official and explicit agency determination, adjudication or rule, or (b) constitutes a material and significant change from a clear, past agency position on the identical subject matter; and (6) reflects a decision on administrative regulatory policy in the nature of the interpretation of law or general policy. These relevant factors can, either singly or in combination, determine in a given case whether the essential agency action must be rendered through rule-making or adjudication.

In *ASG Industries, Inc.*, v. *United States of America and Interstate Commerce Commission*[33] The court held that decisions of an administrative agency could not be disturbed unless they are unsupported by substantial evidence on the record as a whole, or were arrived at in an arbitrary or capricious manner. It also recognized

---

[29] *R & R Marketing LLC* v. *Brown-Forman Corp.* 307 N.J. Super. 474, 204 A.2d 1327 (App. Div. 1998).

[30] *Ibid.*

[31] *Rodriguez* v. *Service Lloyds Insurance Company*, No. 98-0006. Decided: July 1, 1999. 997 S. W.2d 248 (Tex. 1999).

[32] *Matter of Sheriff's Officer (Pc2209j)*, 226 N.J. Super. 17 (1988), 543 A.2d 462.

[33] 548 F.2d 147.

that The Supreme Court has held repeatedly that a court may not substitute its own view of the evidence for that of the Commission. Due deference must be accorded the Commission's expertise as to matters within its special competence.

The findings of a commission cannot be couched in legalese. In the 1997 case of *Attorney General* v. *Canada*,[34] the Canadian Supreme Court held that a commission of inquiry must uphold procedural fairness and substantial legitimate expectancy of the person under inquiry to his rights under the law. In New Zealand courts have increasingly held the right of judicial review over government decisions taken in accordance with findings and recommendations of commissions appointed by the government, if such decisions were ultra vires or beyond the power of government. Judicial review in New Zealand derived from the English common law prerogative writs and the public law manifestations of provisions for declaratory and injunctive relief. These remedies were received into New Zealand law. Commissioners appointed to public commissions by a government have to ensure prudent and ethical conduct on their part. Questions such as: what is the applicable legislation by which this commission is established? Is the commissioner satisfied that the appointing authority provides clear and full authority to complete the mandate as stipulated? Are revisions to the mandate necessary? If so, when and how? Is the commissioner satisfied with the protections afforded his or her "independence" while heading an inquiry at the request of, and upon terms prescribed by the executive branch of government?

In the 1803 seminal case of *Marbury* v. *Madison*[35] in the United States, three basic principles of judicial review were upheld. They were: it is the duty of the courts to pronounce what the law is and to interpret it and inquire whether a law has violated the basic tenets of the Constitution of the country; decisions of the Supreme Court are the final authority on the status and interpretation of the Constitution; and decisions of the Supreme Court are the final word on the Constitution. These principles were endorsed in 1958 (155 years after the handing down of the Marbury decision) in the case of *Cooper* v. *Aaron*[36] which was co-signed by all 9 judges of the Supreme Court.

At administrative law, judicial review hinges on the fundamental doctrine of *ultra vires*, which means that no person or body can act beyond the mandate or powers conferred. This is an immutable fact that has to be followed by any democratic society. For instance, if a rule that derives from main legislation is so outrageous that it goes beyond the scope of the legislation, courts in common law jurisdictions could deem it *ultra vires*.[37] Similarly, an arbitrary rule or regulation could be deemed *ultra vires*.[38] Rules that are manifestly unjust or iniquitous as well

---

[34]*Canada (Attorney General)* v *Canada* (Commission of Inquiry on the Blood System in Canada—Krever Commission, [1997] 3 SCR 440.

[35]5 U.S. 137 (1803).

[36]358 U.S. 1 (1958).

[37]*Customs and Excise Commissioners* v. *Cure & Deeley Ltd.* [1962] 1 Q.B. 340.

[38]See Lord Hodson in *McEldowney* v. *Forde* [1971] A.C. 632.

as those that are *mala fides* (in bad faith) or perceived as interfering with the rights of individuals have also been declared *ultra vires*.[39] In a more recent case decided in 1997[40] certain regulations adopted by The Secretary of State under the Social Security and Contributions Act of 1992 calculated to discourage asylum claims by so called economic migrants were deemed by the court to deny or effectively preclude claims to asylum by the applicants.

In addition to these tests of unreasonableness which could make the judiciary reject rules and by-laws, the courts could also declare invalid rules that are ambiguous or uncertain.[41] In common law jurisdictions, the duty of the judiciary is to ascertain the true meaning of the words used in primary legislation, delegated legislation and rules and regulations including by-laws. This is a sixteenth century principle which holds good today.[42] Courts could also review rules and subordinate legislation hold them invalid or ultra vires on grounds of irrationality, impropriety and illegality even though they are affirmed by resolution of a legislative or executive body.[43]

In The United States case of *Almy* v. *Sebelius* decided in 2012 concerning the judicial interpretation of The Secretary of Health and Human Services' acts under The Medicare Act which was challenged by the plaintiff contested determinations of the Medicare Appeals Council (MAC) refusing to provide coverage for the BIO-1000, a device to treat osteoarthritis of the knee. The plaintiff alleged that the Secretary of Health and Human Services improperly used. The court held that the Secretary could elect to determine the coverage of DME in one of three ways. First, she could make a "national coverage determination" (NCD) binding throughout the Medicare system and not subject to review by administrative law judges. Second, one of the private insurance carriers with whom the Secretary contracts to administer claims could issue a "local coverage determination" (LCD) "respecting whether or not a particular item or service is covered on an intermediary-or carrier-wide basis". Finally, if no NCD or LCD was in place, "contractors may make individual claim determinations," including whether a particular DME met the statutory requirement of being "reasonable and necessary."

The court held that a variety of judicial doctrines require that courts not casually overturn the Secretary's decisions. First, it is well recognized that the Secretary's interpretation of what is "reasonable and necessary" under the Medicare Act is entitled to judicial deference.[44] Court held that:

---

[39] *Kruse* v. *Johnson*, [1898] 2. Q.B. 91 at 99–100 per Lord Russell of Killowen. C.J.

[40] *R.* v. *Secretary of State for Social Security ex parte Joint Council for the Welfare of Immigrants* [1997] 1 W.L.R. 275.

[41] *McEldowney* v. *Forde, supra*, note 26.

[42] *In re. Heydon*, (1584) 3. Co. Rep. 71.

[43] *R (on the application of Asif Javed)* v. *Secretary of State for the Home Department* [2002] Q.B. 129.

[44] See *Chevron U.S.A., Inc.* v. *Natural Res. Def. Council, Inc.*, 467 U.S. 837, 104 S.Ct. 2778, 81 L. Ed.2d 694 (1984).

> Because the Secretary is charged with administering the Medicare Act, we substantially defer to the Secretary's construction of any ambiguous language in the Act, if the Secretary's construction 'is based on a permissible construction of the statute.[45]

Additionally, the court held that the Secretary was also entitled to deference for her interpretation of the regulations that implement the Medicare Act's "reasonable and necessary" standard.[46] This principle required courts to give an agency's view of its own regulations "controlling weight unless it is plainly erroneous or inconsistent with the regulation". It was also noted that The US Supreme Court had emphasized the importance of careful adherence to this standard in the Medicare context, which dealt with "a complex and highly technical regulatory program, in which the identification and classification of relevant criteria necessarily require significant expertise and entail the exercise of judgment grounded in policy concerns".[47]

5.5 Principles of Natural Justice

Rulemaking and judicial review of the process of rulemaking inevitably involve the principles of natural justice: *Audi alteram partem*—no one should be condemned unheard; and *Nemo in propria causa judex, esse debet*—no one should be made a judge in his own cause, or the rule against bias. These principles apply only if an administrative officer acts judicially and not in an administrative capacity.[48] In *Cooper* v. *Wandsworth Board of Works*[49] an owner had failed to give proper notice to the Board they had under an Act of 1855 authority to demolish any building he had erected and recover the cost from him. It was alleged by the plaintiff that the Board had used that power without giving the owner an opportunity of being heard. The Board maintained that their discretion to order demolition was not a judicial discretion and that any appeal should have been to the Metropolitan Board of Works. But the Court decided unanimously in favour of the owner. Erie. C.J. held that the power was subject to a qualification repeatedly recognised that no man is to be deprived of his property without his having an opportunity of being heard and that this had been applied to "many exercises of power which in common understanding would not be at all a more judicial proceeding than would be the act of the district board in ordering a house to be pulled down". Willes, J. said that the

[45]The court cited *MacKenzie Medical Supply, Inc.* v. *Leavitt,* 506 F.3d 341, 346 (4th Cir. 2007) in support of this premise.

[46]In support of this observation, the court cited Bowles v. *Seminole Rock & Sand Co.,* 325 U.S. 410, 65 S.Ct. 1215, 89 L.Ed. 1700 (1945).

[47]As per Th. Jefferson Univ. v. *Shalala,* 512 U.S. 504, 512, 114 S.Ct. 2381, 129 L.Ed.2d 405 (1994).

[48]*Errington* v. *Minister of Health*, [1935] 1 K.B. 249.

[49](1863) 14 C.B.N.S. 180.

rule was "of universal application and founded upon the plainest principles of justice, and Byles, J. said that although there are no positive words in a statute requiring that the party shall be heard yet the justice of the common law will supply the omission of the legislature".[50]

The leading case for *audi alteram partem* is *Ridge* v. *Baldwin*[51] in 1964 where The British House of Lords (which was at that time the highest appellate court in Britain) handed down its decision—that a chief constable who could be dismissed only for just cause could not be so dismissed without his receiving the reasons for dismissal and the right to be heard prior to the dismissal. Lord Morris of Borth-y-Gest said:

'It is well established that the essential requirements of natural justice at least include that before someone is condemned he is to have an opportunity of defending himself, and in order that he may do so that he is to be made aware of the charges or allegations or suggestions which he has to meet... here is something which is basic to our system: the importance of upholding it far transcends the significance of any particular case.[52]

Lord Reid said:

> Sometimes the functions of a Minister or Department may also be of that character, and then the rules of natural justice can apply in much the same way. But more often their functions are of a very different character. If a Minister is considering whether to make a scheme for, say, an important new road, his primary concern will not be with the damage which its con-struction will do to the rights of individual owners of land. He will have to consider all manner of questions of public interest and, it may be, a number of alternative schemes.. . .a Minister cannot do everything himself. His officers will have to gather and sift all the facts, including objections by individuals, and no individual can complain if the ordinary accepted methods of carrying on public business do not give him as good protection as would be given by the principles of natural justice in a different kind of case.[53]

The *Ridge case* embodied the principle that it is the doctrine of ultra vires (acting beyond power granted to a person) that justifies the application of the natural law principles to administrative bodies and that courts would not readily accept the misconception that parliament ascribes to an administrative agency the privilege of arriving at a decision in such a manner as would erode natural justice. The irrefutable premise is that if a particular body does so act, it must be exceeding the powers conferred on it by parliament.

The second principle of natural justice is that no person can be a judge in his own cause. In the seminal case of *Dimes* v. *Grand Junction Canal,*[54] The House of Lords reversed The Lord Chancellor (Lord Cottenham)'s decision to hold legal decrees made pertaining to a company in which The Lord Chancellor held shares. The application of this principle to the context of rulemaking in air transport would

---

[50]Per Lord Reid in *Ridge* v. *Baldwin*, infra note 51.

[51][1964] AC 40, [1963] UKHL 2.

[52]*Id.* 54.

[53]*Id.* 48.

[54](1852) 3 H.L.C. 759.

mean that any rule that is made or implemented by a regulator or person who has authority to do so and has a pecuniary or other interest in that rule would be null and void. In an early case in Britain, it was held that a town committee could not instruct an employee to prosecute a person and have as a judge hearing the case, a member of that town committee.[55]

With regard to the criteria for establishing bias in this limb of natural justice, it has been held that there should be a common criterion based on the real likelihood of bias by a member of a tribunal that would make him or her biased favourably or unfavourably inclined to a person coming before that tribunal.[56] An objective test was established in a later case where it was accepted that the criterion should be based on whether a fair minded and informed observer who had access to all information pertaining to a case would consider the position of a person taking a decision to be biased either to the advantage or disadvantage to the person seeking redress or the person who was being charged.[57] A statute could make an exception to perceived bias as in *Shaw*[58] where under *The Public Health Act* of 1872 a Justice of the Peace was permitted to sit on an inquiry conducted by a local authority although he was a member of that local authority.

5.6 Delegation in the United States and the United Kingdom

A discussion worth having under the subject of judicial review and oversight of rulemaking pertains to the situation in the United States, where, The President and Congress have political interests in pursuing policy and ensuring that the rulemaking process accords with their individual policy interests. Separately, the judiciary takes a different stance in trying o interpret a rule along the lines of the intent of the legislature and the principles enshrined in the United States Constitution. However, judges are a product of the political system and they have their own leanings toward political ideology which makes the federal judiciary in the country a strong legacy of a presidency. At the time of writing, in the aftermath of the death of Justice Scalia of the Supreme court and in the throes of a presidential election, the Republicans were adamant that a replacement by the sitting President (Obama) which was to be a Democratic nomination, would not be supported and that a new appointment should be made after the Presidential election and a new President takes office.

Section 706 of *The Administrative Procedure Act* of the United States prescribes that to the extent necessary to decision and when present, the reviewing court is required to decide all relevant questions of law, interpret constitutional and

[55] *R* v. *Lee ex parte Shaw* [1882] 9 Q.B.D. 394.

[56] *R*. v. *Gough*, [1993] A.C. 646.

[57] *Porter* v. *Magill*, [2002] A.C. 357.

[58] *Supra*, note 55.

statutory provisions, and determine the meaning or applicability of the terms of an agency action. To this end the court is required to: compel agency action unlawfully withheld or unreasonably delayed and to hold unlawful and set aside agency action, findings and conclusions found to be arbitrary (without legal basis or justification), capricious (impulsive), an abuse of discretion, or not otherwise in accordance with the law, contrary to constitutional right, power, privilege or immunity, in excess of statutory jurisdiction, authority or limitations or short of statutory right, without observance of procedure required by law, unsupported by substantial evidence, and unwarranted by facts. The court is required to take into account the full record in the above determinations while taking into account the possibility of prejudicial error.

In the famous *Chevron*[59] decision concerning litigation on air pollution The Court had to determine Congressional intent of a certain provision of the Environment Protection Act and in the process ascertain whether, in passing the statute Congress had taken into consideration a particular issue that arose before the court. The court held that there would be no question if the intent of Congress was clear and that neither the court nor the agency executing the rule in question had any jurisdiction to second guess an unequivocally expressed intent of the Congress. However, if the Congress had not directly addressed the issue, it was not up to the Court to give its own construction. All that the Court could do in an instance such as that would be to determine whether the agency's action was based on a permissible construction of the statute in question.

Any substitution of judgment by a reviewing court with that of an agency would be entirely predicated upon whether the agency in question took its decision regarding the implementation of a rule based on valid assumptions or facts as are reflected in the record. A court would determine whether the agency's acts were rational, substantial and reasonable. In the event of an absence of record the court would ascertain whether the agency considered relevant factors and the facts and evidence the agency ought to have taken into account.[60] There are also instances where an agency may adopt a non-legislative rule—a rule that is not derived from a statute or by law but one that has been adopted for purposes of efficiency and practicality. In such instances, although courts would be precluded from seeking the legal genesis of the rule or intent of the legislature, it could go into whether there was public participation in the adoption of such a rule.

In the broader context, and in general, rulemaking by an administrative body or agency, although it may appear to be legislative, is perceived and treated as essentially an executive function that enables executive power and will be deemed as such by the courts.[61] However, another judicial approach in an earlier decision has suggested that the legislature can delegate its legislative power and authority to a subordinate body such as an administrative agency in certain circumstances.[62]

---

[59] 467 U.S. 637 (1984).

[60] *Massachusetts* v. *EPA* 549 U.S. 497 (2007).

[61] *City of Arlington* v. *FCC* 133 S. ct. (2013) 1863 at 1873.

[62] *Whitman* v. *Am.TrackingAss'ns* 531 U.S. 457 at 472 (2001).

Based on this principle the legislature (Congress in the case of the United States) can delegate legislative power, and in so far as the Agency intends to use that power in rulemaking, the rules that come out of the process could be deemed legislative.[63] As to the intent of the agency to use delegated legislative power, the courts have to defer to an agency's explanation, if persuasive, that the agency had reasonable intent to use such legislative power.[64]

Recent trends in the delegation of power by the legislature to an agency have shown, as in the case of *Mistretta* v. *United States*[65] that "the system of government ordained by the Constitution mandate that Congress generally cannot delegate its legislative power to another Branch".[66] This has been called the "*non-delegation doctrine*" by scholars. The court also recognized in the *Mistretta case* that however, that the separation of powers principle, and the non-delegation doctrine in particular, do not prevent Congress from obtaining the assistance of its coordinate Branches. In *Whitman* v. *American Trucking Ass'ns Inc,*[67] while the court held that no delegated power is constitutionally permissible, it also said that when conferring decision making authority upon agencies, Congress must lay down an intelligible principle to which the person or body authorized to act is directed to conform and that an agency cannot cure an unlawful delegation of legislative power by adopting in its discretion a limiting construction of the statute. The basis for this absolute pronouncement was Article 1 of the American Constitution which stipulates that all legislative power is vested in the Congress of the United States. However, the question arises as to the practicality of this reasoning since Congress routinely, and often with monotonous regularity delegates legislative power on agencies.[68] In the *Whitman* case[69] Stevens J held that the court had two choices: choose to articulate that the court considers the power vested in the agency (in this case the Environment Protection Authority—EPA) had a delegated power which was "legislative" but constitutional; or that the power conferred on the EPA was not legislative, and concluded that the more appropriate and prudent was forward would be to accept the former premise.[70]

All this dichotomous judicial arguments back and forth—from the non-delegation doctrine to the acceptance of the principle that the legislature can actually delegate legislative power to agencies have prompted scholars to suggest that it is time to recognize that, for practical and efficiency purpose as well as for purposes of proper delegation of powers that could prove to be facilitative of

---

[63]*Am. Postal Workers* Union v. U.S. Postal Serv., 707 F2d 548 at 558.

[64]United States v. Mead Corp., 533 U.S. 218, (2001) at 222–227.

[65]488 U.S. 361 (1989).

[66]See *Field* v. *Clark*, 143 U. S. 649, 143 U. S. 692 (1892).

[67]531 U.S. 457 (2001).

[68]The practice of delegation by the Congress has gone on since 1825. See *Wayman* v. *Southard* 23 U.S. (10 Wheat.) (1925) 1 at 42–43.

[69]*Supra.*, note 62.

[70]*Id.* at 488.

governance, legislative power can devolve upon agencies at the behest of the legislature provided there is clear articulation to that effect.[71]

In Britain a fundamental piece of legislation that dealt with judicial review of agencies was the Tribunals and Inquiries Act of 1958. However, there were instances where this statute had to clash with other exclusionary laws that effectively precluded the jurisdiction of the former Act. One such instance was seen in the controversial case of *Anisminic* v. *Foreign Compensation Commission*[72] where determinations of the Foreign Compensations Commission (on claims to compensation out of payments received by the Crown from foreign governments for measures taken by them against the property of British subjects) were excluded from the purview of the 1958 Act. The basis for the *Foreign Compensation Act* of 1950 for excluding the scope of the 1958 Act in this instance was that the payments made by the Foreign Compensation Commission were *ex gratia* and therefore discretionary. The House of Lords disregarded the legislative exclusion of the Parliament and held that the measures taken by the Commission were *ultra vires* and therefore void *ab initio*. Here, the House of Lords also made the point that even if there was a prescriptive limit on such payments and that limit had expired the court had jurisdiction to declare such payments void.

Another concept that the British courts had to grapple with was the "*As if enacted in this Act*" where parliament could bestow legal legitimacy to delegated or subordinated legislation as if enacted in the parent Act. In other words, the subordinate legislation would have equal legislative power as the parent Act seemingly precluding judicial review. Again, the courts disregarded this principle in general on the basis that the agency or authority may be restrained from carrying out an act so authorised if such act were to prove *ultra vires*. A minister, on this principle, could not go beyond his authority irrespective of the "As if enacted" rule.[73]

It must be noted that, when the courts interpret legislation pertaining to conferred powers on an agency, as in other instances of adjudication, the courts do not consider the policy or parliamentary intent behind such legislation but adhere strictly to the meaning of the words in so far as they give effect to the meaning and purpose of the statute.[74] One commentator puts it aptly:

> Meaningful judicial review involves a substantive analysis of the agency's action. The court does not merely ask, "Did the agency provide reasons?" The court queries, "Can good reasons be given for this statute or regulation? Are the reasons adequate? Are the reasons legal?" The "giving reasons" requirement becomes more than a simple procedural formality.40 The "giving reasons" requirement is one of the fundamental means through which a democracy controls the actions of its non-elected government actors.[75]

---

[71]See generally, Watts (2015), pp. 1003–1060, particularly pp. 1059–1060.

[72]1969 2 A.C. 147.

[73]*R*. v. *Minister of Health ex parte Yaffe* [1931] A.C. 494.

[74]*In re*. *Hayden* (1584) 3 Co. Rep. 71.

[75]Tobler (1999, pp. 213–221 at 218.

A closer examination of the two systems: American; and British would reveal that judicial approaches of the former is weighted towards a compelling political perspective, arguably reflective of the appointment process of the judges while the latter hinges on a stronger social context. The one thread that weaves through the fabric of these two structures is democracy.

5.7 Democracy and Administrative Law

The basis of modern democracy is Hobbes' Leviathan, which begins with the premise that the supreme power, whether it be a man, woman or assembly, is called the sovereign. Hobbes (1588–1679), recognized initially that the powers of the sovereign are unlimited, untrammeled and unchallenged. The sovereign has the right of censorship over all expression of opinion, on the basis that the main interest of the sovereign is the preservation of internal peace. Therefore, a true sovereign will not use the power of censorship to suppress the truth, because a doctrine which is at variance with peace cannot be true. Hobbes emphasised that the laws of property should be entirely the purview of the sovereign, for in absolute nature and in its pristine purity, there is no property, as property is created by government.

Hobbes believed that, even if a sovereign were to be despotic, the worst despotism was better than anarchy. The interests of governments become singularly identifiable with the interests of the subjects. Above all, rebellion is wrong: not only because it usually fails; but also, if it succeeds, it sets a bad example.

The most noble of the great philosophers—Spinoza (1632–1677), derived his political philosophy from Hobbes, but differed with Hobbes on the subject of freedom of opinion, which should not, in Spinoza's view, be subject to governmental control. But both Hobbes and Spinoza held the common view that any kind of rebellion was bad against a sovereign.

The influence of the early philosophers on the modern philosophers becomes apparent with the thrust of Aristotle's Politics, which fundamentally held that a government is good when it aimed at the good of the whole community, and bad when it cared only for itself. Aristotle was emphatic when he made the distinction between oligarchy and democracy by using the economic status of the governing party as the only criterion for the distinction: oligarchy is when the rich govern without consideration for the poor; and democracy is when the sovereign gives power to the hands of the poor and needy in initial disregard for the interests of the rich. Aristotle argued that monarchy was better than aristocracy and aristocracy was better than polity. The greatest political sin, according to Aristotle, was the corruption of the best in a political society. He placed tyranny as the worst form of government, next to oligarchy, and placed democracy over both categories. Aristotle concluded that, among actual governments, democracies were the most liked and beneficial.

The Utilitarian School, of which Jeremy Bentham was a protagonist, recognized democracy as being composed of four essential and basic elements: subsistence;

abundance; security and equality. According to Bentham, a good democracy had to ensure these elements for its community. Bentham observed: "wars and storms are best to be read of, but peace and calms are better to endure". The two fundamental postulates which Bentham attributed to good government were equality and security, which to Bentham formed the cornerstone of a balanced sovereign.

The above philosophical beliefs bring one to the inexorable conclusion that democracy is government for all—in equality and unity. The inevitable question which follows is: can a community which, in its constitutional essence, favor a few and require the majority to be content with the second best? Plato and Aristotle answered in the affirmative, purely to support intellectual independence, which was essentially a flawed perception of the era they belonged to, if one were to take their positions literally. If however, one were to interpret the position of these two philosophers as giving the few in power the discretion to decide for the betterment of the entire community with the ultimate aim of ensuring its safety and security, it follows that democracy should focus on a lean executive charged with this task. This interpretation is wholly consistent with religious philosophy and democratic ethics which incontrovertibly hold that the most valuable assets of human life are power and property and that a political system which is unjust in these respects is unacceptable.

Immanuel Kant (1724–1804) who wrote in his Perpetual Peace in 1795, recommending a federation of free States, bound together by a covenant eschewing war, was more emphatic about prohibiting war than considering the virtues of the political clustering of States. Kant viewed war as a problem which only an international government could quell. The group of States, according to Kant, should be republican in civil constitution, with a distinct separation of powers between the executive and the legislature. Kant attacked democracy on the ground that a democracy gave overt and unjust powers to the executive which were invidious to a State. Of course, Kant's theory against democracy, favoring a community of States under one international government, fell into disfavor in his own country in 1933 and has not gained official acceptance since.

John Locke (1632–1704), a moderatist philosopher, deviated from dogma, whilst essentially retaining his faith in the goodness of positive morality. This led to Locke's abiding faith in religious tolerance and parliamentary democracy as the two necessary elements of basic governance. Locke is believed to be the father of empiricism—which was founded on the premise that all knowledge is based on experience. There is evidence in philosophical history that Locke applied the theory of empiricism to parliamentary democracy, ascribing to democracy a certain imperative which brings to bear a compulsive element to democracy. Accordingly, democracy, although reflecting the overall will of the people, would succeed only if practiced with empirical dependence upon past experience. Political negotiations, according to the empirical democracy doctrine, should therefore not be destitute of past experience, whatever the overall will of the community may be.

The wisdom of Locke's empirical democracy is perceived in its application to democracy in the modern context, which is also consistent with the Aristotelian view, that the highest virtue is for the governing few, who could, if the interests of the community dictate, subject conservative and theoretical ethics to political necessity and prudence. Although Aristotle required a president or prime minister to be magnanimous in this regard, the modern interpretation and context of good government does not necessarily require a leader to be magnanimous, but to be different from the average citizen; and to have certain merits connected with his or her status.

The essence of modern practical democracy is to curb unnecessary power of the central government and not to buttress the authority of the State to the point of corruption and self service. The end result is personal freedom and a society which precedes the State. Also, there is a compelling need in a functional democracy for a loyal opposition which does not portend a real threat to national security. This does not, however, mean that democracy should make the executive impotent. On the contrary, a strong and lean executive, as Aristotelian philosophy recommends, is an essential tool of a workable democracy.

The above principles, enunciated by the founding fathers of democracy, eminently accord with the vision that development through democracy is an effective tool of political economics for the next Millennium.

Present day lawyers would define democracy as the form of government in which the sovereign power resides in and is exercised by the whole body of citizens directly or indirectly through a system of representation. Put more simply, the above definition means that democracy is a system where ordinary citizens have a meaningful and compelling role in the affairs of the State, including the formulation of policy and the development and implementation of legislation. A typical democracy as enunciated by the Western philosophers whose views have already been discussed, would separate the State and its instrumentalities from the Church or other religious body. It would be composed of three separate and intrinsic powers, i.e. the Legislature, the Executive and the Judiciary. This separation of powers in a democracy facilitates the sustenance of fundamental human rights of the individual by giving legal protection to a citizen through an independent judiciary. In a social democracy, the protection of the social and economic rights of a person could be very strongly entrenched as an essential principle of the philosophy of government.

In a large ocean there are two neighbouring islands: faultless democracies with full civil and political rights. One island is extremely rich and prosperous, and has ten million inhabitants. The other is extremely poor: it has 100 million inhabitants, who live by subsistence farming. After a bad harvest last year, there are no food stocks, and now the harvest has failed again: 90 million people are facing death by starvation. The democratically elected government of the poor island asks for help, and the democratically elected government of the rich island organises a referendum on the issue. There are three options: Option A is a sharp increase in taxes, to pay for large-scale permanent structural transfers to the poor island. Option B is some increase in taxes, to pay for immediate and sufficient humanitarian aid, so that famine will be averted. Option C is no extra taxes and no aid. When the votes are counted, 100 % of the voters have chosen Option C. After all, who wants to pay more taxes?

So 90 million people starve. Yet all electoral procedures on both islands are free and fair, the media are free, political campaigning is free, there is no political repression of any kind. According to democratic theory, any outcome of this democratic process must be respected. Two perfect democracies have functioned perfectly: if you believe the supporters of democracy, that is morally admirable. But it clearly is not: there is something fundamentally wrong with democracy, if it allows this outcome.

The defect is not hard to find: the people most affected by the decision are excluded from voting. The issue is the composition of the demos, the decision-making unit in a democracy: it is a recurrent theme in the ethics of democracy. Democratic theory can legitimise a political community in the form of an island of prosperity, and then legitimise the selfish decisions of that community. This theoretical possibility corresponds with the real-world western democracies. Millions of people are dying of hunger and preventable disease, yet the electorate in rich democracies will not accept mass transfers of wealth to poorer countries. They will not accept mass immigration from those countries either. A causal relationship has developed at global level, between democracy in the rich countries, and excess mortality elsewhere (famine, epidemics, endemic diseases).

The Greek democracies were not representative governments, they were governments run by the free, male citizens of the city-state. All major government decisions and legislation were made by the Assembly; the closest we've come to such a system is "initiative and referendum," in which legislation is popularly petitioned and then voted on directly by the electorate. The Greek democratic states ran their entire government on such a system. All the members of a city-state were not involved in the government: slaves, foreigners, and women were all disbarred from the democracy. So, in reality, the democratic city-states more closely resembled oligarchies for a minority ruled the state—it was a very large minority, to be sure, but still a minority.

Let us focus more closely on the basic ideals of democracy. First, in a democracy, the people rule. Popular sovereignty implies that all minimally competent adults come together as one body to make decisions about the laws and policies that are to regulate their lives together. Each citizen has a vote in the processes by which the decisions are made and each has the opportunity to participate in the deliberations over what courses of action are to be followed. Second, each citizen has the right to participate as an equal. Political equality implies equality among citizens in the process of decision-making; Third, each citizen has the right to an opportunity to express his or her opinions and supporting reasons to every other citizen as well as a right and duty to hear a wide spectrum of views on subjects of public concern. Each has a right, as well as a duty to participate in open and fair discussion. These are the ideals of democracy.

These ideals are partly realized in features of modern democratic societies. One-person one-vote is observed in the process of electing representatives to the legislative assembly; anyone may run for election to public office; in elections, a number of political parties compete for political power by advocating alternative visions of the society; the political campaigns of candidates and parties consist in large part in discussion and argument over the worth of these opposing views, and everyone is permitted to have a say in this process; and the society tolerates and often encourages vigorous debate on all issues of public interest.

One thing wrong with democracy is that any Tom, Dick or Harry can get themselves elected into power, irrespective of their character, motives and education. In particular, irrespective of whether or not they know or care about the cumulative effect of the individual's wisdom on the affairs and destiny of the nation.

There are many other things wrong with democracy, some of which are more obvious than others. Here are some examples: Whatever motives a political group had when it started out, it eventually becomes a political machine whose prime objective is to win elections and get into power. The integrity of its original mission is compromised; the sort of people who put themselves forward for election are not necessarily going to be the best ones for the job. Wanting to have a position of high office and power is not the same as being the most qualified for it; The appointment of office depends upon the will of the masses. The masses may not necessarily know what constitutes their best interests, and so might not be able to judge accurately who would represent it for them.

References

Craig PP (2003) Administrative law, 5th edn. Thompson, Sweet and Maxwell, London, p. 32

Hamburger P (2013) Is administrative law unlawful? University of Chicago Press, Chicago, p 77

Tobler C (1999) The standard of judicial review of administrative agencies in the US and EU: accountability and reasonable agency action. Boston Coll Int Comp Law Rev 22(1):213–221

Watts KA (2015) Rulemaking as legislating. Georgetown Law J 103:1003–1060

Chapter 6
Interpretation of Air Transport Rules, Treaties and Guidance Material

6.1 Rules and Treaties

6.1.1 Internal Rules

Inasmuch as judicial review of administrative action in pursuance of the implementation of rules is importance so is the interpretation given to rules by the judiciary. In the *Skylink Airways case*[1] the court was requested to determine Section 41102 of Title 49 of The United States Code (The Transportation Code) in the context of whether Skylink Airways (a non operating company incorporated in the State of Delaware), which had applied for an air operator's certificate was "fit, wiling and able to provide" interstate and foreign air transportation for persons and freight the court went into the tripartite test used by the Department of Transportation (DoT) to ascertain the requirements of the rule. The test comprised the elements: whether the applicant had the managerial skills and technical ability to conduct the proposed operations; whether it had resources sufficient to commence and conduct such operations; and whether the applicant would comply with the Transportation Code and regulations imposed by Federal and State Agencies.

The court held that if the applicant airline were to be found fit and eligible for the certificate, it must remain fit to hold that certificate and that it must file a progress report in detail 45 days following the end of the first year of certified operations to The Air Carrier Fitness Division. In the determination of Northwest Airlines' merging with Wings Holdings—a case determined in 1989, it was held that Section 401 r of the Federal Aviation Act required that to provide an air service an operator must continue to satisfy the DoT its ability to sustain that air service through prudent managerial competence and compliance disposition.

[1]Order No. 2005-1-1. See Larson et al. (2006), pp. 176–181.

R. Abeyratne, *Rulemaking in Air Transport*, DOI 10.1007/978-3-319-44657-8_6

In the *DHL Airways Case,*[2] which concerned the interpretation of the term *"US citizen"* in the determination of whether the applicant carrier had fulfilled the requirements of US citizenship the court held that, besides the core requirement,—which stipulated that a citizen of the United States meant a corporation or association organized under the laws of the United States of which the President and at least two thirds of the board of directors or other managing officers are citizens of the United States—the applicant must also satisfy the "actual control" test, thereby bringing to bear the fact that it was not only the words *stricto sensu* of an air transport rule that must be determined but also the various other requirements that the rule brought with it.

When it comes to interpretation of treaties, the seminal case of *Benjamins* v. *British Airways*[3] presented the 2nd Circuit with the question as to whether the Warsaw Convention[4] creates a cause of action in the case of an accident which causes death or injury to a person while on board an aircraft or while in the process of embarkation or disembarkation. The court examined nearly 20 years of decided cases which had decided in the affirmative and held that the fact that the judicial acceptance of a legal proposition over a sustained period of time does not necessarily presuppose a claim to applicability much circumspection was needed in overturning such acceptance. Furthermore, it was held that "the desirability of uniformity in international law can best be recognized by holding that the Convention, otherwise universally applicable, is also the universal source of a right of action".[5]

6.1.2 Treaty Provisions

One of the most interesting developments under the realm of air carrier liability can be seen in the interpretation of Article 17 of the Warsaw Convention of 1929 which has been replaced by Article 17 of the Montreal Convention of 1999.[6] Article 21 of the former states:

> The carrier is liable for damage sustained in the event of the death or wounding of a passenger or any other bodily injury suffered by a passenger, if the accident which caused the damage so sustained took place on board the aircraft or in the course of any of the operations of embarking or disembarking.

Article 2 of the Montreal Convention states:

[2]Order No 2004-5-10, *id.* 189.

[3]572 F.2d 913 (2d Cir. 1978).

[4]Convention on the Unification of Certain Rules Pertaining to International Carriage by Air signed at Warsaw on 10 October 1929.

[5]*Supra*, note 3, at 921.

[6]Convention for the Unification of Certain Rules for International Carriage by Air (Montreal, 28 May 1999).

The carrier is liable for damage sustained in case of death or bodily injury of a passenger upon condition only that the accident which caused the death or injury took place on board the aircraft or in the course of any of the operations of embarking or disembarking.

These two provisions are almost verbatim and certainly convey the same principle. However, there are subtle differences in terminology. For instance, whereas the Warsaw Convention refers to "bodily injury" the Montreal Convention refers to "injury" bringing to bear an argument that the latter may impute liability to the carrier in the event of mental injury being caused to a passenger. The most contentious issue in both treaties has been the interpretation given to *"in the course of any of the operations of embarking or disembarking"*. Both Conventions provide that the accident which causes the damage should take place on board the aircraft or in the course of any of the operations of embarking or disembarking. The first alternative—that of being on board is self explanatory and does not require discussion. The second, which involves the operations of embarking or disembarking has been subject to sustained judicial discussion and analysis. Although *ex facie*, the words on board the aircraft are not problematical, the phrase has been interpreted at least once to engulf time spent by passengers in a hotel consequent to a hijacking.[7] The argument in this case was that the passengers would have been on board if not for the hijacking. This is an extreme interpretation which seems to say that the airline is liable for all accidents within that period of time from the start of the embarkation process to the end of the disembarkation.

Current law on the subject seems to favour the test known as the *Day-Evangelinos* test which was developed as a consequence of a series of terrorist acts on passengers in airport departure lounges. This is a tripartite test which has the three elements of consideration—the location of the passenger, the nature of his activity at the time of the accident and the degree of control exercised by the airline at the relevant time. A number of United States cases have accepted this test.[8] This test clearly establishes the fact that unless the passenger is under the control or direction of the airline at the terminal there is no liability for injury or death caused to the passenger under the provisions of the Warsaw Convention. A case which brings out the significance of this test is *Adler v. Austrian Airlines* where a passenger slipped on some ice and fell between the terminal building and the aircraft by bus. The bus was operated by the airport staff and not by the airline. A Brussels court, applying a test similar to the *Day-Evangelinos* test held that the passenger was not under the control of the airline and was thereby precluded from invoking the provisions of Article 17 of the Convention.

The test itself obviates the need to painstakingly go through every possible exigency in the light of the requirement that the accident should occur during the

[7] *Husserl v. Swiss Air Transport Co. Ltd.* Op cit. See also, *People of the State of Illinois v. Gilberto* 383 NE 2d 977.

[8] *Day v. Trans World Airlines Inc.* 528 F 2d. 31 (2nd Circ. 1975); *Evangelinos v. Trans World Airlines Inc..* 550 F2d 152 (2d. Circ. 1977); *Leppo v. Trans World Airlines Inc.*392 NYS 2d 660 (AD 1977); Rolnick v. *El Al Israel Airlines Ltd.551 Supp. 261 (EDNY 1982).*

process of embarkation or disembarkation. Prior to the adoption of this test there was no uniformity in the judicial reasoning behind the definition of embarkation and disembarkation. It was left to each individual court to determine whether a given situation would fall within the scope of chronology of these two extremities. Now, the tripartite test has made the task of the Courts much easier.

As for mental injury, again, judicial interpretation of the term "injury" has leaned towards physical injury or mental injury caused as a result of physical injury. The issue of compensation for injury caused as a result of an aircraft accident is not one for judicial naiveté, nor is it one for judicial ineptitude and feckless insouciance. For over 83 years, courts have vacillated between a gross disregard for finding the true nature of mental injury, mostly by ignoring its relevance to recovery as a separate head of liability, and claims to pretension that mental injury is something completely comprehensible to the judicial mind as a "non-bodily injury". This article argues that, both in their interpretation of the Montreal Convention's Article 17; its intent, and their gross disregard of medical science, the courts have got their act upside down, and that it is time for a paradigm shift with regard to recovery for mental injury, which should be spearheaded by the judiciary as well as legal and medical experts.

The discussion that follows offers a realistic and practical approach by which mental injury can be categorized and classified based on scientific and medical methodology that could unequivocally result in mental injury being accepted as a compensable element through an inextricable link between mental and bodily injury.

For more than 80 years, courts have largely refused to entertain any claim for mental injury caused in an aircraft accident. The author finds the following statement interesting:

> Although the 1999 Montreal Convention retained "bodily injury' language, a close study of the treaty's history and more importantly, the negotiations among the signatories' delegates suggests that the great majority of nations intended to broaden allowable recovery beyond strict bodily injury and that many had already interpreted the phrase to include mental injury. As a result, courts interpreting "bodily injury" under the new treaty should closely review the intent of the signatories before adopting the previous treaty's precedent.[9]

Indeed, if this were the case, the first measure that could ascertain this statement would be an inquiry into the discussions of the Legal Committee of the Council of ICAO and other groups involved that developed the principles of the Montreal Convention. This article will discuss in chronological and analytical detail the preparatory work of these bodies, as well as the Diplomatic Conference that followed. However, this analysis *per se* would not be sufficient to conclude that the Montreal Convention hints at allowing compensation for mental injury. There has to be an inquiry as to the nature of mental injury and its association with bodily injury. A compelling weakness of judicial determination of this issue is that judges have disregarded the scientific and medical aspects of mental injury and blatantly

[9]Cunningham (2008), available at http://works.bepress.com/mckay_cunningham/1.

ignored the possibility that mental injury could, in some instances, be a physical injury and therefore, recovery could follow.

On the positive side, in the 1999 case of *Weaver* v. *Delta Airlines Inc.*[10] where the plaintiff experienced terror and felt physical manifestations of that terror during an emergency landing, which necessitated her seeking medical treatment for emotional and physical problems attributable to her flight experiences, and she was diagnosed with, and received treatment for post-traumatic stress disorder, the court held that no floodgates of litigation will be opened by allowing for claims such as the plaintiff's, which are based on a definite diagnosis of a disorder that arises from a physical injury that is medically verifiable. The court held that fright alone is not compensable, but brain injury from fright is.

On the negative side, and this has been the prevalent judicial trend, in the case of *In re Crash at Little Rock, Arkansas on 1 June 1999*[11] although the trial judge held that from the evidence presented, it could be accepted that post-traumatic stress disorder is a biological/physical as well as psychological injury, this contention was rejected at the appellate level on the basis that the evidence was not sufficient to establish a physical change to the plaintiff's brain.

The glaring neglect of the judiciary in ascribing to itself the status of expert on mental injury on the presumption that mental injury is simplistically an injury of the mind which is devoid of and completely separate from bodily injury, leaves the question unanswered as to whether a more enlightened approach is called for, if only to involve the medical fraternity in the determination of this issue.

6.1.3 States' Responses to Consumer Protection Under the Warsaw and Montreal Conventions

A unique approach has been taken in Canada where, instead of specific rules that are adopted on the rights of the consumer, a series of decisions issued by the Canadian Transportation Agency addresses the rights of passengers. These form applicable rules of conduct and liability of airlines and are based on the global principles of the aforesaid treaties. The Agency adopts a "circumstance-focused approach" which requires consideration of the particular circumstances surrounding a passenger. The Agency, in five related recent decisions has stated that in some circumstances a delay or cancellation will defeat the purpose of the trip and that, in such cases, the passenger should have the right to choose between continued travel and a full refund. It appears from these decisions that the obligation of an air carrier is not absolute and that its responsibility applies only for delays within its control.

In 2012 The Israeli Knesset enacted the Airline Passenger Rights Law which is applicable to both scheduled and unscheduled (charter) carriers calling for the

[10](1999) 56 F Supp 2d 1190.

[11](2000) 27 Avi 18,428.

provision of assistance in the form of food, drink, phone access in the event of case of flight delays. The passenger has the option of cancelling the reservation and receiving a refund if the duration of the delay is between 5 and 8 h. For longer delays, compensation and accommodation are provided.

In August 2005 The General Authority of Civil Aviation (GACA) of the Kingdom of Saudi Arabia issued a Consumer Protection Regulation (the "GACA Regulation") where Article 5 of the law provides that the Regulation applies to "all domestic and international air carriage of persons, baggage or goods on flights arriving at the [Kingdom of Saudi Arabia] or departing therefrom." Passengers are granted protections in cases of denied boarding due to overbooking, flight cancellations and delays, including assistance and compensation. Article 15 of the GACA Regulation promotes the "principle of utmost transparency in . . .advertisements on flight and services provided" notably by stating that the prices advertised should be considered as "total prices and [that] the air carrier shall not be entitled to add additional fees to such prices, unless such is included explicitly in advertising materials".

The US Department of Transportation on 25 April 2011, adopted a rule enhancing Airline Passengers Protection. This rule applies to: U.S. and foreign air carriers operating passenger service using aircraft of 30 seats or more; and to or from a U.S. airport. ICAO's Manual on the Regulation of International Air Transport,[12] defines "passenger air service" is an air service performed primarily for the transport of passengers. Therefore, this rule does not apply to freight services.[13]

Compensation of up to USD 1300 is due in cases where the passenger is denied boarding due to oversold flights, depending on whether the carrier offers alternate transportation and based on the delay of arrival at final destination. In addition, with respect to domestic flights, a carrier is not permitted to allow an aircraft to remain on the tarmac for more than 3 h before allowing passengers to deplane, subject to security or safety-related circumstances or if air traffic control advises that returning to the gate would significantly disrupt operations. With a view to ensuring price transparency, the price for an airline ticket must be the entire price to be paid. Although charges (e.g. government taxes) can be stated separately, they must be displayed so as to accurately reflect the total price to be paid by the passenger.

EU, Regulation 261/2004 which has already been discussed, was enacted in February 2004. Article 3 provides that the Regulation applies: (a) to passengers departing from an airport located in the territory of a Member State to which the Treaty applies; (b) to passengers departing from an airport located in a third country to an airport situated in the territory of a Member State to which the Treaty applies, unless they received benefits or compensation and were given assistance in that third country, if the operating air carrier of the flight concerned is a Community carrier.

[12]ICAO Manual on the Regulation of International Air Transport (Doc 9626).

[13]*Id.* Sect. 5.3.1.

The second paragraph of Article 3 describes the conditions for application of the Regulation: "(a) passengers must have a confirmed reservation on the flight concerned and, except in the case of cancellation, must present themselves for check-in, as stipulated and at the time indicated in advance and in writing (including by electronic means) by the air carrier, the tour operator or an authorized travel agent, or, if no time is indicated, not later than 45 min before the published departure time; and (b) have been transferred by an air carrier or tour operator from the flight for which they held a reservation to another flight, irrespective of the reason."

The regulation does not apply to passengers travelling free of charge or at a reduced fare not available directly or indirectly to the public. However, it applies to passengers having tickets issued under a frequent flyer programme or other commercial programme by an air carrier or tour operator. Regulation 261/2004 does not apply to other users of air transport, such as users of air freight services, or parties with whom air carriers have a contractual relationship, such as airports, air navigation services providers (ANSPs), or ground-handlers.

Regulation 261/2004 provides different protections to passengers. First, a right to care, or assistance: in case of flight delays and cancellations, the airline must minimize the discomfort to passenger (catering, hotels, communication means, etc.). Second, the Regulation gives passengers a right to compensation, in cases of flight cancellations and depending on flight distance, of up to EUR 600, unless the cancellation is caused by "extraordinary circumstances". It should be noted that the exemption allowed for under "extraordinary circumstances" only applies to compensation obligations, and not to assistance.

The Latin American Civil Aviation Commission (LACAC) recommended in November 2004 that Member States adopt a set of rules protecting passengers with confirmed reservations who have been denied boarding involuntarily. Among the protections provided by the recommended rules is the possibility to choose between substitute transportation and reimbursement. In addition, it is recommended that assistance be provided with respect to communications, refreshments/food, and accommodations for delays exceeding 4 h.

6.2 Guidance Material

6.2.1 Airport Economics Manual Doc 9562

In the field of guidance material, ICAO is the champion, particularly in the field of air transport, as Article 44 of the Chicago Convention circumscribes ICAO to the role of "fostering the development of air transport", leaving ICAO with no authoritative role. As a result, ICAO publishes "manuals" on various subjects such as airport economics, the regulation of air transport and policies on taxation and charges, just to name a few. Doc 9562 (Airport Economics Manual) starts off by saying the objective of the Manual is to provide practical guidance to States, airport managing and operating entities, and designated charging and regulatory authorities, to assist in the efficient management of airports and in implementing ICAO's Policies on Charges for Airports and Air Navigation Services (Doc 9082). It is an irrefutable fact that all ICAO documents start off from provisions of the Chicago Convention. In the instance of Doc 9562 it begins with Article 15 of the Chicago Convention which provides that every airport in a contracting State which is open to public use by its national aircraft shall likewise be open under uniform conditions to the aircraft of all the other contracting States. The like uniform conditions shall apply to the use, by aircraft of every contracting State, of all air navigation facilities, including radio and meteorological services, which may be provided for public use for the safety and expedition of air navigation. Article 15 continues to say that any charges that may be imposed or permitted to be imposed by a Contracting State for the use of such airports and air navigation facilities by the aircraft of any other Contracting State will not be higher, as to aircraft not engaged in scheduled international air services, than those that would be paid by its national aircraft of the same class engaged in similar operations, and as to aircraft engaged in scheduled international air services, than those that would be paid by its national aircraft engaged in similar international air services.

All such charges are required to be published and communicated to ICAO, provided that, upon representation by an interested contracting State, the charges imposed for the use of airports and other facilities will come under the supervisory purview of the ICAO Council, which will then report and make recommendations thereon for the consideration of the State or States concerned. No fees, dues or other charges are to be imposed by any contracting State in respect solely of the right of transit over or entry into or exit from its territory of any aircraft of a contracting State or persons or property thereon.

Following this provision, the Airport Economics Manual and tied to the principle of non discrimination is the statement that a State, in view of the potential abuse of dominant position of airports, is responsible for the economic oversight of their operations. Economic oversight is defined as the function by which a State supervises the commercial and operational practices of an airport. In performing its economic oversight function, a State should, in particular, ensure that airports consult with users and that appropriate performance management systems are in place.

Doc 9562 goes on to recommend certain measures in rulemaking in this regard. It states that States have the flexibility to perform their economic oversight function through legislation or rule-making, or establishment of a regulatory mechanism and similar measures. The mechanism by which economic oversight takes place can direct success in achieving its objectives in an efficient and cost-effective manner. It is important for States to consider carefully the roles, rights and responsibilities of the different parties involved—governments, airports and users—and to exercise their economic oversight function, in particular concerning economic performance management and consultation with users, in an internally consistent manner.

Where the operation of one or more airports is performed by a government entity, the economic oversight function should be functionally separated from the operation and provision of airport services within the administration, and roles and powers should be clearly defined for each function.

A State may, under Doc 9562 take into consideration local considerations and circumstances establish an independent economic oversight entity with the responsibility of reviewing and sanctioning any action on pricing, investments and service quality. An appropriate balance between independence and accountability is required for the economic oversight entity as well as for the airport(s) that it would regulate. In order to hold the regulating entity accountable, the government would need to give it clear objectives, preferably through statute, coupled with sufficient operating autonomy. Without such a balance, there will be a risk to regulatory commitment and credibility.

A State can also use a third party advisory commission as a less formal tool to help perform its economic oversight function. The advisory commission is often considered appropriate when parties concerned do not form cohesive groups and thus have little or no means by which to organize for class action. The advisory commission could comprise air carriers, general aviation, the military, representatives of end-users, and other principal parties concerned. A strong advisory commission would be equipped to engage in meaningful dialogue with the airport management on an ongoing basis and to review specific pricing, investments and service levels proposals.

Another important aspect to be considered is the possible need for additional resources to perform an economic oversight function. Some States may lack the capacity to adequately fulfil their economic oversight responsibilities, given competing priorities on safety, security, environment and liberalization of air transport. For those States, the adoption of a region-wide regulatory framework could be a useful option to pull their resources together in performing their economic oversight function.

When one applies these principles to the contentious situation that arose in December 2005 when a fuel storage tank which provided kerosene to aircraft operating air services into and out of London's airports exploded in Buncefield, forcing a severe shortage of aviation fuel, foreign carriers had to make pit stops so as to cope with the reduced quota issued in London. The issue arose when a larger quota was issued to British national carriers, resulting in alleged discrimination. This was a situation where both Article 15 and Doc 9562 could have been invoked, even if by imputation that there would be no discrimination by a State in terms of the equal access principle enunciated by both documents.[14] Apparently, there were no British rules that internally enforced an equitable distribution of fuel to all

[14] It was reported in *The Guardian* that the flight between London and Sydney had to make an additional stop at Stansted airport in Essex to top up. The additional stop was expected to add around 90 min to the long journey to Australia via Bangkok. South African Airways, which operated from Heathrow to Johannesburg and Cape Town, said it expected one of its evening flights to have to make a refuelling stop. The airline added: "With a loss of one-third of the total fuel supplied to Heathrow,

carriers and the scheme offered by the British authorities differentiated between home base carriers and visiting carriers with base carriers being given higher fuel allocations. Eventually The International Air Transport Association (IATA—the club of member airlines) had to broker a solution that would look after equitably the interests of all 186,000 passengers that flew into and out of Heathrow every day. A voluntary fuel-allocation scheme was implemented immediately following the destruction of the Buncefield facility to make up for the 35 % reduction in fuel supply. Through BAA effort, improvements in supply have since increased the fuel capacity to 78 % of the normal 20–21 million litres per day. The agreement, which took effect on 20 February 2006, eliminated differential treatment for ultra-long haul, long haul and medium haul flights. A differential was maintained for short haul flights. Equity remained the guiding principle and the short haul differential was progressively eliminated as supply increases.[15]

The anomaly in this issue lies in the fact that, although ICAO rules (or at least rules and treaty provisions promulgated by States) were violated, neither States not ICAO were involved in the settlement of the dispute through appropriate interpretation of the applicable provisions.

6.2.2 *ICAO Policies on Charges for Airport and Air Navigation Services: Doc 9082*

Closely linked to Doc 9562 is ICAO's Policies on Charges for Airports and Air Navigation Services which, in Doc 9082 contain the recommendations and conclusions of the Council resulting from ICAO's continuing study of charges in relation to the economic situation of airports and air navigation services provided for international civil aviation. The word "policies" is a euphemism for "guidance" of Contracting States, are founded upon recommendations made in this area by the various conferences on the economics of airports and air navigation services, which are held regularly by ICAO. The last such conference took place in Montréal from 15 to 20 September 2008 (Report of the Conference on the Economics of Airports and Air Navigation Services (CEANS).[16] As per a recommendation adopted by CEANS and endorsed by the ICAO Council, States are encouraged to incorporate the four key charging principles of non-discrimination, cost relatedness, transparency and consultation with users into their national legislation, regulation or policies, as well as into their future air services agreements, in order to ensure compliance by airport operators and air navigation services providers (ANSPs).[17]

---

early indications suggest that the restrictions could run into a period of weeks if not months." See https://www.theguardian.com/business/2005/dec/16/buncefieldfueldepotfire2005.theairlineindustry.

[15]http://www.aviationpros.com/news/10402401/iata-brokers-solution-on-heathrow-fuel-allocation.

[16]*Doc 9908*.

[17]See Abeyratne (2009), pp. 39–46.

Policy is laid out in *limine* in Chapter 1.2 which provides that States permit the imposition of charges only for services and functions which are provided for, directly related to, or ultimately beneficial for, civil aviation operations; and refrain from imposing charges which discriminate against international civil aviation in relation to other modes of international transport. This is immediately followed by the statement that in this regard the ICAO Council is concerned about the proliferation of charges on air traffic and notes that the imposition of charges in one jurisdiction can lead to the introduction of charges in another jurisdiction. A related provision, in sub section 7 of the Chapter says explicitly that whenever an autonomous entity is established, whether by a government or by private interests, to operate an airport(s) and/or provide air navigation services, the State should ensure that all relevant obligations of the State specified in the Chicago Convention, its Annexes and in air services agreements are complied with and that ICAO's policies are observed.

In other words, there should ideally, *de lege ferenda*, be put in place in every State rules that ensure the policies adopted by the ICAO Council, ironically with consensus of all member States of ICAO. But this does not happen in some instances. Granted that ICAO's policies are at best only authoritative in practice and, from a legal perspective, are rendered destitute of effect by the acknowledged lack of enforcement power afflicting them. In this context it is curious that, six decades after the establishment of ICAO some still refer to its powers and functions. There are some others who allude to ICAO's mandate. The fact is that ICAO has only aims and objectives, recognized by the Chicago Convention which established the Organization. Broadly, those aims and objectives are to develop the principles and techniques of international air navigation and to foster the planning and development of international air transport. In effect, this bifurcation implicitly reflects the agreement of the international community of States which signed the Chicago Convention that ICAO could adopt Standards in the technical fields of air navigation and could only offer guidelines in the economic field.

There was discussion during CEANS where some delegations suggested that, in order to "give teeth" to ICAO policy, there be a recommendation in Doc 9082 to the effect that amendment to Doc 9082 should be incorporated by States in their national legislation. It is submitted that such a measure would tantamount to treading uncharted and dangerous ground. While it is one thing to assert that the only way that ICAO policies could be implemented is for States to opt incorporating such principles in their legislation, it is something quite different to recommend that States go ahead and do so.

As a necessary compromise and in order to reach a balance, the Conference broadly recognized the need for economic oversight in the increasingly commercialized and privatized environment for airports and air navigation services. It considered a number of suggestions that were made by the delegates for improving the proposed new text for Doc 9082. The following conclusions were reached by the Conference:

(a) States should bear in mind that economic oversight is the responsibility of States with the objectives, *inter alia*, to prevent the risk that a service provider could abuse its dominant position, to ensure non-discrimination and transparency in the application of charges, to encourage consultation with users, to ensure the development of appropriate performance management systems, and to ascertain that capacity meets current and future demand, in balance with the efforts of the autonomous/private entities to obtain the optimal effects of commercialization or privatization;
(b) States should select the appropriate form of economic oversight according to their specific circumstances, while keeping regulatory interventions at a minimum and as required. When deciding an appropriate form of economic oversight, the degree of competition, the costs and benefits related to alternative oversight forms, as well as the legal, institutional and governance frameworks should be taken into consideration;
(c) States should consider adoption of a regional approach to economic oversight where individual States lack the capacity to adequately perform economic oversight functions; and
(d) ICAO should amend Doc 9082 to clarify the purpose and scope of economic oversight for airports and air navigation services with reference to its different forms and the selection of the most appropriate form of oversight.

Broadly, ICAO policy on charges for airports and air navigation services are geared to ensure that any charging system should, so far as possible, be simple and suitable for general application at international airports; charges should not be imposed in such a way as to discourage the use of facilities and services necessary for safety, such as lighting and navigation aids; charges should be determined on the basis of sound accounting principles and may reflect economic principles as required, provided that these are in conformity with Article 15 of the Chicago Convention other principles in the present policies; charges must be non-discriminatory both between foreign users and those having the nationality of the State in which the airport is located and engaged in similar international operations, and between two or more foreign users.

Furthermore, the policies go on to recommend that, consistent with the form of economic oversight adopted, States should assess, on a case-by-case basis and according to local or national circumstances, the positive and negative effects of differential charges applied by airports. States should ensure that the purpose, creation and criteria for differential charges are transparent. Without prejudice to modulated charging schemes, the costs associated with such differential charges should not be allocated to users not benefiting from them. Charges offered for the purpose of attracting or retaining new air services should only be offered on a temporary basis.

Doc 9082 also states that, in order to avoid undue disruption to users, increases in charges should be introduced on a gradual basis; however, it is recognized that in some circumstances a departure from this approach may be necessary, and that where charges are levied by different entities at an airport, they should, so far as possible, be consolidated for invoicing purposes. The combined revenues should be distributed among the entities concerned as applicable. Maximum flexibility should be maintained in the application of all charging methods to permit introduction of improved techniques as they are developed.

The above notwithstanding, incentive schemes, discrimination and iniquitous imposition of charges is not uncommon. One such case has been reported where, in March 2009, the European Parliament issued the Airport Charges Directive (ACD), intended to establish, as part of national laws, "a common framework regulating the essen-tial features of airport charges" for the larger airports within the European Economic Area and Switzerland.

To be fair, this directive correctly followed the ideal rulemaking process of incorporation of global policy adopted through ICAO in that it essentially codified ICAO's Document 9082, into law and, thus presenting a new and desirable approach to rulemaking in the European Union.

Regrettably, the success that was expected did not come since there was uneven implementation in the member States where the Evaluation of Directive 2009/12/EC on airport charges, a report produced for the European Commission by London based transportation consultants which stated: "there appears to have been little material impact of the Directive on the structure and level of airport charges."[18] Hemant Mistry, IATA Director of Airports and Fuels has commented: "There's been a lot of fragmentation in the way the Directive is being implemented. In many cases, implementation is woefully inadequate," "...the Commission should take a more active role in ensuring it is adequately implemented, advocating for further clarity to address shortfalls through guidelines as well as stronger enforcement by regulators."[19]

The problem has been identified as there being too broad a wording of the Directive, which leaves it open to interpretation. According to Airports Council International (ACI—The Association of Airports) the Directive should have been drafted in more complex and succinct terminology as are notional legislation, rules and regulations.

The problem can be ascribed to a certain extent to the diversely opposed ways in which both IATA and ACI view the issue. ACI favours airport competition and free market forces in the entrepreneurship of airports while IATA interprets the directive as not being clear enough to obviate monopolistic attitudes of the airports.

6.2.3 *ICAO Policies in the Field of Taxation in Air Transport: Doc 8632*

Here again, similar to airport and air navigation charges, the genesis of policy documentation lies in the Chicago Convention. The Convention, in Article 24 (a) provides that that fuel and lubricating oils on board an aircraft of a

[18]Steer Davies Gleave, Airport charges: regulation with teeth, http://airlines.iata.org/analysis/airport-charges-regulation-with-teeth.

[19]*Ibid.*

Contracting State on arrival in the territory of another Contracting State and retained on board on leaving the territory of that State shall be exempt from customs duty, inspection fees or similar national or local duties and charges. The same Article of the Chicago Convention also refers to the temporary admittance, free of duty, of aircraft on a flight to, from or across the territory of another Contracting State and to the exemption from customs duty, etc., of spare parts, regular equipment and aircraft stores.

ICAO goes as far back as 1951 in creating policies along the lines prescribed in Article 24 (a) on taxation where the Council adopted 3 Resolutions and a Recommendation which were published in Doc 7145-C/824. The Council's impetus continued in pursuing Assembly Resolution A15-16 which explored the possibility of a new initiative in this field the Council undertook a comprehensive review of all aspects related to this subject matter and, at the Fourth Meeting of its 59th Session, on 14 November 1966, decided to recast the Resolutions and the Recommendation, taking into account developments since 1951, while reaffirming at the same time their underlying principles. The Council further decided to publish them in the policy document, Doc 8632-C/968, for action by Contracting States and to provide certain explanatory material for guidance to States and international operators.

Basic policy which took its final shape in 1966 was composed of four clauses of a Resolution where aviation fuel was exempted from taxes: exemption from taxation of fuel, lubricants and other consumable technical supplies when an aircraft registered in one State arrives in or departs from a customs territory of another State; exemption from taxation of fuel, lubricants and other consumable technical supplies when an aircraft registered in one State makes successive stops at two or more airports in one customs territory of another State; exemption from taxation of the income and aircraft of international air transport enterprises; and taxes related to the sale or use of international air transport.

The rationale for fuel tax exemption has been inscribed in Doc 8632 as to by-pass the adverse economic and competitive effect that taxation might impose on air transport national or local taxes on the acquisition of fuel, lubricants and consumable technical supplies for use by aircraft in connection with international air transport is imposed by States; as already mentioned Article 24 (a) of the Chicago Convention has clear and unequivocal policy requiring the exemption from taxes on fuel and lubricating oils on board an aircraft of a Contracting State, on arrival in the territory of another Contracting State and retained on board on leaving the territory of that State, shall be exempt from various duties and charges; it is the common practice of many States with respect to aircraft engaged in international transport generally to exempt from taxation all fuel and lubricants on board on arrival in each customs territory and, on a basis of reciprocity, to exempt from or refund taxes on fuel and lubricants taken on board at the final airport in that customs territory; and it is practicable and desirable to extend such exemptions or refunds to other consumable technical supplies, such as de-icing fluid, hydraulic fluid, cooling fluid, etc., which, like fuel and lubricants, are filled into receptacles forming part of the aircraft, are consumed during flight and are essential for that purpose, so that all the exemptions applicable to fuels and lubricants will apply also to such supplies.

On the issues of how States could incorporate these policies in their domestic rules and legislation Doc 8632 is clear. It states that, "in giving effect to the terms of this Resolution, various courses of action are open to Contracting States. Of these, the adoption of legislation granting exemption on a reciprocal basis is undoubtedly the simplest and least time-consuming method of achieving the aims of this Resolution, provided that such legislation can be enacted without undue delays. Some States, on the other hand, find it more practicable to deal with the problem of relief from multiple taxation of air transport enterprises through formal bilateral negotiations of agreements relating to taxation generally or in the context of agreements for the exchange of commercial air transport rights".

IATA has much to say on the imposition of taxation by States. An IATA report on Saudi Arabia states that Jet fuel prices are critical in:

> developing an efficient air transport network, which in turn forms the enabling environment for supporting diversification and spawning higher-value added activities in the economy. □ Moving closer to market based pricing of jet fuel (6 % reduction or equivalent of about 20 US cents per US gallon) will have the following impacts: Air travel and freight costs within, to and from Saudi Arabia reduced: air travel and freight costs will decrease by 1.1 % for international and 1.9 % for domestic travellers and shippers; Improved export competitiveness, higher GDP, and greater employment: Industry's overall contribution to GDP would be higher by about USD 333 million and about 5 thousand new jobs would be supported, with the largest benefits expected in exporting industries; Better off consumers and enabling environment for a diverse economy: Additional economic benefits of USD 343 million per year will accrue to passengers travelling within, to and from Saudi Arabia.[20]

In the Supplement to Doc 8632 published by ICAO in 2013 numerous States have confirmed their compliance by enacting rules enforcing one or more ICAO policies. Just to name a few, Argentina complies *inter alia*, with the Council Resolution contained in Clause 1, with the condition that with reference to the exemptions which the Resolution in Clause 1 of Doc 8632 Argentina establishes with respect to import and export duties, the situations outlined there are free from the payment of such taxes, with the exception of the hypotheses foreseen in its attachment provided to ICAO. Armenia, in accordance with its Law of the Republic of Armenia "On Value-Added Tax", applies a zero rate of VAT in respect of fuel for filling aircraft flying international lines, and the provision of goods intended for use by the crew and passengers on aircraft along the entire route; taxable turnover of services (including air navigation, and take-off and landing), repairs, reequipping the means of transport operating on international routes, as well as services of carriage on international routes for passengers, baggage, freight, and post, and services provided to passengers during transport; taxable turnover of services

[20]IATA Economic Briefing February 2014 Economic Benefits of Moving to Market Based Pricing of Jet Fuel for Saudi Arabia, at http://www.iata.org/whatwedo/Documents/economics/SaudiImpactMktJetPrice.pdf.

(including agency and intermediary services) directly associated with the services indicated in subparagraph b) above and for the providers thereof. A zero rate of VAT applies to resident and non-resident companies.

Australia's policy remains that the taxation of international airlines should be dealt within the context of Australia's overall taxation policy. Australian States and Territories have their own taxing powers, and the Commonwealth does not have the authority to directly override State taxation laws. This is reflected in the fact that Australia's double tax treaties and airline profit agreements do not cover State taxes.

The Kingdom of Bahrain is committed to promote market-based economics and has thus adopted a proactive position within its resources and facilities. Accordingly, it does not levy a corporate tax on companies in all fields of activity including airlines. This is designed to facilitate commercial investment. The State has also concluded several double taxation avoidance agreements in respect of airline activities. Its bilateral air services agreements also contain a special provision exempting airlines from taxes and other charges.

In accordance with Article 24 of the Chicago Convention, Burkina Faso complies with the policies of the ICAO on taxation in the field of international air transport. Burundi applies the provisions of Document 8632 and has no restrictions with respect to the Resolution. Exemption and reciprocity arrangements are specified in the bilateral air transport agreements between Burundi and the country of the air transport company concerned.

Colombia fully agrees that the increase in taxation could have an impact on the growth and development of air transport. It feels that decisions regarding such questions, which are of great importance to any State, should be made based on the knowledge and capacity States deem applicable to matters of taxation, and in compliance with individual fiscal policies.

The above country reports are just a few examples that reflect the overall readiness of ICAO member States to comply with ICAO guidance material. The problem is that ICAO takes these notifications on face value and has no resources to ascertain the veracity of these statements in terms of the extent of their compliance.

References

Abeyratne R (2009) The ICAO conference on the economics of airports and air navigation services. Air Space Law XXXIV(1):39–46

Cunningham M (2008) The Montreal Convention: Can Passengers Finally Recover For Mental Injuries? Phoenix School of Law, From Selected Works of McKay Cunningham. Available at http://works.bepress.com/mckay_cunningham/1

Larson PB, Sweeney JC, Gillick JE (2006) Aviation law, cases and related sources. Transnational, New York, pp 176–181

Chapter 7
Conclusion

Rulemaking in air transport is a serious issue as it hinges on the safety of persons travelling by air without being exploited by commercial interests. The two key words in this context are *standardization* and *harmonization*. The first word means compliance of laws and regulations and the second word denotes consistency of application of rules in a seamless manner. As such legislatures cannot take a chance with rulemaking and at any cost should not relegate the task to the executive alone. This principle, although making eminent sense, carries with it a flaw that has to be addressed. While on the one hand, handing over rulemaking powers to governmental agencies would free the legislature to concentrate on more general policy issues, handing over rulemaking authority to agencies would mean that rules are then made by unelected civil servants, which defeats the philosophy of election and democracy where the people elect their legislators to enact laws for them. The issue then would be, who would be the overall monitor of the rulemaking process in air transport? The answer lies squarely in the State, which has to ensure that rules emanate from the legislature or at least have the stamp of the legislature.

Notwithstanding the above, it must be stated that the mere fact that an agency makes rules without having the power to do so does not make such rules invalid at law, particularly if the capacity to make such rules flow from a discretion granted to the agencies by the legislature. The criterion of validity lies in the judicial requirement that the rules are not too rigidly applied. An inflexible principle in this regard is that such rules should not bypass the legislature, precluding scrutiny by the legislature. Rules promulgated by the executive (or administration) must not be inconsistent with the parent legislation that they emanate from.

Another important factor in administrative rulemaking is that the rule must be promulgated by the person on whom discretion vests to make the rule. This principle is based on the maxim *delegatus non potest delegare* which essentially means that delegated power cannot be re-delegated. Thus a committee, which has been delegated the power by an executive (such as a minister or secretary) cannot

R. Abeyratne, *Rulemaking in Air Transport*, DOI 10.1007/978-3-319-44657-8_7

delegate that power to an officer or group of officers to exercise such discretion.[1] Also, a judicial function—a function that bestows on a body to act judicially, taking decisions, cannot be delegated.[2]

Based on the above reasoning, rulemaking has to involve two vital factors, as the discussion in this book has reflected: public participation; and judicial review of administrative action. The former is left to the State (legislature) to set up. The latter is a matter for the courts, although the courts could not superimpose their stamp on the administration to the extent that would make the administration meaningless. As Lord Shaw said in *Local Government Board* v. *Arlidge*[3]: "[T]hat the judiciary should presume to impose its own methods on administrative or executive officers is a usurpation. And the assumption that the methods of natural justice are ex necessitate those of courts of justice is wholly unfounded".[4]

Coalescing the above principles that have been the result of deconstruction of the core concept of rulemaking, and applying it to air transport, one has to return to the origin of rulemaking in air transport from a general and global perspective, which lies squarely in the hands of ICAO. Backing up even further, one is constrained to examine the meaning and purpose of ICAO in the rulemaking process. A good start is to look at what ICAO is doing (and indeed has been doing for the past 70 years of its existence) with regard to rulemaking. The Organization, along with its member States (which comprise the Assembly and the Council) produces reams of guidance material in the forms of Annexes, Manuals which for persuasive authority and are not compulsory (with the exception of Annex 2 which pertains to rules of the air). ICAO then produces supplements to the Annexes containing information of non-compliance by States of Annex Standards and leaves it at that. In fairness to ICAO, the Organization does not have the resources to monitor whether member States have adopted rules and regulations that accord with such standards and indeed how consistent they are with SARPs of the Annexes.

However, a closer look at ICAO's remit would justify a more involved role by ICAO to guide States in ensuring that firstly, they have adequate rules and regulations that properly implement the Standards and secondly, that States (particularly those that most need ICAO guidance) receive appropriate guidance from ICAO. Article 44 of the Chicago Convention unequivocally identifies, as one of the aims and objectives of the Organization to be to develop principles and techniques of air navigation, which in practicality are contained in all but Annexes 9 (facilitation of air transport) and 17 (security). ICAO has also aim to meet the needs of the people for safe, regular, economical and efficient air transport [as per Article 44(d)] which means that the Organization has not only to produce Annex provisions but also coercive guidance material that would impel States to follow ICAO's lead. This will not attain fruition unless ICAO follows up on States' adherence, through their internal regulations, ICAO policy.

---

[1] *Allingham* v. *Minister of Agriculture* [1948] 1 All. E. R. 780.

[2] *Barnard* v. *National Dock Labour Board* [1953] 2 Q.B. 18.

[3] [1915] A.C. at 120.

[4] *Id.* 138.

An attempt was made as far back as 1956 when the ICAO Council established a Special Implementation Panel to look into problems faced by member States in implementing Standards of the Annexes but this eventually proved too daunting an exercise for the panel and work was abandoned. However, there has been no attempt (perhaps for justifiable reasons of sparse resources) to look into the adequacy of internal rules and regulations in air transport, particularly in States which lack resources and need guidance on rulemaking that would ensure standardization and harmonization in the air transport process in their territories.

In a manner of speaking, ICAO, through its safety and security audits monitors a States' oversight of compliance by those concerned of Standards of the Annexes and identifies any significant concerns. ICAO also has a mechanism where it assists States in addressing and rectifying those concerns. Under ICAO's Universal Safety Oversight Audit Programme (USOAP), States are required to establish a safety programme where aircraft operators, maintenance organizations and services providers implement appropriate safety management systems. Safety Management Systems (SMS) are processes which proactively manage the projected increase in aircraft incidents and accidents brought about by the increase in air traffic movements. SMS require vigilance in the liberalization of air transport and the correspondent increase in capacity. At the Directors General of Civil Aviation Conference on a Global Strategy for Aviation Safety, convened by ICAO in Montreal from 20 to 22 March 2006, Canada defined a Safety Management System as a business-like approach to safety. An SMS is a systematic, explicit and comprehensive process for the management of safety risks that integrates operations and technical systems with financial and human resource management, for all activities related to an air operator as an approved maintenance organization's certificate holder.[5]

The first ICAO safety audit cycle was conducted between 1999 and 2004 where almost all Contracting States (except a few who could not be accessed due to adverse conditions in their territories) were audited. These audits were conducted on the basis of Annexes 1, 6 and 8 of the Chicago Convention. From January 2005, ICAO started its 6-year cycle of audits based on 16 of the 18 ICAO Annexes (all except Annex 9 and Annex 17) and by the end of April 2008 had audited 90 States.

As in safety oversight, ICAO has a security oversight programme called the Universal Security Audit Programme (USAP). The ICAO Universal Security Audit Programme (USAP), launched in June 2002, represents an important initiative in ICAO's strategy for strengthening aviation security worldwide and for attaining commitment from States in a collaborative effort to establish a global aviation security system.

The programme, which is part of the Aviation Security Plan of Action, provides for the conduct of universal, mandatory and regular audits of the aviation security systems in all ICAO member States. The objective of the USAP is to promote global aviation security through the auditing of States on a regular basis to assist

[5]Management of Aviation Safety, Presented by Canada, DGCA/06-WP/15, 4/2/06, at 2.

States in their efforts to fulfil their aviation security responsibilities. The audits identify deficiencies in each State's aviation security system, and provide recommendations for their mitigation or resolution.

Implementation of the programme commenced with the first aviation security audit taking place in November 2002 and between three and four audits were conducted around the world each month thereafter. At the end of December 2007, ICAO had completed the entire initial audit cycle by auditing 182 States. In addition, and in accordance with the programme of audit follow up visits initiated in 2005, 111 audit follow up missions were also being conducted and ICAO is continuing to monitor and validate the implementation of corrective action plans it has recommended to States. A second cycle of security audits has been initiated, and by May 2008 ICAO had audited 5 States in that cycle.

The 35th Session of the Assembly held from 28 September to 8 October 2004 mandated ICAO to maintain strict confidentiality of all State-specific information derived from audits conducted under USAP. However, in order to promote mutual confidence in the level of aviation security between States, the Assembly urged all Contracting States to "share, as appropriate and consistent with their sovereignty, the results of the audit carried out by ICAO and the corrective actions taken by the audited State, if requested by another State"[6]

While noting the importance of continuing bilateral exchanges of information between States, the 36th Session of the Assembly, held from 18 to 28 September 2007, also recognized the value of proposals presented by the Council and Contracting States for the introduction of a limited level of transparency with respect to ICAO aviation security audit results[7] The Assembly directed the Council to consider such an introduction of a limited level of transparency, balancing the need for States to be aware of unresolved security concerns with the need to keep sensitive security information out of the public realm. In doing so, the Assembly emphasized that it was essential that any methodology developed to provide for increased transparency also ensure the appropriate safeguarding of a State's security information in order to prevent specific information that could be used to exploit existing vulnerabilities from being divulged.

However, at these audits internal rules and regulations are not examined in detail, as to whether they would be at the core of those concerns. Granted, ICAO does not have the resources, and indeed will not be given the resources by its member States, to go into all the regulations of all its member States with a view to ascertaining their compatibility with the Standards of the Annexes to the Chicago Convention. However, a start could be made by examining regulations in those States identified as having significant concerns and resources limitations. The Legal Affairs and External Relations Bureau, to the extent of their capability, could be expanded in a limited way to take on this project along with ultimate advice from

[6]A35-9, Appendix E, Resolving Clause 4; and Recommended Practice 2.4.5 of Annex 17—*Security*.

[7]Resolution A36-20, A36-WP/336 and Plenary Action Sheet No. 3.

the Legal Committee of the Council one of the duties of which is to advise the Council on matters relating to the interpretation and amendment of the Chicago Convention referred to it by the Council. The few member States that might need such focus should also be examined in terms of their legal structures and the justification and validity of rulemaking in each State in accordance with the doctrines of ultra vires and delegated legislation and principles of natural justice.

A manual on rulemaking in air transport could follow as justified by Article 55 of the Chicago Convention (permissible functions of the Council) which provides for studies to be conducted by the Council Study on any matters affecting the organization and operation of international air transport, including the international ownership and operation of international air services on trunk routes, and submit to the Assembly plans in relation thereto and investigate, at the request of any contracting State, any situation which may appear to present avoidable obstacles to the development of international air navigation; and, after such investigation, issue such reports as may appear to it desirable.

Appendix A: Extracts of Rulemaking Procedures in the Federal Aviation Administration (USA): Federal Register for 14 CFR Part 11

Title 14 → Chapter I → Subchapter B → Part 11 → Subpart A → §11.3

Aeronautics and Space

§11.3 What is an advance notice of proposed rulemaking?

An advance notice of proposed rulemaking (ANPRM) tells the public that FAA is considering an area for rulemaking and requests written comments on the appropriate scope of the rulemaking or on specific topics. An advance notice of proposed rulemaking may or may not include the text of potential changes to a regulation.

§11.5 What is a notice of proposed rulemaking?

A notice of proposed rulemaking (NPRM) proposes FAA's specific regulatory changes for public comment and contains supporting information. It includes proposed regulatory text.

§11.7 What is a supplemental notice of proposed rulemaking?

On occasion, FAA may decide that it needs more information on an issue, or that we should take a different approach than we proposed. Also, we may want to follow a commenter's suggestion that goes beyond the scope of the original proposed rule. In these cases, FAA may issue a supplemental notice of proposed rulemaking (SNPRM) to give the public an opportunity to comment further or to give us more information.

§11.9 What is a final rule?

A final rule sets out new or revised requirements and their effective date. It also may remove requirements. When preceded by an NPRM, a final rule will also

R. Abeyratne, *Rulemaking in Air Transport*, DOI 10.1007/978-3-319-44657-8

identify significant substantive issues raised by commenters in response to the NPRM and will give the agency's response.

§11.11 What is a final rule with request for comments?

A final rule with request for comment is a rule that the FAA issues in final (with an effective date) that invites public comment on the rule. We usually do this when we have not first issued an ANPRM or NPRM, because we have found that doing so would be impracticable, unnecessary, or contrary to the public interest. We give our reasons for our determination in the preamble. The comment period often ends after the effective date of the rule. A final rule not preceded by an ANPRM or NPRM is commonly called an "immediately adopted final rule." We invite comments on these rules only if we think that we will receive useful information. For example, we would not invite comments when we are just making an editorial clarification or correction.

§11.13 What is a direct final rule?

A direct final rule is a type of final rule with request for comments. Our reason for issuing a direct final rule without an NPRM is that we would not expect to receive any adverse comments, and so an NPRM is unnecessary. However, to be certain that we are correct, we set the comment period to end before the effective date. If we receive an adverse comment or notice of intent to file an adverse comment, we then withdraw the final rule before it becomes effective and may issue an NPRM.

§11.15 What is a petition for exemption?

A petition for exemption is a request to FAA by an individual or entity asking for relief from the requirements of a current regulation.

§11.17 What is a petition for rulemaking?

A petition for rulemaking is a request to FAA by an individual or entity asking the FAA to adopt, amend, or repeal a regulation.

§11.19 What is a special condition?

A special condition is a regulation that applies to a particular aircraft design. The FAA issues special conditions when we find that the airworthiness regulations for an aircraft, aircraft engine, or propeller design do not contain adequate or appropriate safety standards, because of a novel or unusual design feature.

§11.21 What are the most common kinds of rulemaking actions for which FAA follows the Administrative Procedure Act?

FAA follows the Administrative Procedure Act (APA) procedures for these common types of rules:

(a) Rules found in the Code of Federal Regulations;

(b) Airworthiness directives issued under part 39 of this chapter; and

(c) Airspace Designations issued under various parts of this chapter.

§11.23 Does FAA follow the same procedures in issuing all types of rules?

Yes, in general, FAA follows the same procedures for all rule types. There are some differences as to which FAA official has authority to issue each type, and where you send petitions for FAA to adopt, amend, or repeal each type. Assume that the procedures in this subpart apply to all rules, except where we specify otherwise.

§11.25 How does FAA issue rules?

(a) The FAA uses APA rulemaking procedures to adopt, amend, or repeal regulations. To propose or adopt a new regulation, or to change a current regulation, FAA will issue one or more of the following documents. We publish these rulemaking documents in the Federal Register unless we name and personally serve a copy of a rule on every person subject to it. We also make all documents available to the public by posting them in the Federal Docket Management System at http://www.regulations.gov.

(1) An advance notice of proposed rulemaking (ANPRM).

(2) A notice of proposed rulemaking (NPRM).

(3) A supplemental notice of proposed rulemaking (SNPRM).

(4) A final rule.

(5) A final rule with request for comments.

(6) A direct final rule.

(b) Each of the rulemaking documents in paragraph (a) of this section generally contains the following information:

(1) The topic involved in the rulemaking document.

(2) FAA's legal authority for issuing the rulemaking document.

(3) How interested persons may participate in the rulemaking proceeding (for example, by filing written comments or making oral presentations at a public meeting).

(4) Whom to call if you have questions about the rulemaking document.

(5) The date, time, and place of any public meetings FAA will hold to discuss the rulemaking document.

(6) The docket number and regulation identifier number (RIN) for the rulemaking proceeding.

[Doc. No. 1999-6622, 65 FR 50863, Aug. 21, 2000, as amended at 72 FR 68474, Dec. 5, 2007]

§11.27 Are there other ways FAA collects specific rulemaking recommendations before we issue an NPRM?

Yes, the FAA obtains advice and recommendations from rulemaking advisory committees. One of these committees is the Aviation Rulemaking Advisory Committee (ARAC), which is a formal standing committee comprised of representatives of aviation associations and industry, consumer groups, and interested individuals. In conducting its activities, ARAC complies with the Federal Advisory Committee Act and the direction of FAA. We task ARAC with providing us with recommended rulemaking actions dealing with specific areas and problems. If we accept an ARAC recommendation to change an FAA rule, we ordinarily publish an NPRM using the procedures in this part. The FAA may establish other rulemaking advisory committees as needed to focus on specific issues for a limited period of time.

§11.29 May FAA change its regulations without first issuing an ANPRM or NPRM?

The FAA normally adds or changes a regulation by issuing a final rule after an NPRM. However, FAA may adopt, amend, or repeal regulations without first issuing an ANPRM or NPRM in the following situations:

(a) We may issue a final rule without first requesting public comment if, for good cause, we find that an NPRM is impracticable, unnecessary, or contrary to the public interest. We place that finding and a brief statement of the reasons for it in the final rule. For example, we may issue a final rule in response to a safety emergency.

(b) If an NPRM would be unnecessary because we do not expect to receive adverse comment, we may issue a direct final rule.

§11.31 How does FAA process direct final rules?

(a) A direct final rule will take effect on a specified date unless FAA receives an adverse comment or notice of intent to file an adverse comment within the comment period—generally 60 days after the direct final rule is published in the Federal Register. An adverse comment explains why a rule would be inappropriate, or would be ineffective or unacceptable without a change. It may challenge the rule's underlying premise or approach. Under the direct final rule process, we do not consider the following types of comments to be adverse:

(1) A comment recommending another rule change, in addition to the change in the direct final rule at issue. We consider the comment adverse, however, if the commenter states why the direct final rule would be ineffective without the change.

(2) A frivolous or insubstantial comment.

(b) If FAA has not received an adverse comment or notice of intent to file an adverse comment, we will publish a confirmation document in the Federal Register, generally within 15 days after the comment period closes. The confirmation document tells the public the effective date of the rule.

(c) If we receive an adverse comment or notice of intent to file an adverse comment, we will advise the public by publishing a document in the Federal Register before the effective date of the direct final rule. This document may withdraw the direct final rule in whole or in part. If we withdraw a direct final rule because of an adverse comment, we may incorporate the commenter's recommendation into another direct final rule or may publish a notice of proposed rulemaking.

§11.33 How can I track FAA's rulemaking activities?

The best ways to track FAA's rulemaking activities are with the docket number or the regulation identifier number.

(a) Docket ID. We assign a docket ID to each rulemaking document proceeding. Each rulemaking document FAA issues in a particular rulemaking proceeding, as well as public comments on the proceeding, will display the same docket ID. This ID allows you to search the Federal Docket Management System (FDMS) for information on most rulemaking proceedings. You can view and copy docket materials during regular business hours at the U.S. Department of Transportation, Docket Operations, West Building Ground Floor, Room W12-140, 1200 New Jersey Avenue, SE., Washington, DC 20590. Or you can view and download docketed materials through the Internet at http://www.regulations.gov. If you can't find the material in the electronic docket, contact the person listed under FOR FURTHER INFORMATION CONTACT in the document you are interested in.

(b) Regulation identifier number. DOT publishes a semi-annual agenda of all current and projected DOT rulemakings, reviews of existing regulations, and completed actions. This semi-annual agenda appears in the Unified Agenda of Federal Regulations, published in the Federal Register in April and October of each year. The semi-annual agenda tells the public about DOT's—including FAA's—regulatory activities. DOT assigns a regulation identifier number (RIN) to each individual rulemaking proceeding in the semi-annual agenda. This number appears on all rulemaking documents published in the Federal Register and makes it easy for you to track those rulemaking proceedings in both the Federal Register and the semi-annual regulatory agenda.

[Doc. No. 1999-6622, 65 FR 50863, Aug. 21, 2000, as amended at 72 FR 68474, Dec. 5, 2007]

§11.35 Does FAA include sensitive security information and proprietary information in the Federal Docket Management System (FDMS)?

(a) Sensitive security information. You should not submit sensitive security information to the rulemaking docket, unless you are invited to do so in our request for comments. If we ask for this information, we will tell you in the specific document how to submit this information, and we will provide a separate non-public docket for it. For all proposed rule changes involving civil aviation security, we review comments as we receive them, before they are placed in the docket. If we find that a comment contains sensitive security information, we remove that information before placing the comment in the general docket.

(b) Proprietary information. When we are aware of proprietary information filed with a comment, we do not place it in the docket. We hold it in a separate file to which the public does not have access, and place a note in the docket that we have received it. If we receive a request to examine or copy this information, we treat it as any other request under the Freedom of Information Act (5 U.S.C. 552). We process such a request under the DOT procedures found in 49 CFR part 7.

[Doc. No. 1999-6622, 65 FR 50863, Aug. 21, 2000, as amended at 72 FR 68474, Dec. 5, 2007]

§11.37 Where can I find information about an Airworthiness Directive, an airspace designation, or a petition handled in a region?

The FAA includes most documents concerning Airworthiness Directives, airspace designations, or petitions handled in a region in the electronic docket. If the information isn't in the docket, contact the person listed under FOR FURTHER INFORMATION CONTACT in the Federal Register document about the action.

§11.38 What public comment procedures does the FAA follow for Special Conditions?

Even though the Administrative Procedure Act does not require notice and comment for rules of particular applicability, FAA does publish proposed special conditions for comment. In the following circumstances we may not invite comment before we issue a special condition. If we don't, we will invite comment when we publish the final special condition.

(a) The FAA considers prior notice to be impracticable if issuing a design approval would significantly delay delivery of the affected aircraft. We consider such a delay to be contrary to the public interest.

(b) The FAA considers prior notice to be unnecessary if we have provided previous opportunities to comment on substantially identical proposed special conditions, and we are satisfied that new comments are unlikely.

§11.39 How may I participate in FAA's rulemaking process?

You may participate in FAA's rulemaking process by doing any of the following:

(a) File written comments on any rulemaking document that asks for comments, including an ANPRM, NPRM, SNPRM, a final rule with request for comments, or a direct final rule. Follow the directions for commenting found in each rulemaking document.

(b) Ask that we hold a public meeting on any rulemaking, and participate in any public meeting that we hold.

File a petition for rulemaking that asks us to adopt, amend, or repeal a regulation.

§11.40 Can I get more information about a rulemaking?

You can contact the person listed under FOR FURTHER INFORMATION CONTACT in the preamble of a rule. That person can explain the meaning and intent of a proposed rule, the technical aspects of a document, the terminology in a document, and can tell you our published schedule for the rulemaking process. We cannot give you information that is not already available to other members of the public. Department of Transportation policy on oral communications with the public during rulemaking appears in appendix 1 of this part.

§11.41 Who may file comments?

Anyone may file written comments about proposals and final rules that request public comments.

§11.43 What information must I put in my written comments?

(a) Your written comments must be in English and must contain the following:

(1) The docket number of the rulemaking document you are commenting on, clearly set out at the beginning of your comments.

(2) Your name and mailing address, and, if you wish, other contact information, such as a fax number, telephone number, or e-mail address.

(3) Your information, views, or arguments, following the instructions for participation in the rulemaking document on which you are commenting.

(b) You should also include all material relevant to any statement of fact or argument in your comments, to the extent that the material is available to you and reasonable for you to submit. Include a copy of the title page of the document. Whether or not you submit a copy of the material to which you refer, you should indicate specific places in the material that support your position.

§11.45 Where and when do I file my comments?

(a) Send your comments to the location specified in the rulemaking document on which you are commenting. If you are asked to send your comments to the

Federal Document Management System, you may send them in either of the following ways:

(1) By mail to: U.S. Department of Transportation, Docket Operations, West Building Ground Floor, Room W12-140, 1200 New Jersey Avenue, SE., Washington, DC 20590.

(2) Through the Internet to http://www.regulations.gov.

(3) In any other manner designated by FAA.

(b) Make sure that your comments reach us by the deadline set out in the rulemaking document on which you are commenting. We will consider late-filed comments to the extent possible only if they do not significantly delay the rulemaking process.

(c) We may reject your paper or electronic comments if they are frivolous, abusive, or repetitious. We may reject comments you file electronically if you do not follow the electronic filing instructions at the Federal Docket Management System Web site.

[Doc. No. 1999-6622, 65 FR 50863, Aug. 21, 2000, as amended at 72 FR 68474, Dec. 5, 2007]

§11.47 May I ask for more time to file my comments?

Yes, if FAA grants your request for more time to file comments, we grant all persons the same amount of time. We will notify the public of the extension by a document in the Federal Register. If FAA denies your request, we will notify you of the denial. To ask for more time, you must file a written or electronic request for extension at least 10 days before the end of the comment period. Your letter or message must—

(a) Show the docket number of the rule at the top of the first page;

(b) State, at the beginning, that you are requesting an extension of the comment period;

(c) Show that you have good cause for the extension and that an extension is in the public interest;

(d) Be sent to the address specified for comments in the rulemaking document on which you are commenting.

§11.51 May I request that FAA hold a public meeting on a rulemaking action?

Yes, you may request that we hold a public meeting. FAA holds a public meeting when we need more than written comments to make a fully informed decision. Submit your written request to the address specified in the rulemaking document on which you are commenting. Specify at the top of your letter or message that you are requesting that the agency hold a public meeting. Submit your request no later than 30 days after our rulemaking notice. If we find good cause for a meeting, we will notify you and publish a notice of the meeting in the Federal Register.

§11.53 What takes place at a public meeting?

A public meeting is a non-adversarial, fact-finding proceeding conducted by an FAA representative. Public meetings are announced in the Federal Register. We invite interested persons to attend and to present their views to the agency on specific issues. There are no formal pleadings and no adverse parties, and any regulation issued afterward is not necessarily based exclusively on the record of the meeting.

11.61 May I ask FAA to adopt, amend, or repeal a regulation, or grant relief from the requirements of a current regulation?

(a) Using a petition for rulemaking, you may ask FAA to add a new regulation to title 14 of the Code of Federal Regulations (14 CFR) or ask FAA to amend or repeal a current regulation in 14 CFR.

(b) Using a petition for exemption, you may ask FAA to grant you relief from current regulations in 14 CFR.

§11.63 How and to whom do I submit my petition for rulemaking or petition for exemption?

(a) To submit a petition for rulemaking or exemption—

(1) By electronic submission, submit your petition for rulemaking or exemption to FAA through the Internet at http://www.regulations.gov, the Federal Docket Management System Web site. For additional instructions, you may visit http://www.faa.gov/regulations.

(2) By paper submission, send the original signed copy of your petition for rulemaking or exemption to this address: U.S. Department of Transportation, Docket Operations, West Building Ground Floor, Room W12-140, 1200 New Jersey Avenue, SE., Washington, DC 20590.

(b) Submit a petition for rulemaking or exemption from part 139 of this chapter—

(1) To the appropriate FAA airport field office in whose area your airport is, or will be, established; and

(2) To the U.S. Department of Transportation, Docket Operations, West Building Ground Floor, Room W12-140, 1200 New Jersey Avenue, SE., Washington, DC 20590 or by electronic submission to this Internet address: http://www.regulations.gov.

(c) The FAA may designate other means by which you can submit petitions in the future.

(d) Submit your petition for exemption 120 days before you need the exemption to take effect.

[Amdt. 11-50, 69 FR 22386, Apr. 26, 2004, as amended at 72 FR 68474, Dec. 5, 2007; Amdt. 11-55, 74 FR 202, Jan. 5, 2009]

§11.71 What information must I include in my petition for rulemaking?

(a) You must include the following information in your petition for rulemaking:

(1) Your name and mailing address and, if you wish, other contact information such as a fax number, telephone number, or e-mail address.

(2) An explanation of your proposed action and its purpose.

(3) The language you propose for a new or amended rule, or the language you would remove from a current rule.

(4) An explanation of why your proposed action would be in the public interest.

(5) Information and arguments that support your proposed action, including relevant technical and scientific data available to you.

(6) Any specific facts or circumstances that support or demonstrate the need for the action you propose.

(b) In the process of considering your petition, we may ask that you provide information or data available to you about the following:

(1) The costs and benefits of your proposed action to society in general, and identifiable groups within society in particular.

(2) The regulatory burden of your proposed action on small businesses, small organizations, small governmental jurisdictions, and Indian tribes.

(3) The recordkeeping and reporting burdens of your proposed action and whom the burdens would affect.

(4) The effect of your proposed action on the quality of the natural and social environments.

§11.73 How does FAA process petitions for rulemaking?

After we have determined the disposition of your petition, we will contact you in writing about our decision. The FAA may respond to your petition for rulemaking in one of the following ways:

(a) If we determine that your petition justifies our taking the action you suggest, we may issue an NPRM or ANPRM. We will do so no later than 6 months after the date we receive your petition. In making our decision, we consider:

(1) The immediacy of the safety or security concerns you raise;

(2) The priority of other issues the FAA must deal with; and

(3) The resources we have available to address these issues.

(b) If we have issued an ANPRM or NPRM on the subject matter of your petition, we will consider your arguments for a rule change as a comment in connection with the rulemaking proceeding. We will not treat your petition as a separate action.

(c) If we have begun a rulemaking project in the subject area of your petition, we will consider your comments and arguments for a rule change as part of that project. We will not treat your petition as a separate action.

(d) If we have tasked ARAC to study the general subject area of your petition, we will ask ARAC to review and evaluate your proposed action. We will not treat your petition as a separate action.

(e) If we determine that the issues you identify in your petition may have merit, but do not address an immediate safety concern or cannot be addressed because of other priorities and resource constraints, we may dismiss your petition. Your comments and arguments for a rule change will be placed in a database, which we will examine when we consider future rulemaking.

§11.73 How does FAA process petitions for rulemaking?

After we have determined the disposition of your petition, we will contact you in writing about our decision. The FAA may respond to your petition for rulemaking in one of the following ways:

(a) If we determine that your petition justifies our taking the action you suggest; we may issue an NPRM or ANPRM. We will do so no later than 6 months after the date we receive your petition. In making our decision, we consider:

(1) The immediacy of the safety or security concerns you raise;

(2) The priority of other issues the FAA must deal with; and

(3) The resources we have available to address these issues.

(b) If we have issued an ANPRM or NPRM on the subject matter of your petition, we will consider your arguments for a rule change as a comment in connection with the rulemaking proceeding. We will not treat your petition as a separate action.

(c) If we have begun a rulemaking project in the subject area of your petition, we will consider your comments and arguments for a rule change as part of that project. We will not treat your petition as a separate action.

(d) If we have tasked ARAC to study the general subject area of your petition, we will ask ARAC to review and evaluate your proposed action. We will not treat your petition as a separate action.

(e) If we determine that the issues you identify in your petition may have merit, but do not address an immediate safety concern or cannot be addressed because of other priorities and resource constraints, we may dismiss your petition. Your comments and arguments for a rule change will be placed in a database, which we will examine when we consider future rulemaking.

§11.75 Does FAA invite public comment on petitions for rulemaking?

Generally, FAA does not invite public comment on petitions for rulemaking.

§11.77 Is there any additional information I must include in my petition for designating airspace?

In petitions asking FAA to establish, amend, or repeal a designation of airspace, including special use airspace, you must include all the information specified by §11.71 and also:

(a) The location and a description of the airspace you want assigned or designated;

(b) A complete description of the activity or use to be made of that airspace, including a detailed description of the type, volume, duration, time, and place of the operations to be conducted in the area;

(c) A description of the air navigation, air traffic control, surveillance, and communication facilities available and to be provided if we grant the designation; and

(d) The name and location of the agency, office, facility, or person who would have authority to permit the use of the airspace when it was not in use for the purpose to which you want it assigned.

§11.81 What information must I include in my petition for an exemption?

You must include the following information in your petition for an exemption and submit it to FAA as soon as you know you need an exemption.

(a) Your name and mailing address and, if you wish, other contact information such as a fax number, telephone number, or e-mail address;

(b) The specific section or sections of 14 CFR from which you seek an exemption;

(c) The extent of relief you seek, and the reason you seek the relief;

(d) The reasons why granting your request would be in the public interest; that is, how it would benefit the public as a whole;

(e) The reasons why granting the exemption would not adversely affect safety, or how the exemption would provide a level of safety at least equal to that provided by the rule from which you seek the exemption;

(f) A summary we can publish in the Federal Register, stating:

(1) The rule from which you seek the exemption; and

(2) A brief description of the nature of the exemption you seek;

(g) Any additional information, views or arguments available to support your request; and

(h) If you want to exercise the privileges of your exemption outside the United States, the reason why you need to do so.

§11.85 Does FAA invite public comment on petitions for exemption?

Yes, FAA publishes information about petitions for exemption in the Federal Register. The information includes—

(a) The docket number of the petition;

(b) The citation to the rule or rules from which the petitioner requested relief;

(c) The name of the petitioner;

(d) The petitioner's summary of the action requested and the reasons for requesting it; and

(e) A request for comments to assist FAA in evaluating the petition.

§11.87 Are there circumstances in which FAA may decide not to publish a summary of my petition for exemption?

The FAA may not publish a summary of your petition for exemption and request comments if you present or we find good cause why we should not delay action on your petition. The factors we consider in deciding not to request comment include:

(a) Whether granting your petition would set a precedent.

(b) Whether the relief requested is identical to exemptions granted previously.

(c) Whether our delaying action on your petition would affect you adversely.

(d) Whether you filed your petition in a timely manner.

§11.89 How much time do I have to submit comments to FAA on a petition for exemption?

The FAA states the specific time allowed for comments in the Federal Register notice about the petition. We usually allow 20 days to comment on a petition for exemption.

§11.91 How does FAA inform me of its decision on my petition for exemption?

The FAA will notify you in writing about its decision on your petition. A copy of this decision is also placed in the public docket. We will include the docket number associated with your petition in our letter to you.

[Doc. No. FAA-2005-22982, 71 FR 1485, Jan. 10, 2006]

§11.101 May I ask FAA to reconsider my petition for rulemaking or petition for exemption if it is denied?

Yes, you may petition FAA to reconsider your petition denial. You must submit your request to the address to which you sent your original petition, and FAA must receive it within 60 days after we issued the denial. For us to accept your petition, show the following:

(a) That you have a significant additional fact and why you did not present it in your original petition;

(b) That we made an important factual error in our denial of your original petition; or

(c) That we did not correctly interpret a law, regulation, or precedent.

§11.103 What exemption relief may be available to federal, state, and local governments when operating aircraft that are not public aircraft?

The Federal Aviation Administration may grant a federal, state, or local government an exemption from part A of subtitle VII of title 49 United States Code, and any regulation issued under that authority that is applicable to an aircraft as a result of the Independent Safety Board Act Amendments of 1994, Public Law 103-411, if—

(a) The Administrator finds that granting the exemption is necessary to prevent an undue economic burden on the unit of government; and

(b) The Administrator certifies that the aviation safety program of the unit of government is effective and appropriate to ensure safe operations of the type of aircraft operated by the unit of government.

[68 FR 25488, May 13, 2003]

Appendix B: EU Regulations on Air Transport

REGULATION (EC) No 261/2004 OF THE EUROPEAN PARLIAMENT AND OF THE COUNCIL of 11 February 2004 establishing common rules on compensation and assistance to passengers in the event of denied boarding and of cancellation or long delay of flights, and repealing Regulation (EEC) No 295/91 (Text with EEA relevance)

THE EUROPEAN PARLIAMENT AND THE COUNCIL OF THE EUROPEAN UNION,

Having regard to the Treaty establishing the European Community, and in particular Article 80(2) thereof,

Having regard to the proposal from the Commission (1),

Having regard to the opinion of the European Economic and Social Committee (2),

After consulting the Committee of the Regions,

Acting in accordance with the procedure laid down in Article 251 of the Treaty (3), in the light of the joint text approved by the Conciliation Committee on 1 December 2003,

Whereas:

(1) Action by the Community in the field of air transport should aim, among other things, at ensuring a high level of protection for passengers. Moreover, full account should be taken of the requirements of consumer protection in general.

(2) Denied boarding and cancellation or long delay of flights cause serious trouble and inconvenience to passengers.

(3) While Council Regulation (EEC) No 295/91 of 4 February 1991 establishing common rules for a denied boarding compensation system in scheduled air transport (4) created basic protection for passengers, the number of passengers

R. Abeyratne, *Rulemaking in Air Transport*, DOI 10.1007/978-3-319-44657-8

denied boarding against their will remains too high, as does that affected by cancellations without prior warning and that affected by long delays.

(4) The Community should therefore raise the standards of protection set by that Regulation both to strengthen the rights of passengers and to ensure that air carriers operate under harmonised conditions in a liberalised market.

(5) Since the distinction between scheduled and non-scheduled air services is weakening, such protection should apply to passengers not only on scheduled but also on non-scheduled flights, including those forming part of package tours.

(6) The protection accorded to passengers departing from an airport located in a Member State should be extended to those leaving an airport located in a third country for one situated in a Member State, when a Community carrier operates the flight.

(7) In order to ensure the effective application of this Regulation, the obligations that it creates should rest with the operating air carrier who performs or intends to perform a flight, whether with owned aircraft, under dry or wet lease, or on any other basis.

(8) This Regulation should not restrict the rights of the operating air carrier to seek compensation from any person, including third parties, in accordance with the law applicable.

(9) The number of passengers denied boarding against their will should be reduced by requiring air carriers to call for volunteers to surrender their reservations, in exchange for benefits, instead of denying passengers boarding, and by fully compensating those finally denied boarding.

(10) Passengers denied boarding against their will should be able either to cancel their flights, with reimbursement of their tickets, or to continue them under satisfactory conditions, and should be adequately cared for while awaiting a later flight.

(11) Volunteers should also be able to cancel their flights, with reimbursement of their tickets, or continue them under satisfactory conditions, since they face difficulties of travel similar to those experienced by passengers denied boarding against their will.

(12) The trouble and inconvenience to passengers caused by cancellation of flights should also be reduced. This should be achieved by inducing carriers to inform passengers of cancellations before the scheduled time of departure and in addition to offer them reasonable rerouting, so that the passengers can make other arrangements. Air carriers should compensate passengers if they fail to do this, except when the cancellation occurs in extraordinary circumstances which could not have been avoided even if all reasonable measures had been taken.

(13) Passengers whose flights are cancelled should be able either to obtain reimbursement of their tickets or to obtain re-routing under satisfactory conditions, and should be adequately cared for while awaiting a later flight.

(14) As under the Montreal Convention, obligations on operating air carriers should be limited or excluded in cases where an event has been caused by extraordinary circumstances which could not have been avoided even if all reasonable measures had been taken. Such circumstances may, in particular, occur in cases of political instability, meteorological conditions incompatible with the operation of the flight concerned, security risks, unexpected flight safety shortcomings and strikes that affect the operation of an operating air carrier.

(15) Extraordinary circumstances should be deemed to exist where the impact of an air traffic management decision in relation to a particular aircraft on a particular day gives rise to a long delay, an overnight delay, or the cancellation of one or more flights by that aircraft, even though all reasonable measures had been taken by the air carrier concerned to avoid the delays or cancellations.

(16) In cases where a package tour is cancelled for reasons other than the flight being cancelled, this Regulation should not apply.

(17) Passengers whose flights are delayed for a specified time should be adequately cared for and should be able to cancel their flights with reimbursement of their tickets or to continue them under satisfactory conditions.

(18) Care for passengers awaiting an alternative or a delayed flight may be limited or declined if the provision of the care would itself cause further delay.

(19) Operating air carriers should meet the special needs of persons with reduced mobility and any persons accompanying them.

(20) Passengers should be fully informed of their rights in the event of denied boarding and of cancellation or long delay of flights, so that they can effectively exercise their rights.

(21) Member States should lay down rules on sanctions applicable to infringements of the provisions of this Regulation and ensure that these sanctions are applied. The sanctions should be effective, proportionate and dissuasive.

(22) Member States should ensure and supervise general compliance by their air carriers with this Regulation and designate an appropriate body to carry out such enforcement tasks. The supervision should not affect the rights of passengers and air carriers to seek legal redress from courts under procedures of national law.

(23) The Commission should analyse the application of this Regulation and should assess in particular the opportunity of extending its scope to all passengers having a contract with a tour operator or with a Community carrier, when departing from a third country airport to an airport in a Member State.

(24) Arrangements for greater cooperation over the use of Gibraltar airport were agreed in London on 2 December 1987 by the Kingdom of Spain and the United Kingdom in a joint declaration by the Ministers of Foreign Affairs of the two countries. Such arrangements have yet to enter into operation.

HAVE ADOPTED THIS REGULATION:

Article 1

Subject

1. This Regulation establishes, under the conditions specified herein, minimum rights for passengers when:

(a) they are denied boarding against their will;

(b) their flight is cancelled;

(c) their flight is delayed.

2. Application of this Regulation to Gibraltar airport is understood to be without prejudice to the respective legal positions of the Kingdom of Spain and the United Kingdom with regard to the dispute over sovereignty over the territory in which the airport is situated.

1. Application of this Regulation to Gibraltar airport shall be suspended until the arrangements in the Joint Declaration made by the Foreign Ministers of the Kingdom of Spain and the United Kingdom on 2 December 1987 enter into operation. The Governments of Spain and the United Kingdom will inform the Council of such date of entry into operation.

Article 2

Definitions

For the purposes of this Regulation:

(a) 'air carrier' means an air transport undertaking with a valid operating licence;

(b) 'operating air carrier' means an air carrier that performs or intends to perform a flight under a contract with a passenger or on behalf of another person, legal or natural, having a contract with that passenger;

(c) 'Community carrier' means an air carrier with a valid operating licence granted by a Member State in accordance with the provisions of Council Regulation (EEC) No 2407/92 of 23 July 1992 on licensing of air carriers (1);

(d) 'tour operator' means, with the exception of an air carrier, an organiser within the meaning of Article 2, point 2, of Council Directive 90/314/EEC of 13 June 1990 on package travel, package holidays and package tours (2);

(e) 'package' means those services defined in Article 2, point 1, of Directive 90/314/EEC;

(f) 'ticket' means a valid document giving entitlement to transport, or something equivalent in paperless form, including electronic form, issued or authorised by the air carrier or its authorised agent;

(g) 'reservation' means the fact that the passenger has a ticket, or other proof, which indicates that the reservation has been accepted and registered by the air carrier or tour operator;

(h) 'final destination' means the destination on the ticket presented at the check-in counter or, in the case of directly connecting flights, the destination of the last flight; alternative connecting flights available shall not be taken into account if the original planned arrival time is respected;

(i) 'person with reduced mobility' means any person whose mobility is reduced when using transport because of any physical disability (sensory or locomotory, permanent or temporary), intellectual impairment, age or any other cause of disability, and whose situation needs special attention and adaptation to the person's needs of the services made available to all passengers;

(j) 'denied boarding' means a refusal to carry passengers on a flight, although they have presented themselves for boarding under the conditions laid down in Article 3(2), except where there are reasonable grounds to deny them boarding, such as reasons of health, safety or security, or inadequate travel documentation;

(k) 'volunteer' means a person who has presented himself for boarding under the conditions laid down in Article 3(2) and responds positively to the air carrier's call for passengers prepared to surrender their reservation in exchange for benefits.

(l) 'cancellation' means the non-operation of a flight which was previously planned and on which at least one place was reserved.

Article 3

Scope

1. This Regulation shall apply:

(a) to passengers departing from an airport located in the territory of a Member State to which the Treaty applies;

(b) to passengers departing from an airport located in a third country to an airport situated in the territory of a Member State to which the Treaty applies, unless they received benefits or compensation and were given assistance in that third country, if the operating air carrier of the flight concerned is a Community carrier.

2. Paragraph 1 shall apply on the condition that passengers:

(a) have a confirmed reservation on the flight concerned and, except in the case of cancellation referred to in Article 5, present themselves for check-in, — as stipulated and at the time indicated in advance and in writing (including by electronic means) by the air carrier, the tour operator or an authorised travel agent, or, if no time is indicated, — not later than 45 minutes before the published departure time; or

(b) have been transferred by an air carrier or tour operator from the flight for which they held a reservation to another flight, irrespective of the reason.

3. This Regulation shall not apply to passengers travelling free of charge or at a reduced fare not available directly or indirectly to the public. However, it shall apply to passengers having tickets issued under a frequent flyer programme or other commercial programme by an air carrier or tour operator.

4. This Regulation shall only apply to passengers transported by motorised fixed wing aircraft.

5. This Regulation shall apply to any operating air carrier providing transport to passengers covered by paragraphs 1 and 2. Where an operating air carrier which has no contract with the passenger performs obligations under this Regulation, it shall be regarded as doing so on behalf of the person having a contract with that passenger.

6. This Regulation shall not affect the rights of passengers under Directive 90/314/EEC. This Regulation shall not apply in cases where a package tour is cancelled for reasons other than cancellation of the flight.

Article 4

Denied boarding

1. When an operating air carrier reasonably expects to deny boarding on a flight, it shall first call for volunteers to surrender their reservations in exchange for benefits under conditions to be agreed between the passenger concerned and the operating air carrier. Volunteers shall be assisted in accordance with Article 8, such assistance being additional to the benefits mentioned in this paragraph.

2. If an insufficient number of volunteers comes forward to allow the remaining passengers with reservations to board the flight, the operating air carrier may then deny boarding to passengers against their will.

3. If boarding is denied to passengers against their will, the operating air carrier shall immediately compensate them in accordance with Article 7 and assist them in accordance with Articles 8 and 9.

Article 5

Cancellation

1. In case of cancellation of a flight, the passengers concerned shall:

(a) be offered assistance by the operating air carrier in accordance with Article 8; and

(b) be offered assistance by the operating air carrier in accordance with Article 9 (1)(a) and 9(2), as well as, in event of rerouting when the reasonably expected time of departure of the new flight is at least the day after the departure as it was planned for the cancelled flight, the assistance specified in Article 9(1)(b) and 9 (1)(c); and

(c) have the right to compensation by the operating air carrier in accordance with Article 7, unless: (i) they are informed of the cancellation at least two weeks before the scheduled time of departure; or

(ii) they are informed of the cancellation between two weeks and seven days before the scheduled time of departure and are offered re-routing, allowing them to depart no more than two hours before the scheduled time of departure and to reach their final destination less than four hours after the scheduled time of arrival; or (iii) they are informed of the cancellation less than seven days before the scheduled time of departure and are offered re-routing, allowing them to depart no more than one hour before the scheduled time of departure and to reach their final destination less than two hours after the scheduled time of arrival.

2. When passengers are informed of the cancellation, an explanation shall be given concerning possible alternative transport.

3. An operating air carrier shall not be obliged to pay compensation in accordance with Article 7, if it can prove that the cancellation is caused by extraordinary circumstances which could not have been avoided even if all reasonable measures had been taken.

4. The burden of proof concerning the questions as to whether and when the passenger has been informed of the cancellation of the flight shall rest with the operating air carrier.

Article 6

Delay

1. When an operating air carrier reasonably expects a flight to be delayed beyond its scheduled time of departure:

(a) for two hours or more in the case of flights of 1500 kilometres or less; or

(b) for three hours or more in the case of all intra-Community flights of more than 1500 kilometres and of all other flights between 1500 and 3500 kilometres; or

(c) for four hours or more in the case of all flights not falling under (a) or (b), passengers shall be offered by the operating air carrier: (i) the assistance specified in Article 9(1)(a) and 9(2); and

(ii) when the reasonably expected time of departure is at least the day after the time of departure previously announced, the assistance specified in Article 9(1) (b) and 9(1)(c); and

(iii) when the delay is at least five hours, the assistance specified in Article 8(1)(a).

2. In any event, the assistance shall be offered within the time limits set out above with respect to each distance bracket.

Article 7

Right to compensation

1. Where reference is made to this Article, passengers shall receive compensation amounting to:

(a) EUR 250 for all flights of 1500 kilometres or less;

(b) EUR 400 for all intra-Community flights of more than 1500 kilometres, and for all other flights between 1500 and 3500 kilometres;

(c) EUR 600 for all flights not falling under (a) or (b).

In determining the distance, the basis shall be the last destination at which the denial of boarding or cancellation will delay the passenger's arrival after the scheduled time.

2. When passengers are offered re-routing to their final destination on an alternative flight pursuant to Article 8, the arrival time of which does not exceed the scheduled arrival time of the flight originally booked:

(a) by two hours, in respect of all flights of 1500 kilometres or less; or

(b) by three hours, in respect of all intra-Community flights of more than 1500 kilometres and for all other flights between 1500 and 3500 kilometres; or

(c) by four hours, in respect of all flights not falling under (a) or (b), the operating air carrier may reduce the compensation provided for in paragraph 1 by 50 %.

4. The compensation referred to in paragraph 1 shall be paid in cash, by electronic bank transfer, bank orders or bank cheques or, with the signed agreement of the passenger, in travel vouchers and/or other services.

5. The distances given in paragraphs 1 and 2 shall be measured by the great circle route method.

Article 8

Right to reimbursement or re-routing

1. Where reference is made to this Article, passengers shall be offered the choice between:

(a) — reimbursement within seven days, by the means provided for in Article 7 (3), of the full cost of the ticket at the price at which it was bought, for the part or parts of the journey not made, and for the part or parts already made if the flight is no longer serving any purpose in relation to the passenger's original travel plan, together with, when relevant, — a return flight to the first point of departure, at the earliest opportunity;

(b) re-routing, under comparable transport conditions, to their final destination at the earliest opportunity; or

(c) re-routing, under comparable transport conditions, to their final destination at a later date at the passenger's convenience, subject to availability of seats.

1. Paragraph 1(a) shall also apply to passengers whose flights form part of a package, except for the right to reimbursement where such right arises under Directive 90/314/EEC.

2. When, in the case where a town, city or region is served by several airports, an operating air carrier offers a passenger a flight to an airport alternative to that for which the booking was made, the operating air carrier shall bear the cost of transferring the passenger from that alternative airport either to that for which the booking was made, or to another close-by destination agreed with the passenger.

Article 9

Right to care

1. Where reference is made to this Article, passengers shall be offered free of charge:

(a) meals and refreshments in a reasonable relation to the waiting time;

(b) hotel accommodation in cases — where a stay of one or more nights becomes necessary, or — where a stay additional to that intended by the passenger becomes necessary;

(c) transport between the airport and place of accommodation (hotel or other).

1. In addition, passengers shall be offered free of charge two telephone calls, telex or fax messages, or e-mails.

2. In applying this Article, the operating air carrier shall pay particular attention to the needs of persons with reduced mobility and any persons accompanying them, as well as to the needs of unaccompanied children.

Article 10

Upgrading and downgrading

1. If an operating air carrier places a passenger in a class higher than that for which the ticket was purchased, it may not request any supplementary payment.

2. If an operating air carrier places a passenger in a class lower than that for which the ticket was purchased, it shall within seven days, by the means provided for in Article 7(3), reimburse

(a) 30 % of the price of the ticket for all flights of 1500 kilometres or less, or

(b) 50 % of the price of the ticket for all intra-Community flights of more than 1500 kilometres, except flights between the European territory of the Member States and the French overseas departments, and for all other flights between 1500 and 3500 kilometres, or

(c) 75 % of the price of the ticket for all flights not falling under (a) or (b), including flights between the European territory of the Member States and the French overseas departments.

Article 11

Persons with reduced mobility or special needs

1. Operating air carriers shall give priority to carrying persons with reduced mobility and any persons or certified service dogs accompanying them, as well as unaccompanied children.

2. In cases of denied boarding, cancellation and delays of any length, persons with reduced mobility and any persons accompanying them, as well as unaccompanied children, shall have the right to care in accordance with Article 9 as soon as possible.

Article 12

Further compensation

1. This Regulation shall apply without prejudice to a passenger's rights to further compensation. The compensation granted under this Regulation may be deducted from such compensation.

2. Without prejudice to relevant principles and rules of national law, including case-law, paragraph 1 shall not apply to passengers who have voluntarily surrendered a reservation under Article 4(1).

Article 13

Right of redress

In cases where an operating air carrier pays compensation or meets the other obligations incumbent on it under this Regulation, no provision of this Regulation may be interpreted as restricting its right to seek compensation from any person, including third parties, in accordance with the law applicable. In particular, this Regulation shall in no way restrict the operating air carrier's right to seek reimbursement from a tour operator or another person with whom the operating air carrier has a contract. Similarly, no provision of this Regulation may be interpreted as restricting the right of a tour operator or a third party, other than a passenger, with whom an operating air carrier has a contract, to seek reimbursement or compensation from the operating air carrier in accordance with applicable relevant laws.

Article 14

Obligation to inform passengers of their rights

1. The operating air carrier shall ensure that at check-in a clearly legible notice containing the following text is displayed in a manner clearly visible to passengers: 'If you are denied boarding or if your flight is cancelled or delayed for at least two hours, ask at the check-in counter or boarding gate for the text stating your rights, particularly with regard to compensation and assistance'.

2. An operating air carrier denying boarding or cancelling a flight shall provide each passenger affected with a written notice setting out the rules for compensation and assistance in line with this Regulation. It shall also provide each passenger affected by a delay of at least two hours with an equivalent notice. The contact details of the national designated body referred to in Article 16 shall also be given to the passenger in written form.

3. In respect of blind and visually impaired persons, the provisions of this Article shall be applied using appropriate alternative means.

Article 15

Exclusion of waiver

1. Obligations vis-à-vis passengers pursuant to this Regulation may not be limited or waived, notably by a derogation or restrictive clause in the contract of carriage.

2. If, nevertheless, such a derogation or restrictive clause is applied in respect of a passenger, or if the passenger is not correctly informed of his rights and for that reason has accepted compensation which is inferior to that provided for in this Regulation, the passenger shall still be entitled to take the necessary proceedings before the competent courts or bodies in order to obtain additional compensation.

Article 16

Infringements

1. Each Member State shall designate a body responsible for the enforcement of this Regulation as regards flights from airports situated on its territory and flights from a third country to such airports. Where appropriate, this body shall take the measures necessary to ensure that the rights of passengers are respected. The Member States shall inform the Commission of the body that has been designated in accordance with this paragraph.

2. Without prejudice to Article 12, each passenger may complain to any body designated under paragraph 1, or to any other competent body designated by a Member State, about an alleged infringement of this Regulation at any airport situated on the territory of a Member State or concerning any flight from a third country to an airport situated on that territory. 3. The sanctions laid down by

Member States for infringements of this Regulation shall be effective, proportionate and dissuasive.

Article 17

Report

The Commission shall report to the European Parliament and the Council by 1 January 2007 on the operation and the results of this Regulation, in particular regarding: — the incidence of denied boarding and of cancellation of flights, — the possible extension of the scope of this Regulation to passengers having a contract with a Community carrier or holding a flight reservation which forms part of a 'package tour' to which Directive 90/314/EEC applies and who depart from a third-country airport to an airport in a Member State, on flights not operated by Community air carriers, — the possible revision of the amounts of compensation referred to in Article 7(1).

The report shall be accompanied where necessary by legislative proposals.

Article 18 Repeal

Regulation (EEC) No 295/91 shall be repealed.

Article 19

Entry into force

This Regulation shall enter into force on 17 February 2005.

This Regulation shall be binding in its entirety and directly applicable in all Member States.

Done at Strasbourg, 11 February 2004.

REGULATION (EC) No 300/2008 OF THE EUROPEAN PARLIAMENT AND OF THE COUNCIL of 11 March 2008

on common rules in the field of civil aviation security and repealing Regulation (EC) No 2320/2002

(Text with EEA relevance)

THE EUROPEAN PARLIAMENT AND THE COUNCIL OF THE EUROPEAN UNION,

Having regard to the Treaty establishing the European Community, and in particular Article 80(2) thereof,

Having regard to the proposal from the Commission,

Having regard to the opinion of the European Economic and Social Committee (1),

Having consulted the Committee of the Regions,

Acting in accordance with the procedure laid down in Article 251 of the Treaty (2), in the light of the joint text approved by the Conciliation Committee on 16 January 2008.

Whereas:

(1) In order to protect persons and goods within the European Union, acts of unlawful interference with civil aircraft that jeopardise the security of civil aviation should be prevented by establishing common rules for safeguarding civil aviation. This objective should be achieved by setting common rules and common basic standards on aviation security as well as mechanisms for monitoring compliance.

(2) It is desirable, in the interests of civil aviation security generally, to provide the basis for a common interpretation of Annex 17 to the Chicago Convention on International Civil Aviation of 7 December 1944.

(3) Regulation (EC) No 2320/2002 of the European Parliament and of the Council of 16 December 2002 establishing common rules in the field of civil aviation security (3) was adopted as a result of the events of 11 September 2001 in the United States. A common approach is needed in the field of civil aviation security and consideration should be given to the most effective means of offering assistance following terrorist acts that have a major impact in the transport field.

(4) The content of Regulation (EC) No 2320/2002 should be revised in the light of the experience gained, and the Regulation itself should be repealed and replaced by this Regulation seeking the simplification, harmonisation and clarification of the existing rules and the improvement of the levels of security.

(5) Given the need for more flexibility in adopting security measures and procedures in order to meet evolving risk assessments and to allow new technologies to be introduced, this Regulation should lay down the basic principles of what has to be done in order to safeguard civil aviation against acts of unlawful interference without going into the technical and procedural details of how they are to be implemented.

(6) This Regulation should apply to airports serving civil aviation located in the territory of a Member State, to operators providing services at such airports and to entities providing goods and/or services to or through such airports.

(7) Without prejudice to the Convention on offences and certain other acts committed on board aircraft, Tokyo, 1963, the Convention for the suppression of unlawful seizure of aircraft, The Hague, 1970, and the Convention for the suppression of unlawful acts against the safety of civil aviation, Montreal, 1971, this Regulation should also cover security measures that apply on board an aircraft, or during a flight, of Community air carriers.

(8) Each Member State retains the competence to decide whether to deploy in-flight security officers on aircraft registered in that Member State and on flights of air carriers licensed by it as well as to ensure, in accordance with paragraph 4.7.7 of Annex 17 to the Chicago Convention on International Civil Aviation and under the terms of that Convention, that such officers are government personnel who are specially selected and trained, taking into account the required security and safety aspects on board an aircraft.

(9) The various types of civil aviation do not necessarily present the same level of threat. In setting common basic standards on aviation security, the size of the aircraft, the nature of the operation and/or the frequency of operations at airports should be taken into account with a view to permitting the grant of derogations.

(10) Member States should also be allowed, on the basis of a risk assessment, to apply more stringent measures than those laid down in this Regulation.

(11) Third countries may require the application of measures that differ from those laid down in this Regulation in respect of flights from an airport in a Member State to, or over, that third country. However, without prejudice to any bilateral agreements to which the Community is a party, it should be possible for the Commission to examine the measures required by the third country.

(12) Even though, within a single Member State, there may be two or more bodies involved in aviation security, each Member State should designate a single authority responsible for the coordination and monitoring of the implementation of security standards.

(13) In order to define responsibilities for the implementation of the common basic standards on aviation security and to describe what measures are required by operators and other entities for this purpose, each Member State should draw up a national civil aviation security programme. Furthermore, each airport operator, air carrier and entity implementing aviation security standards should draw up, apply and maintain a security programme in order to comply both with this Regulation and with whichever national civil aviation security programme is applicable.

(14) In order to monitor compliance with this Regulation and with the national civil aviation security programme, each Member State should draw up and ensure the implementation of a national programme to check the level and quality of civil aviation security.

(15) In order to monitor the application by Member States of this Regulation, and also to make recommendations to improve aviation security, the Commission should conduct inspections, including unannounced inspections.

(16) As a general rule, the Commission should publish measures that have a direct impact on passengers. Implementing acts setting out common measures and procedures for the implementation of the common basic standards on aviation security which contain sensitive security information, together with

Commission inspection reports and the answers of the appropriate authorities should be regarded as EU classified information within the meaning of Commission Decision 2001/844/EC, ECSC, Euratom of 29 November 2001 amending its internal rules of procedure (4). Those items should not be published and should be made available only to those operators and entities with a legitimate interest.

(17) The measures necessary for the implementation of this Regulation should be adopted in accordance with Council Decision 1999/468/EC of 28 June 1999 laying down the procedures for the exercise of implementing powers conferred on the Commission (5).

(18) In particular, the Commission should be empowered to adopt general measures amending non-essential elements of the common basic standards by supplementing them, set criteria allowing Member States both to derogate from the common basic standards and to adopt alternative security measures, and adopt specifications for national quality control programmes. Since those measures are of general scope and are designed to amend non-essential elements of this Regulation by supplementing it with new non-essential elements, they must be adopted in accordance with the regulatory procedure with scrutiny provided for in Article 5a of Decision 1999/468/EC.

(19) When, on imperative grounds of urgency, the normal time-limits for the regulatory procedure with scrutiny cannot be complied with, the Commission should be able to apply the urgency procedure provided for in Article 5a(6) of Decision 1999/468/EC for the adoption of common rules for safeguarding civil aviation.

(20) The goal of 'one-stop security' for all flights within the European Union should be advanced.

(21) Furthermore, it should not be necessary to rescreen passengers or their baggage arriving on flights from third countries that have aviation security standards equivalent to those laid down by this Regulation. Therefore, without prejudice to the right of each Member State to apply more stringent measures, or to the respective competences of the Community and Member States, decisions of the Commission, and, where necessary, agreements between the Community and third countries, which recognise that the security standards applied in the third country are equivalent to the common standards, should be encouraged since these further one-stop security.

(22) This Regulation is without prejudice to the application of rules on aviation safety, including those relating to the transport of dangerous goods.

(23) Penalties should be provided for infringements of the provisions of this Regulation. Those penalties, which may be of a civil or administrative nature, should be effective, proportionate and dissuasive.

(24) The Ministerial Statement on Gibraltar Airport, agreed in Cordoba on 18 September 2006 during the first Ministerial meeting of the Forum of Dialogue on Gibraltar, will replace the Joint Declaration on Gibraltar Airport made in London on 2 December 1987, and full compliance with it will be deemed to constitute compliance with the 1987 Declaration.

(25) Since the objectives of this Regulation, namely to safeguard civil aviation against acts of unlawful interference and to provide a basis for a common interpretation of Annex 17 to the Chicago Convention on International Civil Aviation, cannot be sufficiently achieved by the Member States and can therefore, by reason of the scale and effects of this Regulation, be better achieved at Community level, the Community may adopt measures, in accordance with the principle of subsidiarity as set out in Article 5 of the Treaty. In accordance with the principle of proportionality, as set out in that Article, this Regulation does not go beyond what is necessary in order to achieve those objectives,

HAVE ADOPTED THIS REGULATION:

Article 1

Objectives

1. This Regulation establishes common rules to protect civil aviation against acts of unlawful interference that jeopardise the security of civil aviation.

It also provides the basis for a common interpretation of Annex 17 to the Chicago Convention on International Civil Aviation.

2. The means of achieving the objectives set out in paragraph 1 shall be:

(a) the setting of common rules and common basic standards on aviation security;

(b) mechanisms for monitoring compliance.

Article 2

Scope

1. This Regulation shall apply to the following:

(a) all airports or parts of airports located in the territory of a Member State that are not exclusively used for military purposes;

(b) all operators, including air carriers, providing services at airports referred to in point (a);

(c) all entities applying aviation security standards that operate from premises located inside or outside airport premises and provide goods and/or services to or through airports referred to in point (a).

2. The application of this Regulation to the airport of Gibraltar is understood to be without prejudice to the respective legal positions of the Kingdom of Spain

and the United Kingdom with regard to the dispute over sovereignty over the territory in which the airport is situated.

Article 3

Definitions

For the purposes of this Regulation:

1. 'civil aviation' means any air operation carried out by civil aircraft, excluding operations carried out by State aircraft referred to in Article 3 of the Chicago Convention on International Civil Aviation;

2. 'aviation security' means the combination of measures and human and material resources intended to safeguard civil aviation against acts of unlawful interference that jeopardise the security of civil aviation;

3. 'operator' means a person, organisation or enterprise engaged, or offering to engage, in an air transport operation;

4. 'air carrier' means an air transport undertaking holding a valid operating licence or equivalent;

5. 'Community air carrier' means an air carrier holding a valid operating licence granted by a Member State in accordance with Council Regulation (EEC) No 2407/92 of 23 July 1992 on licensing of air carriers (6);

6. 'entity' means a person, organisation or enterprise, other than an operator;

7. 'prohibited articles' means weapons, explosives or other dangerous devices, articles or substances that may be used to commit an act of unlawful interference that jeopardises the security of civil aviation;

8. 'screening' means the application of technical or other means which are intended to identify and/or detect prohibited articles;

9. 'security control' means the application of means by which the introduction of prohibited articles may be prevented;

10. 'access control' means the application of means by which the entry of unauthorised persons or unauthorised vehicles, or both, may be prevented;

11. 'airside' means the movement area of an airport, adjacent terrain and buildings or portions thereof, access to which is restricted;

12. 'landside' means those parts of an airport, adjacent terrain and buildings or portions thereof that are not airside;

13. 'security restricted area' means that area of airside where, in addition to access being restricted, other aviation security standards are applied;

14. 'demarcated area' means an area that is separated by means of access control either from security restricted areas, or, if the demarcated area itself is a security restricted area, from other security restricted areas of an airport.,

15. 'background check' means a recorded check of a person's identity, including any criminal history, as part of the assessment of an individual's suitability for unescorted access to security restricted areas;

16. 'transfer passengers, baggage, cargo or mail' means passengers, baggage, cargo or mail departing on an aircraft other than that on which they arrived;

17. 'transit passengers, baggage, cargo or mail' means passengers, baggage, cargo or mail departing on the same aircraft as that on which they arrived;

18. 'potentially disruptive passenger' means a passenger who is either a deportee, a person deemed to be inadmissible for immigration reasons or a person in lawful custody;

19. 'cabin baggage' means baggage intended for carriage in the cabin of an aircraft;

20. 'hold baggage' means baggage intended for carriage in the hold of an aircraft;

21. 'accompanied hold baggage' means baggage, carried in the hold of an aircraft, which has been checked in for a flight by a passenger travelling on that same flight;

22. 'air carrier mail' means mail whose origin and destination are both an air carrier;

23. 'air carrier materials' means materials either whose origin and destination are both an air carrier or that are used by an air carrier;

24. 'mail' means dispatches of correspondence and other items, other than air carrier mail, tendered by and intended for delivery to postal services in accordance with the rules of the Universal Postal Union;

25. 'cargo' means any property intended for carriage on an aircraft, other than baggage, mail, air carrier mail, air carrier materials and in-flight supplies;

26. 'regulated agent' means an air carrier, agent, freight forwarder or any other entity who ensures security controls in respect of cargo or mail;

27. 'known consignor' means a consignor who originates cargo or mail for its own account and whose procedures meet common security rules and standards sufficient to allow carriage of cargo or mail on any aircraft;

28. 'account consignor' means a consignor who originates cargo or mail for its own account and whose procedures meet common security rules and standards sufficient to allow carriage of that cargo on all-cargo aircraft or mail on all-mail aircraft;

29. 'aircraft security check' means an inspection of those parts of the interior of the aircraft to which passengers may have had access, together with an inspection of the hold of the aircraft in order to detect prohibited articles and unlawful interferences with the aircraft;

30. 'aircraft security search' means an inspection of the interior and accessible exterior of the aircraft in order to detect prohibited articles and unlawful interferences that jeopardise the security of the aircraft;

31. 'in-flight security officer' means a person who is employed by a state to travel on an aircraft of an air carrier licensed by it with the purpose of protecting that aircraft and its occupants against acts of unlawful interference that jeopardise the security of the flight.

Article 4

Common basic standards

1. The common basic standards for safeguarding civil aviation against acts of unlawful interference that jeopardise the security of civil aviation shall be as laid down in the Annex.

Additional common basic standards not foreseen at the entry into force of this Regulation should be added to the Annex in accordance with the procedure referred to in Article 251 of the Treaty.

2. General measures, designed to amend non-essential elements of the common basic standards referred to in paragraph 1 by supplementing them, shall be adopted in accordance with the regulatory procedure with scrutiny referred to in Article 19(3).

These general measures shall concern:

(a) methods of screening allowed;

(b) categories of articles that may be prohibited;

(c) as regards access control, grounds for granting access to airside and security restricted areas;

(d) methods allowed for the examination of vehicles, aircraft security checks and aircraft security searches;

(e) criteria for recognising the equivalence of security standards of third countries;

(f) conditions under which cargo and mail shall be screened or subjected to other security controls, as well as the process for the approval or designation of regulated agents, known consignors and account consignors;

(g) conditions under which air carrier mail and air carrier materials shall be screened or subjected to other security controls;

(h) conditions under which in-flight supplies and airport supplies shall be screened or subjected to other security controls, as well as the process for the approval or designation of regulated suppliers and known suppliers;

(i) criteria for defining critical parts of security restricted areas;

(j) criteria for staff recruitment and methods of training;

(k) conditions under which special security procedures or exemptions from security controls may be applied; and

(l) any general measures designed to amend non-essential elements of the common basic standards referred to in paragraph 1 by supplementing them not foreseen at the date of entry into force of this Regulation.

On imperative grounds of urgency, the Commission may use the urgency procedure referred to in Article 19(4).

3. Detailed measures for the implementation of the common basic standards referred to in paragraph 1 and the general measures referred to in paragraph 2 shall be laid down in accordance with the regulatory procedure referred to in Article 19(2).

These shall include:

(a) requirements and procedures for screening;

(b) a list of prohibited articles;

(c) requirements and procedures for access control;

(d) requirements and procedures for the examination of vehicles, aircraft security checks and aircraft security searches;

(e) decisions to recognise the equivalence of security standards applied in a third country;

(f) as regards cargo and mail, procedures for the approval or designation of, and the obligations to be fulfilled by, regulated agents, known consignors and account consignors;

(g) requirements and procedures for security controls of air carrier mail and air carrier materials;

(h) as regards in-flight supplies and airport supplies, procedures for the approval or designation of, and the obligations to be fulfilled by, regulated suppliers and known suppliers;

(i) definition of critical parts of security restricted areas;

(j) staff recruitment and training requirements;

(k) special security procedures or exemptions from security controls;

(l) technical specifications and procedures for approval and use of security equipment; and

(m) requirements and procedures concerning potentially disruptive passengers.

4. The Commission shall, by amending this Regulation through a decision in accordance with the regulatory procedure with scrutiny referred to in Article 19 (3), set criteria to allow Member States to derogate from the common basic standards referred to in paragraph 1 and to adopt alternative security measures that provide an adequate level of protection on the basis of a local risk assessment. Such alternative measures shall be justified by reasons relating to the size of the aircraft, or by reasons relating to the nature, scale or frequency of operations or of other relevant activities.

On imperative grounds of urgency, the Commission may use the urgency procedure referred to in Article 19(4).

The Member States shall inform the Commission of such measures.

5. Member States shall ensure the application in their territory of the common basic standards referred to in paragraph 1. Where a Member State has reason to believe that the level of aviation security has been compromised through a security breach, it shall ensure that appropriate and prompt action is taken to rectify that breach and ensure the continuing security of civil aviation.

Article 5

Security costs

Subject to the relevant rules of Community law, each Member State may determine in which circumstances, and the extent to which, the costs of security measures taken under this Regulation to protect civil aviation against acts of unlawful interference should be borne by the State, the airport entities, air carriers, other responsible agencies, or users. If appropriate, and in conformity with Community law, Member States may contribute with users to the costs of more stringent security measures taken under this Regulation. As far as may be practicable, any charges or transfers of security costs shall be directly related to the costs of providing the security services concerned and shall be designed to recover no more than the relevant costs involved.

Article 6

More stringent measures applied by Member States

1. Member States may apply more stringent measures than the common basic standards referred to in Article 4. In doing so, they shall act on the basis of a risk assessment and in compliance with Community law. Those measures shall be relevant, objective, non-discriminatory and proportional to the risk that is being addressed.

2. Member States shall inform the Commission of such measures as soon as possible after their application. Upon reception of such information, the Commission shall transmit this information to the other Member States.

3. Member States are not required to inform the Commission where the measures concerned are limited to a given flight on a specific date.

Article 7

Security measures required by third countries

1. Without prejudice to any bilateral agreements to which the Community is a party, a Member State shall notify the Commission of measures required by a third country if they differ from the common basic standards referred to in Article 4 in respect of flights from an airport in a Member State to, or over, that third country.

2. At the request of the Member State concerned or on its own initiative, the Commission shall examine the application of any measures notified under paragraph 1 and may, in accordance with the regulatory procedure referred to in Article 19(2), draw up an appropriate response to the third country concerned.

3. Paragraphs 1 and 2 shall not apply if:

(a) the Member State concerned applies the measures concerned in accordance with Article 6; or

(b) the requirement of the third country is limited to a given flight on a specific date.

Article 8

Cooperation with the International Civil Aviation Organisation

Without prejudice to Article 300 of the Treaty, the Commission may conclude a Memorandum of Understanding concerning audits with the International Civil Aviation Organisation (ICAO) in order to avoid duplicate monitoring of Member States' compliance with Annex 17 to the Chicago Convention on International Civil Aviation.

Article 9

Appropriate authority

Where, within a single Member State, two or more bodies are involved in civil aviation security, that Member State shall designate a single authority (hereinafter referred to as the appropriate authority) to be responsible for the coordination and monitoring of the implementation of the common basic standards referred to in Article 4.

Article 10

National civil aviation security programme

1. Every Member State shall draw up, apply and maintain a national civil aviation security programme.

That programme shall define responsibilities for the implementation of the common basic standards referred to in Article 4 and shall describe the measures required by operators and entities for this purpose.

2. The appropriate authority shall make available in writing on a 'need to know' basis the appropriate parts of its national civil aviation security programme to operators and entities which it deems to have a legitimate interest.

Article 11

National quality control programme

1. Every Member State shall draw up, apply and maintain a national quality control programme.

That programme shall enable the Member State to check the quality of civil aviation security in order to monitor compliance both with this Regulation and with its national civil aviation security programme.

2. The specifications for the national quality control programme shall be adopted by amending this Regulation through the addition of an annex in accordance with the regulatory procedure with scrutiny referred to in Article 19(3).

On imperative grounds of urgency, the Commission may use the urgency procedure referred to in Article 19(4).

The programme shall allow for the swift detection and correction of deficiencies. It shall also provide that all airports, operators and entities responsible for the implementation of aviation security standards that are located in the territory of the Member State concerned shall be regularly monitored directly by, or under the supervision of, the appropriate authority.

Article 12

Airport security programme

1. Every airport operator shall draw up, apply and maintain an airport security programme.

That programme shall describe the methods and procedures which are to be followed by the airport operator in order to comply both with this Regulation and with the national civil aviation security programme of the Member State in which the airport is located.

The programme shall include internal quality control provisions describing how compliance with these methods and procedures is to be monitored by the airport operator.

2. The airport security programme shall be submitted to the appropriate authority, which may take further action if appropriate.

Article 13

Air carrier security programme

1. Every air carrier shall draw up, apply and maintain an air carrier security programme.

That programme shall describe the methods and procedures which are to be followed by the air carrier in order to comply both with this Regulation and with the national civil aviation security programme of the Member State from which it provides services.

The programme shall include internal quality control provisions describing how compliance with these methods and procedures is to be monitored by the air carrier.

2. Upon request, the air carrier security programme shall be submitted to the appropriate authority, which may take further action if appropriate.

3. Where a Community air carrier security programme has been validated by the appropriate authority of the Member State granting the operating licence, the air carrier shall be recognised by all other Member States as having fulfilled the requirements of paragraph 1. This is without prejudice to a Member State's right to request from any air carrier details of its implementation of:

(a) the security measures applied by that Member State under Article 6; and/or

(b) local procedures that are applicable at the airports served.

Article 14

Entity security programme

1. Every entity required under the national civil aviation security programme referred to in Article 10 to apply aviation security standards shall draw up, apply and maintain a security programme.

That programme shall describe the methods and procedures which are to be followed by the entity in order to comply with the national civil aviation security programme of the Member State in respect of its operations in that Member State.

The programme shall include internal quality control provisions describing how compliance with these methods and procedures is to be monitored by the entity itself.

2. Upon request, the security programme of the entity applying aviation security standards shall be submitted to the appropriate authority, which may take further action if appropriate.

Article 15

Commission inspections

1. The Commission, acting in cooperation with the appropriate authority of the Member State concerned, shall conduct inspections, including inspections of airports, operators and entities applying aviation security standards, in order to monitor the application by Member States of this Regulation and, as appropriate, to make recommendations to improve aviation security. For this purpose, the appropriate authority shall inform the Commission in writing of all airports in its territory serving civil aviation other than those covered by Article 4(4).

The procedures for conducting Commission inspections shall be adopted in accordance with the regulatory procedure referred to in Article 19(2).

2. Commission inspections of airports, operators and entities applying aviation security standards shall be unannounced. The Commission shall in good time before an inspection inform the Member State concerned thereof.

3. Each Commission inspection report shall be communicated to the appropriate authority of the Member State concerned, which shall, in its answer, set out the measures taken to remedy any identified deficiencies.

The report, together with the answer of the appropriate authority, shall subsequently be communicated to the appropriate authority of the other Member States.

Article 16

Annual report

Every year the Commission shall present a report to the European Parliament, the Council and the Member States informing them of the application of this Regulation and of its impact on improving aviation security.

Article 17

Stakeholders' Advisory Group

Without prejudice to the role of the Committee referred to in Article 19, the Commission shall establish a Stakeholders' Advisory Group on Aviation Security, composed of European representative organisations engaged in, or directly affected by, aviation security. The role of this group shall be solely to advise the Commission. The Committee referred to in Article 19 shall keep the Stakeholders' Advisory Group informed during the entire regulatory process.

Article 18

Dissemination of information

As a general rule, the Commission shall publish measures that have a direct impact on passengers. However, the following documents shall be regarded as

EU classified information within the meaning of Decision 2001/844/EC, ECSC, Euratom:

(a) measures and procedures as referred to in Articles 4(3), 4(4), 6(1) and 7(1), if containing sensitive security information;

(b) the Commission inspection reports and the answers of the appropriate authorities referred to in Article 15(3).

Article 19

Committee procedure

1. The Commission shall be assisted by a Committee.

2. Where reference is made to this paragraph, Articles 5 and 7 of Decision 1999/468/EC shall apply, having regard to the provisions of Article 8 thereof.

The period laid down in Article 5(6) of Decision 1999/468/EC shall be set at one month.

3. Where reference is made to this paragraph, Article 5a(1) to (4) and Article 7 of Decision 1999/468/EC shall apply, having regard to the provisions of Article 8 thereof.

4. Where reference is made to this paragraph, Article 5a(1), (2), (4), and (6) and Article 7 of Decision 1999/468/EC shall apply, having regard to the provisions of Article 8 thereof.

Article 20

Agreements between the Community and third countries

When appropriate, and in conformity with Community law, agreements recognising that the security standards applied in a third country are equivalent to Community standards could be envisaged in aviation agreements between the Community and a third country in accordance with Article 300 of the Treaty, in order to advance the goal of 'one-stop security' for all flights between the European Union and third countries.

Article 21

Penalties

Member States shall lay down the rules on penalties applicable to infringements of the provisions of this Regulation and shall take all measures necessary to ensure that they are implemented. The penalties provided for must be effective, proportionate and dissuasive.

Article 22

Commission report on financing

The Commission will report, no later than 31 December 2008, on the principles of the financing of the costs of civil aviation security measures. That report will consider what steps need to be taken in order to ensure that security charges are used exclusively to meet security costs, and to improve the transparency of such charges. The report will also address the principles necessary to safeguard undistorted competition between airports and between air carriers, and the different methods to ensure consumer protection as regards the distribution of the costs of security measures between taxpayers and users. The Commission report will be accompanied, if appropriate, by a legislative proposal.

Article 23

Repeal

Regulation (EC) No 2320/2002 is hereby repealed.

Article 24

Entry into force

1. This Regulation shall enter into force on the 20th day following its publication in the Official Journal of the European Union.

2. It shall apply as from the date specified in the implementing rules adopted in accordance with the procedures referred to in Article 4(2) and (3), but not later than 24 months after the entry into force of this Regulation.

3. By way of exception to paragraph 2, Articles 4(2), 4(3), 4(4), 8, 11(2), 15 (1) second subparagraph, 17, 19 and 22 shall apply from the date of entry into force of this Regulation.

This Regulation shall be binding in its entirety and directly applicable in all Member States.

Done at Strasbourg, 11 March 2008.

Index

R. Abeyratne, *Rulemaking in Air Transport*, DOI 10.1007/978-3-319-44657-8

Printed in the United States
By Bookmasters